LEARNING IN SPORTS COACHING

The facilitation of learning is a central feature of coaches' and coach educators' work. Coaching students and practitioners are, as a result, being expected to give increasing levels of thought towards how they might help to develop the knowledge and practical skills of others. *Learning in Sports Coaching* provides a comprehensive introduction to a diverse range of classic, critical and contemporary theories of learning, education and social interaction and their potential application to sports coaching. Each chapter is broadly divided into two sections. The first section introduces a key thinker and the fundamental tenets of his or her scholarly endeavours and theorising. The second considers how the theorist's work might influence how we understand and attempt to promote learning in coaching and coach education settings. By design this book seeks to promote theoretical connoisseurship and to encourage its readers to reflect critically on their beliefs about learning and its facilitation. This is an essential text for any pedagogical course taken as part of a degree programme in sports coaching or coach education.

Lee Nelson is a Senior Lecturer in Sports Coaching at Edge Hill University and an Honorary Senior Research Fellow at the University of Hull, UK. His research and teaching interests include micro-politics, emotions and learning in coaching and coach education contexts. Lee was the lead editor for the recent title *Research Methods in Sports Coaching* (Routledge).

Ryan Groom is a Senior Lecturer in Sports Coaching and Programme Director for the M.A./ M.Sc. Exercise and Sports degrees at Manchester Metropolitan University, UK. A lead tutor on the M.A. Coaching Studies degree, his main teaching and research interests focus on the use of qualitative research methodologies and social theory to explore power, identity, education and interaction. Ryan was a co-editor for the title *Research Methods in Sports Coaching* (Routledge).

Paul Potrac is a Professor of Sports Coaching at Edge Hill University and an Honorary Professor at the University of Hull, UK. His research and teaching interests focus on exploring the social complexity of sports coaching and coach education, with a particular emphasis on the political and emotional nature of practice. Paul has led and contributed to the completion of a number of book projects including *Research Methods in Sports Coaching, The Sociology of Sports Coaching, Understanding Sports Coaching*, the *Routledge Handbook of Sports Coaching*, and *Sports Coaching Cultures* (all published by Routledge).

LEARNING IN SPORTS COACHING

Theory and application

Edited by Lee Nelson, Ryan Groom and Paul Potrac

Routledge
Taylor & Francis Group

LONDON AND NEW YORK

First published 2016
by Routledge
2 Park Square, Milton Park, Abingdon, Oxon OX14 4RN

and by Routledge
711 Third Avenue, New York, NY 10017

Routledge is an imprint of the Taylor & Francis Group, an informa business

British Library Cataloguing in Publication Data
A catalogue record for this book is available from the British Library

Library of Congress Cataloging in Publication Data
Names: Nelson, Lee. | Groom, Ryan. | Potrac, Paul, 1974–
Title: Learning in sports coaching : theory and application / edited by
Lee Nelson, Ryan Groom and Paul Potrac.
Description: New York : Routledge, 2016. | Includes bibliographical references.
Identifiers: LCCN 2015031447| ISBN 9781138816565 (Hardback) |
ISBN 9781138816572 (Paperback) | ISBN 9781315746012 (eBook)
Subjects: LCSH: Coaching (Athletics) | Coaching (Athletics)--Study and
teaching.
Classification: LCC GV711 .L426 2016 | DDC 796.07/7--dc23
LC record available at http://lccn.loc.gov/2015031447

ISBN: 978-1-138-81656-5 (hbk)
ISBN: 978-1-138-81657-2 (pbk)
ISBN: 978-1-315-74601-2 (ebk)

Typeset in Bembo
by Taylor & Francis Books

Lee Nelson: To Emma and Isabelle.
Ryan Groom: To my parents Neil and Sue, and my wife Angela, thank you for your support in all I do. To our sons James and Jack.
Paul Potrac: To Susi, Megan, and Abigail.

CONTENTS

ILLUSTRATIONS

Figures

Tables

Boxes

ACKNOWLEDGEMENT

We would like to thank Simon Whitemore and the team at Routledge for commissioning and supporting the realisation of this project. Our thanks also go to those scholars and practitioners that authored the various chapters contained in this book. And finally we would like to thank Ben Ives for helping us with formatting duties.

CONTRIBUTORS

Tristan Coulter is a Lecturer in Sport and Exercise Psychology at Queensland University of Technology, Australia. His research and teaching interests focus on understanding personality in sport and physical activity and the social and personal factors associated with mental toughness.

Diane Culver is an Associate Professor in the School of Human Kinetics, University of Ottawa, Canada. Her research interests include coach development and qualitative research. In her teaching, research and consulting she is particularly interested in social learning theory and building social learning capability in sport.

Chris Cushion is Professor of Coaching and Pedagogy at Loughborough University, UK. His research interests are in understanding coach learning, coaching practice and coach behaviour, within a framework of developing a sociology of coaching.

Dave Day is a Reader in Sports History at Manchester Metropolitan University, UK. His research interests focus on the history of sports coaching and training, the life courses of elite coaches, and the importance of traditional craft knowledge in the working lives of coaching practitioners.

Jim Denison is an Associate Professor in the Faculty of Physical Education and Recreation at the University of Alberta, Canada. A sport sociologist and coach developer, his research examines the formation of coaches' practices through a Foucauldian lens.

Christian Edwards is a Lecturer in Sports Coaching at the Cardiff School of Sport, Cardiff Metropolitan University, UK. His (ongoing) doctoral work examines the social significance of humour, and its use as a crucial component in the negotiation of coaching relationships. A former professional footballer, Christian is also the Director of Men's Football at Cardiff Met.

Tatiane da Silva Pires Felix is a Ph.D. student at UNESP (Universidade Estadual Paulista Júlio de Mesquita Filho), Presidente Prudente, Brazil. Her research involves an exploration into children's affective development from a cultural-historical activity theory (CHAT) perspective.

Brian Gearity is the founding Director of the Master of Arts in Sport Coaching programme at the University of Denver, USA. His research interests include coach development and coach quality.

Megan Gilchrist is a Research Assistant and Ph.D. student at the University of Queensland, Australia. Her teaching and research interests include understanding coaching behaviours within a particular organisational culture.

Kerry Harris is a Senior Lecturer in Sports Coaching at Cardiff Metropolitan University, UK. Her research and teaching interests include learning theory, social interaction in sport coaching and the development of professional practice in sport coaching and pedagogy through the use of action research.

Luke Jones is a Lecturer in the Department of Sport, Health and Exercise Science at the University of Hull, UK. His research concentrates upon problematising overtly disciplinary coaching practices common to elite sport.

Robyn L. Jones is a Professor of Sport and Social Theory at the Cardiff School of Sport, Cardiff Metropolitan University, UK, a Visiting Professor (II) at the Norwegian School of Sport Sciences, Oslo, Norway, and a Visiting Associate Principal Lecturer (Research) at Hartpury College, UK. He has (co-)published numerous articles and books on sports coaching and pedagogy. Robyn is also the General Editor of the Taylor & Francis journal *Sports Coaching Review*.

Clifford J. Mallett is a Professor of Sport Psychology and Coaching at the University of Queensland, Australia, and an Honorary Professor in Sports Coaching at Edge Hill University, UK. His research and teaching focuses on coaches' motivation and behaviours, mental toughness, coach learning and development.

Jenny McMahon is a Lecturer in Sports Coaching, Physical Pursuits, and Health and Physical Education at the University of Tasmania, Australia. Her research interests include sport development, coach education, athlete well-being, creative analytical practices, and sporting culture. Her teaching areas include sports coaching, sports pedagogy, and health and physical education.

Aidan Moran is Professor of Cognitive Psychology and Director of the Psychology Research Laboratory at University College, Dublin, Ireland. He has published widely in areas related to concentration, mental imagery and expertise in sport performers.

Kevin Morgan is a Senior Lecturer in Sport Coaching and Physical Education in the School of Sport at Cardiff Metropolitan University, UK. He is Programme Director for the M.Sc. in Sport Coaching and his primary research interests are in pedagogy, motivational climate and coach education.

Christine Nash is Deputy Head of the Institute for Sport, Physical Education and Health Sciences at the University of Edinburgh UK, and Programme Director of the M.Sc. in Sport Coaching and Performance. Her research interests are expertise in sports coaching.

Rūtenis Paulauskas works at Lithuanian University of Educational Sciences and Lithuania Sports University. His central areas of teaching and research pertain to coaching high performance basketball players, teaching sport concepts and skills, and the physical fitness of youth and adolescents.

Laura Purdy is a Senior Lecturer in Sports Coaching at Edge Hill University, UK. Her research focuses on high performance sporting cultures and the everyday realities of coaches and athletes who operate in these contexts. Specifically, she looks at the construction of, and relationship between, coaches' and athletes' social worlds and identities.

Jean-Paul Richard has over 20 years of experience in coaching. Between 2011 and 2014 he was the World Cup coach for Canada's Freestyle ski team, working with the women's mogul team. At the Olympic Games in Sochi, he led the team to winning two medals, one gold and silver medal, plus a 10th and 12th place finish. Jean-Paul is currently the Manager, Team Services for the Canadian Olympic Committee. He has a university degree in Kinesiology and is certified Level 4 by the National Coaching Certification Program.

Chris Rowley is a Lecturer in Sport and Exercise Psychology at Leeds Trinity University, and an Associate Lecturer with The Open University. His main teaching and research interests include sport psychology, reflective practice, the impact of contextual complexity on applied practice, and the implementation of student-led enquiry within higher education.

Brett Smith is a Professor in Physical Activity and Health at Birmingham University, UK. His research and teaching interests include qualitative research, narrative inquiry, and disability. He is editor-in-chief of the international journal *Qualitative Research in Sport, Exercise and Health*.

William G. Taylor is a Senior Lecturer in the Department of Exercise and Sport Science, Manchester Metropolitan University, UK, where he is the research lead for the 'Cluster for Research into Coaching'. His research interests centre on postmodern critiques of coaching structures and practice, coaching in the 'risk society', and the development of professionalism and professional identity among sports coaches.

Gethin Ll. Thomas is a Lecturer in Sports Coaching in the School of Sport at Cardiff Metropolitan University, UK. His primary research interests are in pedagogy for sports coaching, coach education, and game-centred coaching approaches.

John Toner is a Lecturer in the Department of Sport, Health and Exercise Science at the University of Hull, UK. His research and teaching interests include skill acquisition, expertise in sport performers and pedagogy in sports coaching.

Pierre Trudel is a Professor in the School of Human Kinetics, University of Ottawa, Canada. His research and teaching interests focus on exploring how sport coaches learn to coach. He is also a consultant for many sport organizations, developing programmes based on social learning systems.

Irineu Tuim Viotto Filho is a Professor and former age-grade national Brazilian water polo coach. He is currently the Postgraduate Education Coordinator at the Department of Physical Education, UNESP-Presidente Prudente, Brazil. His research interests include the study and application of Vygotskyan thought to current pedagogical practice.

1

INTRODUCTION

Towards a theoretical connoisseurship of learning in sports coaching

Lee Nelson, Ryan Groom and Paul Potrac

Introduction and aim

The decision to edit this book largely stemmed from our experiences of leading or contributing to the delivery of pedagogy modules on sports coaching degree programmes. As educators of undergraduate and postgraduate students, we found that there were very few resources on which to base the content, delivery, and assessment of learning in sports coaching. In response to this situation, we each found ourselves turning to mainstream books and research articles on learning and its facilitation. Engaging with these texts certainly helped to advance our respective understandings of different and useful theoretical perspectives regarding teaching and learning, and subsequently shaped our thoughts about coaching and coach education. Indeed, like Jones (2006), we certainly believe that the field of sports coaching could learn a great deal from the theorizing that has taken place in education. However, we often yearned for a text that was specific to sports coaching. Similarly, we also found that some students found it difficult to understand and translate the information contained in these mainstream educational texts to the practices of coaching and coach education, while others appeared reluctant to read academic material that did not directly relate to sports coaching. It was in light of these experiences that we decided to compile this edited text.

The purpose of this book, then, is to present a broad range of theoretical perspectives on teaching and learning, and to think about what these might mean for how coaching students, scholars, and practitioners think about the practices of coaching and coach education. We aim to achieve this objective by presenting the work of seventeen theorists of learning, education, and social interaction. While drafting the list of possible theorists to include proved relatively straightforward, deciding on which to remove was a much more difficult task. Like other similar texts in sports coaching (e.g. Jones et al. 2011), space restrictions meant that our initial 'wish list' had to be pragmatically reduced. The omission of certain scholars was an unfortunate reality that we had to accept. Eventually, we opted to include both classic and contemporary theorists in an effort to maximize the range of perspectives presented in this text as a standalone resource. As such, we hope that this book proves to be a useful introductory resource for students, scholars, and practitioners interested in learning and for the education and development of sports coaches.

Connoisseurship

As indicated above, it has been our experience that sports coaching students can be ambivalent about theory, especially theorizing drawn from disciplines outside of coaching. When attempting to introduce students to such frameworks some state 'I don't like theory!' whereas others ask 'Why have we got to learn about theory? What's theory got to do with practice?' At times, some students have (passionately) argued that theory is redundant or unnecessary in the practical doing of coaching. Often, these same people view the learning of others to be a somehow straightforward, technical, and homogeneous activity. While we appreciate that grappling with theory can be a challenging intellectual exercise, we find these responses perplexing as, like Lewin (1951: 169), we are of the belief that 'there is nothing more practical than a good theory'. Indeed, from our perspective at least, theory plays an important role in helping students to move beyond the mindless reproduction of alleged 'gold standard' coaching behaviours, as it can provide them with a firm foundation for developing their capacity to engage with learning and learners in both critical and creative ways (Jones et al. 2011).

When helping students to think about the relationship between theory and practice, we find ourselves returning to Thompson's (2000, 2010) discussions of *the fallacy of theoryless practice*. Thompson (2010: 6) reminds us that attempts to divorce theory from practice are essentially flawed as they mistakenly assume that practitioners operate 'without drawing on some sort of framework of understanding – in other words, a theory'. Underpinning this fallacy is the assumption that theory refers only to formal 'book theory', a perspective that fails to acknowledge the role of informal, personal, theories of practice that are generated through socialization processes and applied practice experiences (Thompson 2000).

Whether or not we are aware of it then, each of us has underpinning theoretical understandings that shape and guide our pedagogical practices: beliefs that are influenced by our respective learning biographies both inside and outside of sport. As practitioners, it is not only important to acknowledge this fact but to reflect on how our personal values, beliefs, and ideas shape our teaching and learning decisions, practices, and interactions. Rather than viewing theory and practice as separate entities then, instead we would encourage all coach educators and coach learners to recognize that these concepts are, in reality, inextricably intertwined (Cassidy et al. 2009; Jones et al. 2011).

We have each come to appreciate the value of reading about formal theories of learning, education, and interaction and the importance attached to such activities within education. Acquiring an understanding of these theories has, for example, encouraged us to think about our own practices and practice contexts in new and insightful ways, and to experiment with novel pedagogical approaches. While we think that much could be learnt from such theorizing, it is important to recognize that discussions about learning, education, and social interaction are far from unified. As will become evident, significant differences exist between orientations and the works of individual theorists, and the field of sports coaching would benefit from developing a more nuanced appreciation of those differences.

In many ways then, asking coaches and coach educators to grasp the subtleties of these various learning orientations and the propositions expressed by each of the theorists in this text calls for the qualities of connoisseurship: a line of thinking that Sparkes and Smith (Sparkes 2009; Sparkes and Smith 2009, 2013) have called for in the sports sciences more broadly. While connoisseurship should be considered the art of appreciation, that appreciation should not be conflated with 'a liking or preference for what one has encountered, but rather an awareness of its characteristics and qualities' (Eisner 1975: 6). To help bring this concept to life Eisner presents the example of wine connoisseurship:

> The wine connoisseur has through long and careful attention to wine developed a gustatory palate that enables him [or her] to discern its most subtle qualities. When he [or she] drinks wine it is done with an intention to discern, and with a set of techniques that he [or she] employs to examine the range of qualities within the wine upon which he [or she] will make his [or her] judgments. Body, color, nose, aftertaste, bite, flavor, these are some of the attributes to which the wine connoisseur attends ... It is through his [or her] refined palate, his [or her] knowledge of what to look for, his [or her] backdrop of previous experience with wines other than those he [or she] is presently drinking that differentiates his [or her] level of discernment from that of an ordinary drinker of wine.
>
> *(Eisner 1975: 6–7)*

It is our belief that coaching students, scholars, and practitioners would benefit a great deal from becoming connoisseurs of theory relating to learning, education, and interaction. Like Eisner (1985: 92), we are of the opinion that good theory 'does not replace intelligence and perception and action'; rather it helps us to see more by providing 'some of the windows through which intelligence can look out into the world'. We hope that the content of this text will help you to refine your own 'gustatory palate' not only by introducing you to a broad overview of theoretical positions and perspectives, but also by identifying some of the concepts and attributes that the connoisseur of pedagogical theory, from our perspective at least, needs to consider. That said, we acknowledge that becoming a connoisseur is not an easy task. Many of the theoretical concepts encountered in this book may seem 'foreign' and confusing at first. To overcome this challenge, we encourage readers to relish, where necessary, the opportunity to expand their theoretical vocabularies and understandings. While similarities certainly exist between theoretical positions, some frameworks stand in stark contrast to each other. The identification of such distinctions can prove to be quite disconcerting for the developing connoisseur. For example, reading about certain theories could prove somewhat unsettling, especially if they directly challenge your existing understandings and beliefs. Connoisseurship, then, involves 'risking one's prejudices when encountering something new or unfamiliar' (Sparkes and Smith 2013: 204). Despite the potential challenges that might be encountered, we encourage readers to use this text to help familiarize themselves with the broad range of theoretical perspectives that are presented and to think critically about how such theorizing might apply to the practice of coaching and coach education.

The structure and use of the book

Following this editors' introduction (Chapter 1), the theorizing of seventeen prominent learning and educational thinkers is presented (Chapters 2–18) across six sections, namely: (1) behaviourist and social cognitivist theorists, (2) experiential theorists, (3) humanist theories, (4) constructivist theorists, (5) critical and post-structuralist theorists, and (6) social and ethical theorists. More specifically, the chapters in this section of the book cover the work of Burrhus Frederic Skinner (Chapter 2), Albert Bandura (Chapter 3), John Dewey (Chapter 4), Donald Schön (Chapter 5), Abraham Maslow (Chapter 6), Carl Rogers (Chapter 7), Jean Piaget (Chapter 8), Lev Vygotsky (Chapter 9), Yrjö Engeström (Chapter 10), Ivor Goodson (Chapter 11), Paulo Freire (Chapter 12), Jack Mezirow (Chapter 13), Robin Usher (Chapter 14), Herbert Blumer (Chapter 15), Jean Lave (Chapter 16), Peter Jarvis (Chapter 17), and Nel Noddings (Chapter 18).

Most chapters comprise the following thematic format: (i) a short biography (i.e. a concise biography of the theorist's life and career), (ii) key concepts (i.e. an exploration of the key tenets of the scholar's theorizing), (iii) application to sports coaching (i.e. consideration of how such work might be applied to the context of sports coaching), (iv) practitioner commentary (i.e. a commentary by a coaching practitioner reflecting on the utility of the theorist's work), and (v) critical questions (i.e. questions for readers to consider to check their understanding). The book concludes with a chapter that discusses some identifiable tensions in theorizing about learning, education, and interaction.

In keeping with our call for connoisseurship we sought to design a text that could be read in its entirety. We acknowledge, however, that texts such as this are invariably utilized in contrasting ways. For some readers, this might be their first encounter with theorizing in this area; such individuals might want to work their way through the book from start to finish. For others, this book might provide an additional source of information on a known theory or an opportunity to learn about the work of a theorist whose ideas they have not previously encountered. Equally, some coach educators might want to use the content of this book to inform their course content and assessments. However the text is utilized, we hope that it provides a useful foundation for considering the dimensions of, and possibilities for, learning in sports coaching.

References

Cassidy, T., Jones, R. L. and Potrac, P. (2009) *Understanding sports coaching: The social, cultural and pedagogical foundations of coaching practice* (2nd edn), London: Routledge.

Eisner, E. W. (1975) *The perceptive eye: Towards the reformation of educational evaluation*, Occasional papers of the Stanford Evaluation Consortium. Stanford, CA: Stanford University Press.

Eisner, E. W. (1985) *The art of educational evaluation: A personal view*, London: Falmer Press.

Jones, R. L. (2006) 'How can educational concepts inform sports coaching?', in R. L. Jones (ed.) *The sports coach as educator: Re-conceptualising sports coaching*, London: Routledge, 3–13.

Jones, R. L., Potrac, P., Cushion, C. and Ronglan, L. T. (2011) *The sociology of sports coaching*, London: Routledge.

Lewin, K. (1951) *Field theory in social science: Selected theoretical papers*, New York: Harper & Row.

Sparkes, A. C. (2009) 'Novel ethnographic representations and the dilemmas of judgement', *Ethnography and Education*, 4(3): 301–319.

Sparkes, A. C. and Smith, B. (2009) 'Judging the quality of qualitative inquiry: Criteriology and relativism in action', *Psychology of Sport and Exercise*, 10(5): 491–497.

Sparkes, A. C. and Smith, B. (2013) *Qualitative research methods in sport, exercise and health: From process to product*, London: Routledge.

Thompson, N. (2000) *Theory and practice in human services*, Buckingham: Open University Press.

Thompson, N. (2010) *Theorizing social work practice*, Basingstoke: Palgrave Macmillan.

SECTION 1

Behaviourist and social cognitivist theorists

2

BURRHUS FREDERIC SKINNER

Environmental reinforcement in coaching

Ryan Groom, Lee Nelson and Paul Potrac with Andy Coyles

Burrhus Frederic Skinner: a short biography

Burrhus Frederic Skinner was born on 20 March 1904 in Susquehanna, Pennsylvania, USA. Skinner originally studied for a B.A. in English Literature at Hamilton College, Clinton, New York. He graduated in 1926 and set out to become a writer, although ultimately he considered himself to be a failed writer, or at least that literature had failed him as a method for his work (Skinner 1976). A major turning point for Skinner was reading Bertrand Russell's (1927) text *An Outline of Philosophy*. It was here that Skinner came across John B. Watson's behaviourism and its epistemological implications. In reading the work of Russell, Skinner was further introduced to the scientific study of learning in animals and the work of Edward Thorndike (1874–1949) and Ivan Pavlov (1849–1936). Thorndike's (1911) work, *Animal Intelligence: Some Experimental Studies*, outlined the method of manipulating the presence of a stimulus to generate a desired response (the stimulus–response relationship). Inspired by Russell, Skinner (1976: 299) stated that 'it would be a long time before I saw the mistakes which Russell and Watson were making … the course of psychology was to follow the unproductive path of stimulus-response psychology for many years'.

Skinner received his M.A. in 1930 and his Ph.D. in 1931 from Harvard University. He then worked at the University of Minnesota and the University of Indiana before returning to Harvard in 1947 as William James Lecturer, and joining the Department of Psychology the following year as Professor in 1948. A prolific writer, Skinner published 180 articles and 21 books, including: *The Behavior of Organisms* (1938); *Walden Two* (1948); *Science and Human Behavior* (1953); *Verbal Behavior* (1957); *Schedules of Reinforcement* (1957) with C. B. Ferster; *The Analysis of Behavior* (1961); *The Technology of Teaching* (1968); *Contingencies of Reinforcement* (1969); *Beyond Freedom and Dignity* (1971); *About Behaviorism* (1974), and three autobiographical texts.

He became Professor Emeritus at Harvard in 1964, and is widely regarded as one of the most influential psychologists. During his fifty-year career, Skinner was the recipient of a large number of awards, such as the *Warren Medal of the Society of Experimental Psychology* in 1942, the *Distinguished Scientific Contribution Award* of the American Psychological Society in 1958, the *Edward Thorndike Award* in Education in 1966, and the *National Medal of Science* in 1968. Skinner lived to the age of 86, and died in 1990 in Cambridge, Massachusetts.

Burrhus Frederic Skinner: key concepts

Understanding contrasting philosophical approaches within psychology

To understand Skinner's work we must first appreciate the type of scientific project that he proposed. In his 1974 text, *About Behaviorism*, Skinner argued that 'behaviorism is not the science of human behavior; it is the philosophy of that science' (Skinner 1974: 3). It follows then that to understand Skinner's work we must also explore contrasting philosophical approaches to psychology. A number of prominent psychological approaches such as psychoanalysis, humanistic psychology, cognitive psychology, and neuropsychology follow the *Cartesian* paradigm (i.e. 'that external reality consists only of the internal mental representations'), through a dualistic separation of *mind–body* where behaviour is an indicator of hypothetical mental processes that are internal to the individual (Moss 2001: 11). Palmer and Donahoe (1992) noted that such an approach follows the *Essentialist* paradigm, where behavioural phenomena are explained by inventing a property of the organism responsible for the phenomena (i.e. the mind). Alternatively, behaviourism follows a *Selectionist* paradigm, by characterizing the units of analysis in behaviour as genetic in nature, where the behaviour of the organism develops as a result of the selection of responses by contingencies of reinforcement (Palmer and Donahoe 1992).

The evolution of methodological behaviourism

Methodological *behaviourism*, evident in the early work of John Watson (1878–1958), endeavoured to avoid those problems associated with attempting to explain the cause of behaviour as internal mental process and feelings. Skinner explained that:

> Methodological behaviorism might be thought of as a psychological version of logical positivism or operationism, but they are concerned with different issues. Logical positivism or operationism holds that since no two observers can agree on what happens in the world of the mind, then from the point of view of physical sciences mental events are 'unobservable'; there can be no *truth* by agreement, and we must abandon the examination of mental events and turn instead to how they are studied.

(Skinner 1974: 15)

Methodological behaviourism, following logical positivism (see Smith and Smoll 2014), shifted the focus of understanding behaviour away from *mentalism* and from feelings, sensations, ideas, or the introspection of inner life and towards genetic and environmental antecedents and *truth* commitments.

The ontology and epistemology of methodological behaviourism and radical behaviourism

Behaviourism follows three primary ontological commitments: (1) *ontological realism*, which assumes that there is a single reality which can be known; (2) *ontological determinism*, in that human and animal behaviour are governed by natural laws, and there are no such things as free will or volition in human behaviour (Skinner 1971); and (3) *ontological materialism*, where reality is composed only of physical matter, thus concepts such as memory and mind are 'theoretical' abstracts (McDonald et al. 2005; Boghossian 2006). Epistemologically, behaviourism follows both *epistemological objectivism*, in that there is a single reality external to the individual, and *epistemological empiricism*, in that there are no innate mental precepts or ideas and that knowledge or behaviour is gradually constructed through sensory experiences of physical matter (McDonald et al. 2005; Boghossian 2006). The philosophical difference between methodological behaviourism and radical behaviourism lies in radical behaviourism's acceptance that private events are behavioural in character, and that they can contribute to discriminative control over behaviour. Therefore, 'the ontology of private events as physical, material and behavioral is one of the distinguishing features of Skinner's radical behaviorism' (Moore 2001: 241–242).

Radical behaviourism, self and free will

When discussing the person or self within radical behaviourism, Skinner (1974: 164) stated that 'a self or personality is at best a repertoire of behaviour imparted by an organized set of contingencies'. Consistent with his views on behaviour, Skinner's version of radical behaviourism focuses upon the human as an organism with an acquired repertoire developed through contingencies of reinforcement. Skinner (1974) wrote:

> The person who asserts his freedom by saying 'I determine what I shall do next,' is speaking of freedom in or from a current situation: the 'I' who thus seems to have an option is the product of a history from which it is not free and which in fact determines what it will do now.
>
> *(Skinner 1974: 185)*

Skinner's conception of the self has important practical implications for the act of teaching when compared with humanistic views of the self. For example, Swaim (1972) highlighted that the deterministic assumptions within Skinner's work are useful because they cause the educator to look for the environmental cause of behaviour within the classroom, as opposed to Rogers (see Chapter 7), who believed that students are governed by some inner faculty. Thus, Skinner's work is premised upon *environmental determinism*, in that there is no such thing as free will (Swaim 1972).

Radical behaviourism, self and self-knowledge

While *mentalism* kept attention away from the external antecedents of events, and methodological behaviourism did just the reverse (i.e. focusing upon the external antecedents away from internal events), radical behaviourism restores some kind of balance: 'it does not insist upon *truth* by agreement and therefore considers events taking place in the private *world within the skin*. It does not call these events unobservable, and it does not dismiss them as subjective. It simply questions the nature of the object observed and the reliability of the observations' (Skinner 1974: 18).

Radical behaviourism, the body, verbal behaviour and introspection

Skinner (1974) explained that we respond to our body through the nervous system, and we use the verb 'feel' to describe our interactions with this system. Skinner (1974) suggested that the *verbal community* (i.e. other human beings) enables us to describe and report things felt, and through language we are able to learn how to identify and describe events, thus circumventing the restrictions imposed by *privacy* (e.g. internal thought and private stimuli such as pain and hunger). Indeed, in discussing his 1957 book entitled *Verbal Behavior*, Skinner illustrated that pre-verbal organisms would not be able to ask: 'Why did I do that?' Pre-verbal organisms 'do things' and if they are successful they 'do them again' otherwise they 'do other things' (Skinner 1988). The answer to such questions, Skinner suggested, must have come through self-introspection regarding the way the person felt, their state of mind, and their thoughts, which are all verbal constructs.

Radical behaviourism and innate behaviour

In following on from the work of Darwin, Skinner conceived that 'the human species, like all other species, is the product of natural selection' (Skinner 1974: 37). Skinner acknowledged the complex organic, anatomical and physiological components of the human being. However, in this view, rather than being content with describing behaviour itself, we must investigate the conditions under which it occurs (Skinner, 1974). One kind of relationship between behaviour and stimulation is known as a *reflex*; for example, the removal of a hand from a hot stove. Other behaviours are better described as *instincts*. Examples include: courting, nesting, mating, and caring for young. Instinctive behaviours present more complex phenomena for physiologists than *reflex* behaviours.

Radical behaviourism and operant behaviour

A very different way that a person comes to deal with a new environment is through *operant conditioning*. While many of the previously described behaviours are critical for survival, throughout the process of operant conditioning certain behaviours become more likely to occur (Skinner 1974). The behaviour is said to be *strengthened* by its consequence and for that reason the consequences themselves are called *reinforcers*. Thus, 'when hungry organisms exhibit behavior that produces food, the behavior is reinforced by that consequence and is therefore more likely to reoccur' (Skinner 1974: 44). The typical distinction between *reflex behaviours* and *operant behaviours* is that one is involuntary and the other is voluntary (Skinner, 1974). Here, in this regard, Skinner (1968) described his most famous work, the Skinner Box:

> Once we have arranged the particular type of consequences called a reinforcement, our techniques permit us to shape the behavior of organisms almost at will. It has become routine exercise to demonstrate this in classes in elementary psychology by conditioning such organisms as a pigeon. By simply presenting food to a hungry pigeon at the right time it is possible to shape three well-defined responses in a single demonstration period – such responses as turning around, pacing the floor in the pattern of a figure eight, standing still in a corner of the demonstration apparatus, stretching the neck, or stamping the foot. Extremely complex performance may be reached through successive stages in the shaping process, the contingencies of reinforcement being changed progressively in the direction of the required behavior.
>
> *(Skinner 1968: 10)*

The basic premise of operant conditioning is that where behaviours have consequences that are reinforcing, they are more likely to occur again. A positive reinforcer strengthens any behaviour that produces it, whereas a negative reinforcer strengthens any behaviour that reduces or terminates it (Skinner 1974: 51). Skinner (1953: 185) suggested that 'both [positive and negative reinforcers] are reinforcers in the literal sense of reinforcing or *strengthening* a response'.

Shaping and maintaining behaviour through schedules of reinforcement

Skinner (1974) highlighted that the probability of a person responding in a particular way is influenced by their history of operant reinforcement, and that the associated bodily responses can be felt and observed introspectively; for example, a footballer with a feeling of confidence because they report that they practise a particular skill or technique 'until they feel confident' (thus the skill or technique has been reinforced).

Fixed and variable interval schedules of reinforcement

If behaviour is reinforced at regular intervals (i.e. time-contingent), termed *interval* reinforcement, it can be shaped by a nearly constant rate of responding, determined by the frequency of reinforcement. For example, when discussing the findings of his laboratory results and their application to human behaviour, Skinner (1953: 100) explained that 'if we reinforce it every minute, the animal responds rapidly; if every five minutes, much more slowly. A similar effect on the probability of response is a characteristic of human behavior.' Indeed, Skinner highlighted that behaviour that appears under *fixed interval* reinforcement is especially stable; however, the size and rate of the reinforcement affect the rate at which operant behaviours occur (Skinner 1953). In addition, different kinds of reinforcers yield different rates; therefore, reinforcers may be thought of as variable and thus ranked in their effectiveness (Skinner 1953). The rate also varies with the immediacy of the rein-forcer, with a delay in reinforcement reducing the overall response rate (Skinner 1953). Optimal schedules of reinforcement are of great practical value, as small regular tokens of reinforcement following the desired behaviour may be more effective than large blocks of reinforcement following a number of completed behaviours. An alternative to fixed interval reinforcement (i.e. reinforcement every five minutes) is *variable interval* reinforcement, where behaviours are reinforced 'on average' during a specified period of time (i.e. on average every five minutes, but sometimes sooner and sometimes later). Again, performance under such schedules is incredibly stable and uniform and 'it is usually very difficult to extinguish a response after such a schedule' (Skinner 1953: 102).

Fixed and variable ratio schedules of reinforcement

For Skinner (1953), *ratio* reinforcement depends upon the behaviour of the organism (i.e. frequency contingent), where reinforcement is provided after every x number of responses. *Fixed ratio* reinforcement generates a very high rate of response (Skinner 1953), but criticisms of such schedules include that they produce a dangerously high level of activity and a period of intense reinvestment following completion. Alternatively, within *variable ratio* schedules, reinforcement occurs after a given average number of responses but the next response to be reinforced cannot be predicted (Skinner 1974). A favourable history in which the average is slowly increased is said to increase willpower (Skinner 1974). Under *ratio* reinforcement schedules and *fixed intervals* reinforcement schedules, behaviour demonstrates a low probability of reinforcement because reinforcement has just been received (Skinner 1953).

Combined schedules of reinforcement

Other schedules include a *combined* schedule where *ratio* and *interval* reinforcement are determined by both the passage of time and the number of responses. The combination of frequency of responses (*ratio*) over a set period of time (*interval*) can generate high response rates (i.e. reinforcement provided after every five behaviours within ten seconds).

Aversive stimuli and punishment

Aversive stimuli, which generate a host of bodily conditions felt or introspectively observed, are the stimuli which function as reinforcers when they are reduced or terminated. Punishment is easily confused with negative reinforcement, sometimes called aversive control; however, punishment is designed to remove behaviour from a repertoire, whereas negative reinforcement generates behaviour through the removal of the stimuli (Skinner 1974). While many often think of Skinner's work as based in the Pavlovian condition through the presentation of punishment (electric shocks to pigeons, rats, etc.), Skinner's theoretical position is in fact the opposite. This is perhaps the main misunderstanding of his radical behaviourism, where he considered punishment to be an ineffective long-term way to reinforce behaviour, with serious consequences associated with its application:

> Severe punishment unquestionably has an immediate effect in reducing a tendency to act in a given way. This result is no doubt responsible for its widespread use ... In the long run, however, punishment does not actually eliminate behavior from a repertoire, and its temporary achievement is obtained at tremendous cost in reducing the overall efficiency and happiness of the group.
>
> *(Skinner 1953: 190)*

Control of self and control of others

Skinner did not deny the possibility of self-knowledge but he asserted that this is of social origin through the *verbal community* (i.e. other human beings), where it becomes important to individuals to manage or control themselves. For Skinner, the control of self, similar to the control of others, is reliant upon the environment and contingencies of reinforcement. For example, with children, behaviour can be modified through a reward system (e.g. tokens and praise), which over time can be self-administered and made autonomous through behavioural contracts (Skinner 1976). Indeed, Skinner believed that culture, the social environment of a group, can be shaped to ensure that individuals are much more successful and *effective* (Skinner 1948, 1977). Skinner suggested that certain environments bring out the best in people while other environments suppress people (Skinner 1948, 1977).

Critiques of Skinner's radical behaviourism

In reflecting upon the famous Rogers–Skinner debate of 1956, Rogers (1974: 118) emphasized that while he respected the contribution of Skinner and his achievements in promoting 'certain types of learning', he also cautioned that 'I have come to realize that the basic difference between a behavioristic and a humanistic approach to human beings is a *philosophical* choice'. Rogers (1974) further outlined the specific issue that placed his humanistic views at odds with the type of behaviourism proposed by Skinner:

> if the environment, which is part of a causal sequence, is the sole determiner of the individual's behavior, which is thus again an unbreakable chain of cause and effect. All the things that I do, or that Skinner does, are simply inevitable results of our conditioning ... My experience in therapy and in groups makes it impossible for me to deny the reality and significance of human choice.
>
> *(Rogers 1974: 118)*

Noam Chomsky was also critical of Skinner's work. In his review entitled 'The case against B. F. Skinner', Chomsky (1971: 1) wrote that Skinner has been accused of immorality, 'attacking fundamental human values, demanding control in the place of defense of freedom and dignity'. Thus many pose philosophical and ethical questions about Skinner's ideas: Who decides what good behaviour is? Who controls the reinforcement? How is this different from a dictatorship? Even when the intentions are to create good behaviour, many critics find Skinner's ideas, particularly regarding cultural control, to be against democratic human values.

Burrhus Frederic Skinner: applications to sports coaching

The previous section discussed the key concepts of Skinner's radical behaviourism, but what might these concepts mean for learning in the context of sports coaching? The following section explores what Skinner's work might mean for coaches, particularly regarding the design of effective coaching environments.

The role of the teacher/coach in reinforcing learning in radical behaviourism

For Skinner (1968) there are three central conditions under which learning takes place:

1. An occasion upon which behaviour occurs (i.e. a practice setting or game);
2. The behaviour itself (i.e. a technique or skill);
3. The consequences of the behaviour (i.e. the type of reinforcement received).

They have direct implications for the role of the coach within a coaching context. As Swaim (1972) succinctly highlighted:

> [Skinner's] educational theory, as does his general theory of behavior, centers in the concept of control. If learning is seen merely as the changing of

behavior patterns according to environmental stimuli, then teaching is necessarily seen as the manipulation of the stimuli to control the change.

(Swaim 1972: 13)

Skinner's conception of the role of the educator, when applied to coaching, is therefore one of providing an environment where behaviours can be reinforced effectively through schedules of reinforcement.

The use of positive reinforcement and punishment in sports coaching

Positive reinforcement (i.e. reward) from a coach includes behaviours such as verbal praise, a smile of approval or a pat on the back to encourage athletes' behaviours to be continued (Huber 2013). Negative reinforcement (i.e. relief) might include a glare of disapproval which when removed encourages behaviour to continue, while punishment (i.e. reprimand) can be mild or harsh, using verbal or non-verbal responses from a coach such as raising the voice or shaking a finger at an athlete to eradicate behaviour (Huber 2013). Observational studies of coaches have revealed that most coaches use both positive and aversive forms of control (Cushion and Jones 2006; Groom et al. 2012). However, as discussed above, Skinner (1953) suggested that positive reinforcement should be used in preference to aversive forms of control to achieve long-term benefits. Indeed, when discussing the impact of punishment on sports coaching, Smith (2015) highlights that such behaviours may negatively impact the coach–athlete relationship, creating a sort of cohesion of hatred in the athletes against the coach. Smith (2015) further highlighted that the effective use of reinforcement to strengthen behaviour requires the coach to:

a   find a reinforcer that works for a particular athlete.
b   make the occurrence of the reinforcement dependent on the performance of the desired behaviour.
c   make sure the athlete understands why the reinforcement is being given.

(Smith 2015: 45)

Schedules of reinforcement in sports coaching

Although the work of Skinner (1974) explored a number of different ways to manipulate the schedule of reinforcement a coach might use (e.g. *interval, ratio* or *combined* schedules), the application of such schedules by a coach depends on a number of factors. For example, Smith (2015) highlighted that during the initial stages of behaviour shaping, reinforcement is best given with higher frequency schedules. Once a behaviour has been acquired in a repertoire, research has demonstrated that reinforcement should be reduced, as behaviour persists for longer in the absence of reinforcement (Smith 2015). For Skinner (1968), the temporal nature of the behaviour–reinforcement relationship is essential, as a delay of a few seconds, for example while the teacher is working with another pupil in class, may destroy most of the effect of the reinforcement. Indeed, to shape the education of a child, Skinner (1968) suggested that reinforcement should be provided at each step of the process, therefore reinforcement on blocks of practice are unhelpful in shaping learning towards a desired behavioural goal (see the example of the Skinner Box in the previous section). Alternatively for Skinner, 'educational environments should be arranged so the student will be constantly, consistently, and immediately reinforced for the socially desired behavior' (Swaim 1972: 15). Therefore, coaches must seek to provide environments where desired behaviours can be positively reinforced as close to the behavioural response as possible, and thus the probability of their response rate increased.

Burrhus Frederic Skinner: a practitioner commentary by Andy Coyles

As a qualified physical education teacher with an M.A. in Exercise and Sports Coaching, and a Union of European Football Associations (UEFA) Advanced License coach, I have always been interested in learning and teaching, particularly regarding my main sport of soccer. At present, I teach sports coaching at a university while also coaching a Premier League Academy U14 team. At the university, the majority of my teaching consists of coaching-related subject matter, and as such I am familiar with some elements of Skinner's work. As an academy coach, my work often consists of five initial phases before we move into a small-sided game (SSG). For example: (1) a player-led warm-up, (2) a short discussion with the players (e.g. aims and objectives), (3) a 15-minute ball mastery session, (4) a 15-minute technical practice (e.g. passing and receiving), and finally (5) a 15-minute mini-opposed practice (e.g. developing the topic with passive and active opponents). After these five initial practices, the technique or skill is integrated into an SSG with specific planned conditions (e.g. game restrictions), with the aim of applying the technique or skill in a game situation.

Following on from reading this chapter, I can see that elements of my coaching practice in the *technical practice* can at times follow a similar approach to Skinner's ideas regarding shaping behaviour (i.e. the occasion). For example, I often look to reinforce the *body positioning and shape* (i.e. the behaviour) of players when receiving the ball and the communication that players convey following the pass. Typically, in these sessions, the idea is to keep the session moving quickly, giving the players lots of opportunities to practise the skill, while *positively reinforcing* the good technical executions or behaviours as close to performance as possible (i.e. the consequences of the behaviour), with the aim of encouraging the behaviours in the future. Skinner's ideas regarding positive reinforcement appear to mirror how I develop these skills as a coach. In coaching this way, I have come to recognize that the players I work with respond very well and very quickly to instant praise based on their performance. Particularly at their age, the attention and reinforcement that I provide seems to encourage these athletes to behave in a way that I desire.

Typically, I find that this can carry on into the next practice or skill progression, in a relatively permanent manner. I find that using positive reinforcement immediately after skill execution can also act as a way of reinforcing the speed and tempo of a session. For example, I often use key trigger words or phrases such as 'passing good', 'body shape superb', and 'communication excellent' to reinforce behaviour. Thus perhaps, in Skinner's view, I am simply shaping the athletes' behaviour and the performance environment. Alternatively, when I see performance during the sessions at a standard below what I would expect from the group, I occasionally express mild forms of verbal disapproval of the players' efforts (i.e. punishment) as a method of eradicating behaviour. While I have seen other soccer coaches use punishment frequently, I am very cautious of using such an approach with the athletes as I know this can be detrimental to our relationship. I must admit that in my role as a coach I very rarely use negative reinforcement with players (i.e. the removal of a negative coaching behaviour such as a look of disapproval), and that positive reinforcement is my preferred method of shaping player behaviour.

In planning a technical session that allows me to provide instant positive reinforcement to the players, it is important that I consider the physical space and distance from coach to player while the skills are performed. Typically, I will design and set up a session in a small area, perhaps a 20 x 20 yard diamond with 4 players per station (16 players in total), with my assistant coach and me observing and reinforcing behaviour. Often I will be in close proximity to the players, sometimes circling the practice area, or even in the middle of the diamond, using trigger words to shape performance in the session. I will ask my assistant to observe the session from outside the area and pick up individual players for immediate reinforcement, thus reinforcing the session aims. Sometimes I will incorporate myself into the practice as an opposing player, to apply pressure on the skill execution. Again, I will aim to provide reinforcement as soon as the skill has been executed correctly. A key aim for me is to give players the opportunity to practise skills and techniques by reinforcing good play without stopping performance to highlight errors and thus reduce practise time. However, I am also cautious of the players becoming overly dependent upon my reinforcement, so I will often look to reduce the frequency and ratio of my reinforcement.

While reading this chapter, I have been able to relate some of Skinner's ideas regarding the shaping of behaviour to some of my practices as a coach, but I certainly would not class myself as a behaviourist (or even a radical behaviourist in Skinner's mould!). Although it is relatively easy for me to look at my own practices (or snapshots of my practices), particularly in a fairly closed skill, and identify with some of Skinner's ideas, when I consider my practice as a whole there are many important elements of it that, as a coach, I feel Skinner's work does not fully explore. My training as a physical education teacher and my repertoire of coaching experience have greatly influenced my ideas regarding pedagogy, sports coaching, and athlete learning. For example, I place great value on talking to the players individually and asking questions to generate dialogue and to check understanding, as well as using demonstrations. I am also concerned with what the athletes are thinking during performance and their game understanding. Therefore, although reading this chapter has made me more aware of my implicit coaching practices, and therefore perhaps enabled me to ensure I reinforce behaviours immediately in technical practices, I find that Skinner's work can only offer a limited perspective on the much more complex learning process involved when working with athletes.

Burrhus Frederic Skinner: critical questions

1. What types of athlete behaviours do you see in your coaching practice that you would reinforce?
2. What techniques would you use to reinforce these behaviours?
3. What types of athlete behaviours do you see in your coaching practice that you would extinguish?
4. What techniques would you use to extinguish these behaviours?
5. What would be the likely consequences of these different types of reinforcement for your relationship with your athlete and learning situation from your coaching practice?

References

Boghossian, P. (2006) 'Behaviorism, constructivism, and Socratic pedagogy', *Educational Philosophy and Theory*, 38(6): 713–722.

Chomsky, N. (1971) 'The case against BF Skinner', *New York Review of Books*, 30 December: 1–12.

Cushion, C. and Jones, R. L. (2006) 'Power, discourse and symbolic violence in professional youth soccer: The case of Albion F.C.', *Sociology of Sport Journal*, 23(2): 142–161.

Ferster, C. B. and Skinner, B. F. (1957) *Schedules of reinforcement*, New York: Appleton-Century.

Groom, R., Cushion, C. and Nelson, L. (2012) 'Analysing coach-athlete "talk in interaction" within the delivery of video-based performance feedback in elite youth soccer', *Qualitative Research in Sport, Exercise and Health*, 4(3): 439–458.

Huber, J. (2013) *Applying educational psychology in coaching athletes*, Champaign, IL: Human Kinetics.

McDonald, J. K., Yanchar, S. C. and Osguthorpe, R. T. (2005) 'Learning from programmed instruction: Examining implications for modern instructional technology', *Education Technology Research and Development*, 53(2): 84–98.

Moore, J. (2001) 'On distinguishing methodological from radical behaviorism', *European Journal of Behavior Analysis*, 2: 221–244.

Moss, D. (2001) 'The roots and genealogy of humanistic psychology', in K. J. Schneider, J. F. T. Buental and J. F. Pierson (eds) *The handbook of humanistic psychology: Leading edges in theory, research and practice*, London: Sage, 5–20.

Palmer, D. C. and Donahoe, J. W. (1992) 'Essentialism and selectionism in cognitive science and behavior analysis', *American Psychologist*, November: 1345–1358.

Rogers, C. R. (1974) 'In retrospect: Forty-six years', *American Psychologist*, February: 115–123.

Russell, B. (1927) *An outline of philosophy*, London: George Allen & Unwin.

Skinner, B. F. (1938) *The behavior of organisms*, New York: Appleton-Century.

Skinner, B. F. (1948) *Walden two*, Cambridge, MA: Hackett.

Skinner, B. F. (1953) *Science and human behaviour*, New York: The Free Press.

Skinner, B. F. (1957) *Verbal behaviour*, New York: Copley.

Skinner, B. F. (1961) *The analysis of behaviour*, New York: McGraw-Hill.

Skinner, B. F. (1968) *The technology of teaching*, New Jersey: Prentice-Hall.

Skinner, B. F. (1969) *Contingencies of reinforcement*, New York: Appleton-Century.

Skinner, B. F. (1971) *Beyond freedom and dignity*, Cambridge: Hackett.

Skinner, B. F. (1974) *About behaviourism*, New York: Alfred A. Knopf.

Skinner, B. F. (1976) *Particulars of my life*, New York: Alfred A. Knopf.

Skinner, B. F. (1977) *Psychology of human relations: About behaviourism*, MATC College On the Air Interview.

Skinner, B. F. (1988) *An informal talk about human behavior and its determinant: Interview with Eve Segal*, San Diego State University.

Smith, R. (2015) 'A positive approach to coaching effectiveness and performance enhancement', in J. M. Williams and V. Krane (eds) *Applied sport psychology: Personal growth to peak performance*, New York: McGraw-Hill, 40–56.

Smith, R. E. and Smoll, F. L. (2014) 'Logical positivism', in L. Nelson, R. Groom and P. Potrac (eds) *Research methods in sports coaching*, London: Routledge, 18–30.

Swaim, E. E. (1972) 'B. F. Skinner and Carl R. Rogers on behavior and education', *Oregon ASCD Curriculum Bulletin*, 324: 1–45.

Thorndike, E. L. (1911) *Animal intelligence: Some experimental studies*, New York: Macmillan.

3

ALBERT BANDURA

Observational learning in coaching

Gethin Thomas, Kevin Morgan and Kerry Harris

Albert Bandura: a short biography

Albert Bandura was born on 4 December 1925 in Mundare, Alberta, Canada. His primary and secondary education took place at the one and only school in Mundare, and as a result of this meagre academic environment he soon discovered that learning is largely a social and self-directed endeavour. Following secondary school, he attended the University of British Columbia in Vancouver, where he initially studied psychology as a 'filler course', but later became enamoured with the subject. Bandura received his B.A. in psychology in 1949, excelling in the subject and winning the Bolocan Award in the process. Following his undergraduate degree, he moved to the United States for his graduate studies at the University of Iowa, where, he received his M.A. in 1951 and his Ph.D. in clinical psychology in 1952. Following a postdoctoral internship at the Wichita Guidance Center, he began his teaching career in the Department of Psychology at Stanford University in 1953 (Bandura 2014), where he remains to this day in his current position as the David Starr Jordan Professor Emeritus of Social Science in Psychology.

Bandura is one of the most well-known and widely cited scholars in both psychology and education (Gordon et al. 1984). He was elected president of the American Psychological Society (APA) in 1974, and in 1998, was honoured with the E. L. Thorndike Award of the APA for his research influence on educational psychology, research that has contributed significantly to knowledge, theory and practice in the field. In 2006, he was honoured by the APA with a Gold Medal Award for Distinguished Lifetime Contribution to Psychological Science.

Bandura is widely published and highly recognized for his work in social learning theory, social cognitive theory and self-efficacy. Although it is difficult to pinpoint a single accomplishment that stands above all others, his 1961 Bobo doll experiment certainly ranks near the top of the list. At that time behaviourist theories of learning were prominent, resulting in the belief that learning was a result of reinforcement. In the Bobo doll experiment Bandura presented children with social models of violent behaviour or non-violent behaviour towards an inflatable Bobo doll. The children who viewed the violent behaviour were in turn violent towards the doll; the control group was rarely violent towards the doll. This experiment demonstrated that observation and social modelling is a very effective way of learning, and moved psychological thinking away from previously limited conceptions in which learning required overt actions.

Albert Bandura: key concepts

Reciprocal determinism

The core theoretical assumptions of social learning are explained in Albert Bandura's book *Social Learning Theory* (SLT) (Bandura 1977). A key concept of SLT is reciprocal determinism, which dismisses the explanation of human behaviour in terms of one-sided determinism. This view is in contrast to the behaviourist standpoint of behaviour being controlled by the environment, and to the humanist and existential viewpoints of people as free agents (Wulfert 2005). SLT supports a triadic reciprocal determinism where interacting determinants such as internal personal factors, behavioural patterns, and environmental influences impact each other bidirectionally (Bandura 1986). From this standpoint, reciprocal determinism recognizes that external determinants of behaviour, such as rewards or punishments, and internal determinants, such as thoughts and beliefs, form an interlinking system that influences behaviour and other elements of the system. Reciprocal determinism, therefore, indicates that the examination of the interaction between an individual's cognitive processes, behaviour and environment provides the most effective approach to explaining human learning and behaviour (Wulfert 2005). Within this model of reciprocal causation, these different sources of influence are not of equal strength; some may be stronger than others, while these influences do not happen simultaneously. Individuals are not free agents within this system nor do not react passively to external pressures; they have some degree of control, through self-regulatory processes, over their own actions. People can affect their own behaviour, for example, through goal setting, generating cognitive strategies, and evaluating goal attainment. According to the model, initially these self-regulatory processes are learned through external rewards and punishments; however, despite their external origin, once internalized they play a part in determining behaviour.

Learning through modelling

Reciprocal determinism underpins the concept of observational learning or learning through modelling, which is a key element of SLT understanding of human behaviour (Bandura 1977, 1986). Prior to the development of SLT, the dominant theoretical assumption in classical and operant learning theories was that social learning was the consequence of trial and error (Wulfert 2005). Through these approaches it was theorized that an individual could only learn by performing responses that were followed by reinforcement or punishment. In comparison, Bandura (1977, 1986) highlighted that social behaviour is not attained as the result of trial and error but through symbolic modelling. People, therefore, learn from both their own experiences and also through watching others. Observing others forms rules of how to behave, and it is this coded information that guides future actions (Bandura 1986). A response, however, is not required for an individual to have learned, and this is why symbolic modelling is considered to be learning without trial. This approach to learning is regarded as highly efficient in transmitting information when compared to trial and error learning, as it bypasses the needless repetition and reinforcement to gradually shape the behaviour of individuals. With observational learning, the simultaneous learning of complex behaviours can be taught to many individuals through a single model. According to Bandura learning is mostly an information-processing activity where individuals acquire new behaviours through four component processes of observational learning: Attention, Retention, Production, Motivation (Bandura 1977).

Processes of observational learning

Attentional processes

Individuals cannot learn through observation alone if they do not attend to, or recognize accurately the key features of the modelled behaviour (Bandura 1977). Attentional processes, therefore, are essential component functions of learning by example. Through this process individuals decide what elements of the modelled behaviour to observe and what is gained from these experiences.

According to Bandura one of the main factors to determine observational experiences are associational preferences. This commonly emerges within groups of social acquaintances where an individual's learning will be heavily influenced by repeated exposure to regular modelled behaviours. For example, opportunities for students to observe models of delinquent behaviour are more likely to occur in schools where there is a high occurrence of exclusions and suspensions when compared to schools where there are none.

Another key factor within these social groups is that certain individuals will command greater attention than other members. The effectiveness of the behaviours used by these individuals will have a significant impact on whether their behaviour will be closely observed and modelled, or ignored. Interpersonal attraction is an important attentional element in this instance, as models with desired behavioural qualities will be identified and those without discounted. An individual's capability to process information will also influence the degree and level of benefit to be gained from observational learning. Past experiences and situational needs will shape what is gained from observations and the interpretation of what is seen and heard.

In contemporary society, modelled behaviour has greatly expanded from being solely a social group activity. As Bandura highlighted, one of the most effective methods of capturing the attention of people of all ages for extended periods is symbolic modelling through the mass media. Television and the Internet provide children and adults with an abundance of models where a variety of behaviours can be observed and learnt. This type of modelling is intrinsically rewarding and can capture the attention of all ages for a prolonged period of time.

Retention processes

Although individuals may observe a model's behaviour, they need to remember these actions in order to be influenced by them. The second key component of observational learning is the long-term retention of activities that have been modelled on one occasion or another (Bandura 1977). If an individual is to reproduce a model's behaviour at a later date without the presence of the latter, these patterns need to be embodied in symbolic form through the imaginal and verbal representational systems. Once modelled behaviours have been converted into these images and verbal symbols, the subsequent actions are guided by these conceptions (Bandura 1986).

Within the imaginal system, images of modelled performances can be accessed following repeated exposure to the modelling stimuli. These are not simply mental images of past observations but imaginal abstractions of previous events (Bandura 1986). Individuals build a general conception of the modelled skill that includes key aspects varying around the basic pattern. This involves a constructive process rather than a matching template of the desired skill. Consequently, when a physical activity has been repeatedly observed, for example, throwing a ball, the associated image can usually be produced by that person. According to Bandura, visual imagery plays a crucial role in observational learning, especially during early developmental periods where individuals lack appropriate verbal skills or when verbal coding is problematic. The throwing motion, for example, is easier to visualize than to describe.

Observational learning and retention is further supported by verbally coding a significant amount of information in an easily stored structure. Despite being a key aspect of the modelling process, verbal symbols are often difficult to distinguish from images (Bandura 1986). Once modelled activities are changed into images they are usually accompanied by verbal symbols which act as memory codes to reproduce the desired behaviour. Alongside symbolic coding, a combination of mentally rehearsing and actually performing modelled patterns of behaviour are key aspects in the process of retaining knowledge efficiently. Although motor rehearsal alone provides some degree of knowledge recollection, it is through combining symbolic rehearsal and physical rehearsal that modelled behaviour is learned most effectively. According to Bandura, the highest level of observational learning is best achieved through, first, organizing the modelled behaviour mentally, and second, alternating symbolic rehearsal with motor performance.

Reproduction processes

The third element of modelling consists of transforming symbolic representations into motor behaviours (Bandura 1977). Bandura highlights that these motor reproductions can be split into four parts: cognitive organization of responses, their instalment, monitoring, and refinement based on informative feedback given. Starting at the cognitive level, even if the modelled activities are acquired and retained, individuals can only reproduce these behaviours if they have the ability to execute the required skills. Therefore, if these elements are missing the complex skill has to be developed first through modelling and practice. Even when the person has the ability to produce the skill, physical limitations may restrict their ability to reproduce the required behaviour. A further barrier to motor reproduction is the inability of individuals to completely observe the actions they take, for example when executing a basic step in dance. In these situations it is difficult to personally identify and correct complex behaviour and individuals must rely on verbal feedback from observers to refine their skills. According to Bandura, in most learning situations people usually produce an uneven likeness to the newly developed skills through modelling, and it is only through observation and feedback from performance that refinement and adaption of behaviours occurs.

Reinforcement and motivational processes

The final key element of learning through observation is that a person needs to be motivated to apply the modelled behaviour (Bandura 1977). The theory distinguishes between acquisition and performance, as people, despite having the capability to execute the modelled behaviour, do not always perform or act on everything they learn. Modelled behaviour is more likely to be used if it results in favourable consequences as opposed to unfavourable or punishing effects. According to Bandura (1986), observationally learned behaviour is influenced by external reinforcement, vicarious reinforcement and self-reinforcement. External incentives influence the performance of modelled actions, where through observed consequences behaviours associated with effective outcomes for others are favoured over those that have negative outcomes. Individuals also observe reactions to their own behaviours and evaluate these responses in order to decide which learned behaviours to apply in specific situations (vicarious reinforcement). Personal standards of conduct (self-reinforcement), according to Bandura, provide a further motivational source, where people regulate their own behaviour based on the consequences of their own actions.

Albert Bandura: applications to sports coaching

Attentional phase

The first phase of observational learning is paying attention to a model (Bandura 1977). Athletes cannot learn by observation if they do not attend to or recognize the essential features of a technique or skill. Gaining the attention of the learners in order to model behaviour is therefore crucial in sport coaching situations. In order to achieve this, coaches use an array of strategies which might include raising their voice, waiting for silence, the use of humour, or other more intrinsically rewarding methods such as the use of video, to gain and hold the learner's attention.

The coach's positioning in relation to the learners, and any other attention-demanding activities going on around them, is also important in order to engage the learners and ensure their attention is maintained. Furthermore, the level of discipline and control that the coach demands, as well as the interpersonal relationships and level of rapport they have with the athletes, will impact on the ability to gain and maintain attention. Simply using an athlete's name, for example, is an effective strategy to gain their attention, particularly in the early stages of getting to know a group.

Observational learning is not limited to the athletes observing the coach. Indeed, athletes observing each other in coaching situations can facilitate a significant amount of social learning. Linking this to associational preferences, it is important for the coach to consider how they group athletes in order to maximize their learning opportunities. Varying the grouping arrangements within and between coaching sessions will, therefore, expose the learners to a wider range of observational experiences and broaden the potential for observational and social learning. Inevitably, some group members are more influential and command greater respect and attention than others. Orchestrating the coaching environment to utilize individuals who possess influential and winsome qualities can, therefore, assist the coach in achieving greater levels of attention.

Retention phase

Athletes cannot be influenced by observing a model if they have no memory of it (Bandura 1977). Therefore, once the coach has the attention of the athletes, the next phase of observational learning is to model or demonstrate the behaviour, so that it is retained in their memory. Demonstration is estimated to be the most commonly used mode of instruction in skill acquisition (Magill 2007), and is seen as an effective means of transferring information from coach to learner. This can be achieved by the coach in different ways; for example, modelling the skill themselves accompanied by instructions, or using another learner in the group to act as the model whilst commentating on the key aspects to be retained. Both of these methods use visual and verbal representational systems to enhance retention and both have their merits and challenges. If the coach alone models the behaviour the athletes cannot observe themselves in action and may, therefore, be presenting a less than technically accurate model. Ensuring that the model is a skilled and accurate representation of what the athletes should be retaining is a crucial element of this phase of learning (Magill 2007). Identifying an able performer to present an accurate model of performance whilst commentating on it may, therefore, prove to be a more reliable modelling process than coach demonstrations. However, it has also been found that beginners can derive learning benefits from observing other beginners (Magill 2007). Regardless of who performs the demonstration, from a skill acquisition perspective, Magill (2007) states that it is beneficial to demonstrate before the observer starts to practise and that the model should continue to be demonstrated during practice as frequently as possible.

Increasingly, the use of technology and visual learning methods such as video, are becoming commonplace in sport coaching. Such methods can be intrinsically motivating and an effective way of facilitating athlete's retention of information. The advantage of this type of modelling is the accuracy of the modelled perfor- mance and the opportunity to pause and replay the video to identify and discuss different aspects with the learners. Other visual methods for modelling skills or desired behaviours could include posters or wall charts, which are available for a wide variety of sporting techniques and activities.

Once the modelled behaviours have been transformed into images, verbal symbols can be used to help retain and represent this information, for example, a 'call' for a set move in a game of rugby, or a verbal cue for a specific aspect of technique in a golf swing. This is known as 'symbolic coding' which can enhance observational learning. Observers who code the modelled activities into words, concise labels, or vivid imagery retain the behaviours better than those who simply observe. Further, people who mentally rehearse (i.e. symbolic rehearsal) or actually perform modelled patterns of behaviour (i.e. motor rehearsal) are less likely to forget them than are those who neither think about nor practise what they have seen (Bandura 1977, 1986). Therefore, in addition to mental rehearsal, athletes require time to practise the technique or skill during this retention phase of the learning process.

Reproduction phase

The third component of modelling is concerned with motor reproduction and involves converting symbolic representations into appropriate actions (Bandura 1977). According to Bandura, to achieve behavioural reproduction the learner must put together a given set of responses according to a modelled pattern. Acquiring the component skills of a modelled pattern of behaviour will determine the amount of observational learning that can be exhibited behaviourally. Bandura (1977) contends that if the learner possesses the constituent elements of a skill, these can easily be integrated to produce new patterns of behaviour. If, on the other hand, the different response components are lacking, the behavioural reproduction will be lacking. The message for coaches here is that more complex skills should be broken down into constituent parts and practised until they are acquired, before they can be developed into more complex skills.

Although the sub-skills of a modelled behaviour may be acquired and retained, physical limitations may mean that the individual is unable to coordinate various actions in the modelled pattern and sequence. For example, a young child can learn observationally to take a corner kick in football and be adept at executing the component parts of the skill, but they may not have the power to take a good corner on a full size football pitch with a full size ball. It is, therefore, imperative to adapt the skills of sport to the age and levels of physical development of the participants in order to optimize their learning opportunities.

A further impediment at the behavioural level of reproducing motor skills is that performers cannot see the responses they are making at the actual time of performance (i.e. performance ambiguity). They are, therefore, dependent upon the feedback of others (particularly the coach) to correct and adjust their motor patterns. The ability to accurately observe and guide learners to refine their behaviours is, therefore, a crucial skill for coaches to develop. The learner usually has to self-correct on the basis of informative feedback, so unless this feedback is being given, and to a high level of accuracy and corrective information, learning is unlikely to occur. As already referred to in the attention and retention phases, modern technology allows for the use of video feedback during coaching sessions, and from an observational learning perspective can be utilized to enhance learning opportunities.

Reinforcement and motivation phase

According to Bandura (1977), human behaviour is extensively controlled by its consequences. Behaviours that result in unrewarding or punishing effects tend to be discarded, whereas those that produce rewarding consequences are generally strengthened. Reinforcement control is, therefore, an important factor in understanding human behaviour. Whilst acknowledging the importance of extrinsic feedback (i.e. external reinforcement) in reinforcing behaviour, social learning theory posits that individuals also regulate their behaviour on the basis of observed consequences (i.e. vicarious reinforcement) and consequences they create for themselves (i.e. self-reinforcement). These three different forms of reinforcement control are now considered.

In accordance with SLT, athletes do not enact everything they learn in coaching settings and are more likely to imitate behaviours because they believe that doing so will increase their chances of being positively reinforced by the coach (i.e. external reinforcement). Furthermore, a coach who repeatedly demonstrates desired responses, instructs others to reproduce them, physically prompts the behaviour when it fails to occur, and then administers rewards for successful execution will eventually elicit matching responses in most athletes. This process may require multiple demonstrations of the desired behaviours and external reinforcement, but if the coach persists the behaviour will eventually be evoked (Bandura 1977). Although the major focus is on specific motor skills, attitudes can also be acquired through observation. The coach should, therefore, exemplify and reward good standards of behaviour, attitudes and moral behaviour, if these are expectations they have of the learners. For example, if a coach expects punctuality and politeness, they should demonstrate and reinforce those behaviours. In cooperative situations (e.g. teams) the success of the group may be dependent on the peer models in that group; it is therefore just as important to identify and praise athletes with a high work ethic and motivation to learn as it is to recognize athletes with high ability levels, as these behaviours will be imitated by the group.

An athlete can acquire, retain, and possess the capabilities for skilful execution of modelled behaviour, but may rarely be activated into performing that behaviour if it is unfavourably received or negatively sanctioned by the coach. In contrast, when a positive incentive is provided by the coach, observational learning which may have previously remained unexpressed is promptly translated into action (Bandura 1965). Thus, unsurprisingly, athletes are more likely to adopt modelled behaviour if it results in positive rewards, feedback or praise by the coach (i.e. external reinforcement), than if it has unrewarding or punishing effects. This is consistent with a behaviourist approach (see Chapter 2) to coaching, but where social learning goes further is in its claim that observed consequences of behaviour influence model conduct in much the same way as actual behaviour. This is known as vicarious learning, i.e. the change in behaviour of observers resulting from the emotional responses of another person, as conveyed through facial, vocal and postural manifestations (i.e. vicarious reinforcement) (Bandura 1977), or indeed, a lack of these reactions. Thus, for example, if poor discipline or low levels of commitment and engagement go unpunished by the coach, other athletes are more likely to imitate these poor behaviours and diminish the quality of the coaching sessions. In contrast, if the coach wants certain behaviours to be replicated, they need to reinforce these behaviours with praise and rewards in order to evoke a positive emotional response from the performer, so that others will be more likely to replicate these behaviours. The observed consequences of behaviours are, therefore, important for social learning.

The notion that behaviour is controlled by its consequences can be interpreted to mean that actions are at the mercy of situational influences, whereas, behaviour is extensively self-regulated. Thus, athletes can observe their own behaviour, judge it against their own standards and reinforce or punish themselves (i.e. self-reinforcement). They therefore need to have expectations of their own performance and self-regulation strategies, both of which can be developed by the coach. Athletes learn to evaluate their behaviour partly on the basis of how the coach reacts to it. Coaches promote certain norms of what constitutes a worthy performance and are generally pleased when athletes achieve these standards and disappointed when they do not. As a consequence, athletes come to respond to their own behaviours in self-approving or self-critical ways, depending on how they compare with their coach's standards.

In conclusion, it is important to note that athletes do not passively absorb standards of behaviour from coaches and other athletes. Rather, the theory acknowledges the interrelationship between the individual, the environment and behaviour, known as reciprocal determinism (Bandura 1977). Thus expectations, self-perceptions, goals, and physical abilities all combine to direct behaviour in sport coaching contexts.

Albert Bandura: a practitioner commentary by Kerry Harris

Kerry is performance director and head coach at Cardiff Metropolitan University Women's Football Club. Kerry, a UEFA B license holder, is also a graduate of the university who later took a master's degree and subsequently a Ph.D. in sports coaching. She currently combines coaching with her lecturing role at Cardiff Met. Since she took over in 2003 the club has been successful in winning several British Universities and Colleges Sport (BUCS) league and championship titles, Football Association of Wales (FAW) domestic league and cup titles, and also twice securing a place in the Union of European Football Associations (UEFA) Women's Champions' League competition. Kerry has juggled the role with other coaching appointments such as assistant coach for the Great Britain women's football team at the World University Games in 2009.

Before reading this chapter I was already vaguely familiar with Bandura's work through my own academic study and teaching. However, I had only ever given superficial consideration to the implications for, and how it might be applied to, practice. Indeed, providing this commentary has been a beneficial experience in the sense that I was compelled to really think about and reflect on my practice in light of some of the more intricate aspects of SLT and modelling.

I initially stumbled on the notion of reciprocal determinism. It seemed a logical and certainly appropriate view of learning and behaviour. I agree with the shift away from the one-dimensional 'carrot and stick' approach of behaviourism and the humanist viewpoint of personal agency, or the exercise of free will, being the crux of determining behaviour. Learning is complex, certainly non-linear and whilst we often assume it's about individuals, I do not think we can escape the reality that it largely involves others. Personally, I've learnt more about coaching through observing and interacting with other coaches than I ever did through studying it on my own.

For me, modelling is an important aspect of my delivery as I'm sure it is for most other coaches. The very fact that this modelling can be a 'highly efficient' way of getting information across is a big 'selling point' and thus, makes it an attractive addition to most coaches' armoury. Indeed, I'm often 'on the clock' and our fixture schedule has a very quick turnaround and I do not always have enough time to spend on trial and error learning.

In the attentional phase, it can be extremely frustrating when you start a practice after instruction and demonstration, and it becomes apparent that players were not fully concentrating. I find myself constantly changing position and moving the group away from visual distractions and often, trying to bring to a halt 'the mothers meeting' taking place between players. Sometimes I use humour or a stern word or two, which works just as effectively. Beyond using an athlete's name, I think that questioning is also a good strategy for maintaining attention and keeping players focused and 'on their toes'. This section has also made me think about the other strategies I use to gain attention. I regularly use other audible cues, for example a loud-to-softer countdown of 3-2-1, or a sharp, high-pitched whistle. I find in relation to specific skills such as pressing, trigger words are also useful – something simple and easily remembered but also descriptive, such as 'touch-tight' to encourage the correct distance between the defender and the attacker. Linking it to the next aspect of modelling, the retention phase, players will remember these trigger words, verbal cues or 'calls' more so than long descriptions.

In relation to visual and verbal representations, I will sometimes demonstrate the skill myself or use another player. Doing the latter enables me to explain whilst the demonstration is taking place, and also ensure that those observing are giving the model their full attention. I am sometimes guilty of always using the same players to model practice, but those players are technically more capable than others, so naturally will provide the most accurate model.

Moving to the reproduction phase, here I would argue that the important thing is that players do not become bored, which often occurs when anything we do is rehearsed or repeated over and over again. The repetitive drill approach is something I include in all of my sessions. Despite its criticisms, I feel it is crucial especially for developmental players who I work with, who often come in to the club technically very 'raw'. I will usually incorporate these sorts of 'fine-tuning' activities either after, or as part of, the warm-up. Rarely are techniques ever mastered in a single session (no matter how good the model is) so they are often revisited in subsequent sessions. I strongly agree with the point that if players cannot perform isolated techniques then larger, more complex, skills will undoubtedly break down. However, I think it is important that the players understand where these skill components apply in a game; as they need to see the functional relevance. Additionally, in order to prevent boredom and maintain motivation, players need to be challenged.

I also agree that the application of modern technology can support the reproduction phase and self-evaluation, whilst also helping to motivate players. Symbolic modelling through the mass media can be an effective method of capturing attention. I'm in a fortunate position to be able to use modern technology through the equipment and support staff we have at the university. An excellent example of this is when we decided to apply a new aggressive defensive strategy in preparation for a major tournament. Using Atlético Madrid as an example of this defensive strategy saved hours of technical delivery, explanation and persuasion. Players were encouraged to use this match as a reference point. We asked them to watch and pay particular attention to what Atlético did when out of possession.

Albert Bandura: critical questions

1. What self-regulatory processes can athletes use to affect their own behaviour in sport coaching situations, and how are these processes learned?
2. What practical strategies might you use to gain the attention of a group of young athletes in order to teach them a skill or technique?
3. How can a coach use modern technology to enhance learning, and what are the advantages and disadvantages of this in comparison to coach or player demonstrations?
4. What is a component skill based approach to motor reproduction, and what are the potential issues associated with applying the skill in game situations?
5. From a reinforcement and motivational perspective, what can coaches do to get athletes to imitate desired behaviours?

References

Bandura, A. (1965) 'Influence of models' reinforcement contingencies on the acquisition of imitative responses', *Journal of Personality and Social Psychology*, 1: 589–595.

Bandura, A. (1977) *Social learning theory*, Englewood Cliffs, NJ: Prentice Hall.

Bandura, A. (1986) *Social foundations of thought and action: A social cognitive theory*, Englewood Cliffs, NJ: Prentice Hall.

Bandura, A. (2014) Albert Bandura's web page, Stanford University, retrieved 11 November 2014 from: http://stanford.edu/dept/psychology/bandura/

Gordon, N. J., Nucci, L. P., West, C. K., Hoerr, W. A., Uguroglu, M. E., Vukosavich, P. and Tsai, S. L. (1984) 'Productivity and citations of educational research: Using educational psychology as the data base', *Educational Researcher*, 13(7): 14–20.

Magill, R. A. (2007) *Motor learning and control: Concepts and applications* (8th edn), Boston: McGraw-Hill.

Wulfert, E. (2005) 'Social learning theory: Albert Bandura', in N. A. Piotrowski (ed.) *Psychology Basics*, Pasadena, CA: Salem Press, 787–793.

SECTION 2
Experiential theorists

4

JOHN DEWEY

Experience, inquiry, democracy, and community in coaching

David Day with Jackie Newton

John Dewey: a short biography

The originator of experimentalist philosophy and one of the most influential educational thinkers of the twentieth century, John Dewey was born on 20 October 1859, in Burlington, Vermont. Aged just fifteen, he enrolled at the University of Vermont, where he studied philosophy under H. A. P. Torrey. After graduating second in his class he taught at a seminary in Pennsylvania and at a private school in Vermont before studying philosophy and psychology at Johns Hopkins with George Sylvester Morris and G. Stanley Hall. Following this, he gained his doctorate in 1884 and became an assistant professor at the University of Michigan. He then went to the University of Minnesota in 1888 as a professor of philosophy, returning to Michigan the following year before being made head of the philosophy department at the University of Chicago in 1894.

At Chicago, he began his systematic study of the philosophy of education by establishing a department of pedagogy and founding the University Laboratory School as a site for experiments in educational thinking. Drawing on his findings, Dewey published several influential works, including *Interest in Relation to Training of the Will* (1896), *My Pedagogic Creed* (1897), *The School and Society* (1900), and *The Child and the Curriculum* (1902), in which he set out his practical pedagogy and explained the psychological and philosophical foundations on which it was based. His educational theories were informed by his belief that America's evolution from an agricultural to an industrial society should be reflected in its schools, and that an emphasis on the transmission of vocational skills and the development of discipline was no longer appropriate. Schools should be sites of interaction with the emergent technological culture, and the specific interests of the child, in finding out about things, in making things, and in artistic expression, should be encouraged.

Dewey resigned from Chicago in 1904 and accepted a joint appointment on the faculty of philosophy and the faculty of Teachers College at Columbia University in New York City. He continued to develop his educational theorising in works that included *Moral Principles in Education* (1909), *How We Think* (1910), *Democracy and Education* (1916), and *Experience and Education* (1938). During the 1920s and 1930s, Dewey lectured on educational reform all over the world, despite having formally retired in 1930. He remained an active member of educational organizations and was an advocate of professional teachers' unions. On 1 June 1952, Dewey died of pneumonia, aged 92, in New York.

John Dewey: key concepts

Dewey published more than 1,000 works covering psychology, educational theory, culture, religion, politics and philosophy, many of which were informed by his reading of the work of philosopher and psychologist William James. His philosophical stance was also influenced by German philosopher G. W. F. Hegel's argument that societies are in constant flux and that progress occurs as the result of a reconstructive synthesis of opposing trends and ideas. In time, however, Dewey rejected Hegel's view that progress occurs on a grand scale and he argued instead that progress tended to be piecemeal, resulting from individuals and groups engaging in a conscious reconstruction of their environment. An effective education system is critical because it provides an important primary tool for social reconstruction.

Dewey's philosophy of experimentalism, the notion that learning occurs through problem solving, or instrumentalism, the usefulness of scientific theories in predicting future events, largely centred on human experience and regarded ideas as tools for experimentation. For Dewey, humans generally behave out of habit and change leads to unexpected outcomes since it forces people to think creatively in order to maintain control of their shifting environment. An education based on the principle of learning through doing is essential in enabling people to abandon their habits and think creatively. Dewey also rejected the prevailing notion of the mind as only being relevant at the individual level, arguing instead that it is a function of social life. Mind was not a fixed entity but a process of engagement in discourse with, and participation in, civil society, through which the individual developed. Influenced by James, who published *The Principles of Psychology* in 1890, he suggested that psychology should not be restricted to solely dealing with knowledge because emotion and action also play an important role in learning. A continuous interaction between intellect and feelings, rather than solely relying on facts and logic, characterized the human psychological condition.

Dewey was influenced significantly by the naturalism of Charles Darwin, and it was from *The Origin of Species* (1859) that Dewey acquired his concept of the human being as a highly complex organism that continually accommodates itself to some environmental circumstances while altering others to meet its needs. Dewey conceived of education as evolutionary and without any firm rules, preferring instead to view it as an ongoing experiment in which the teacher leads the student to discover ways of adjusting to novel circumstances. In contrast to those Social Darwinists who held that the rich were the product of natural selection, Dewey interpreted individualism in terms of social cooperation and argued that a society could free the pupil from developmental constraints through its education system. Children could be guided at school to develop their own latent talents and capacities, which would prepare them to cope with life in the wider society. This Darwinian naturalism contributed to Dewey's adoption of several highly controversial views, such as arguing for equal education for women and co-educational classrooms at a time when many considered women intellectually inferior and co-education was believed to distract young men and lower standards. Equally controversial was his view that manual training should be integrated into education because learning involves the coordination of all human capacities, not just the intellect. Children should be taught weaving, carpentry, cooking, and gardening not only as examples of problem solving but also because such skills are fundamental to the notion of knowledge and provide tools for further discovery and learning. As a result, Dewey rejected the two-track system of education proposed by some educators who suggested that children should be tested and then directed into either 'vocational' or 'academic' schools. For Dewey, this separation would create a social chasm and merely reinforce the worst practices of the industrial system.

Experience, reflection, and pragmatic inquiry

Dewey's most concise statement on education, *Experience and Education* (1938), reflected how he had reformulated his ideas because of his educational experiences and in the light of critiques of his theories. His educational philosophy, as expressed here, proposes an orderly and dynamic educational system based on a learning environment that is both historical and social and one that respects all sources of experience. This philosophical perspective is grounded in Dewey's notion that people learn from experiences and their reflection on those experiences (Dewey 1902). He argued that education was a process of 'living and not a preparation for future living' (Dewey 1897: 78) and that learners must be actively engaged in domain-related practices (Dewey 1938). He conceived of education as a 'continuing reconstruction of experience' (Dewey 1897: 79) and believed that learners should be active participants functioning in a cyclical, transactional manner with their environments (Burden 2000: 467).

For Dewey, there was no intellectual growth without some 'reconstruction', i.e the rethinking and re-examining of old concepts and experiences in order to deal with the demands of the present (Vazir 2006: 445–446). He saw reflection as a further dimension of thought and defined reflective thinking as an active, careful, and persistent reconsideration of beliefs and knowledge (Dewey 1933). Reflection is a rational and purposeful act, and the purpose of any interaction is to derive learning from experience through reflective thinking, which led to inquiry through a scientific method, a process of experimentation that resulted in the formulating and testing of theory.

This represented an extension of themes first suggested by James and other American pragmatists such as Charles Sanders Peirce, who believed that inquiry should be undertaken in a controlled and experimental manner. Like other pragmatists, Dewey argued that all inquiry is initiated by doubt, an uneasy state in which equilibrium is lost. He outlined his own version of the pragmatic theory of inquiry in *How We Think* (1910), arguing that a five-step experimental method of inquiry is apparent wherever true thinking and learning occur.

1. First, there is an organic, emotional response to an unsettled or threatening situation. When circumstances inhibit a normal course of action, this triggers a search for alternatives in order to regain equilibrium.
2. Then there is an intellectual response when there is an attempt to collate the emotional responses and immediate suggestions to the confused situation into a precise formulation of the problem. Certain facts and interpretations are selected as appropriate to the situation and others rejected as irrelevant. While there are no selection rules, individuals can be helped to assess the relevance or irrelevance of data and their interpretation by teaching them good habits of inquiry in which alertness (being mentally responsive to situations), flexibility (being adaptable to change in the environment), and curiosity (being keen to explore the mental and physical landscape) are essential tools.
3. After the problem has been clarified, some hypothesis must be produced which could lead to a resolution. This has to be formulated carefully and based on the analysis undertaken in phase two. It must be testable, and it is critical that children be taught the distinction between a haphazard and unregulated suggestion based on an emotional response and a carefully formulated hypothesis.
4. The hypothesis is then subjected to reasoning, during which its possible consequences are worked out and its value relative to competing hypotheses calculated. Dewey thought that quantitative analysis often plays an important role at this stage since quantification allows generalization to and from other, better-known cases.
5. Finally, once the hypothesis has been subjected to reasoning, then the inquiry is devoted to tests that involve overt action. If results turn out as predicted, new habits of action are produced and doubt dissipates. Importantly, Dewey believed that even if the experiments fail, the process could still prove instructive.

Although critics accused Dewey of promoting 'scientism', the view that the scientific method should serve as the exemplar for all types of thinking, he replied that inquiry within the arts and humanities is also experimental. In history, for example, the researcher gathers information, synthesizes the material to postulate a theory or narrative of the past and then tests that perspective against further evidence. The result is that versions of the past are rarely uncontested and they often change as new 'data' emerges. Whatever the field, inquiry contributes to an overarching general method through which the various disciplines can communicate with one another.

The role of the teacher

Teachers are the agents through which knowledge and skills are communicated and rules of conduct enforced (Dewey 1938), and the role of the teacher is critical in educating a pupil into the five-step inquiry method. Dewey addressed this on a number of occasions as he responded to the positions taken by proponents and opponents of his educational philosophy. A number of Dewey's students were working in schools by the 1920s and their construction of child-centred curricula, which marginalized knowledge-based components, led to 'progressive education' becoming synonymous with 'self expression'. Dewey criticized some of his former students for their pedagogical extremism, a situation exacerbated further during the 1930s when the traditionalists called for a return to the fundamentals of the 'three Rs'. Their opponents argued that dividing the curriculum into subjects was inappropriate and that children should have freedom to decide what to study.

Dewey was aware that pedagogy tends to oscillate between these two extremes, with educators at one end of this continuum having little concern for the development of a child's experiences but seeing education as the rote memory of facts. Discipline was central to their view of education but, for Dewey, this approach lacked the active experimentation that allowed pupils to discover their own individual talents and most appropriate learning techniques. He argued that advocates of this approach were in danger of interpreting indoctrination as education and implementing a programme that would leave students poorly equipped to assess the wider context of their lives in a technological society. He was equally critical of those at the other pedagogical extreme, who considered the independent self-expression of the child, and not the mastery of subject matter, as the main goal of education. They abdicated their responsibilities by not providing guidance for their pupils and Dewey argued that, like a good gardener or metalworker, the good teacher cultivated and developed potential. The raw materials of the child's interests required skilful reconstruction and refinement and the teacher must play an active role by directing energies away from negative influences, focusing attention on important themes and problems, and helping the learner develop the tools needed to play a full role in society.

Dewey recognized that not all experiences are equally educational and everything depended on the quality of the experience, which could be enhanced through the choice of activities and the way in which it was structured (Cooperstein and Kocevar-Weidinger 2004: 145). As he pointed out, 'the central problem of an education based on experience is to select the kind of present experiences that live fruitfully and creatively in subsequent experiences' (Dewey 1938: 25–28). For Dewey, the teacher is critical to the educative process, although he or she should act as a facilitator in enabling students to solve problems, not as an instructor aiming to achieve specific, pre-determined goals (Burden 2000). The teacher needs to 'provide the materials and the conditions by which organic curiosity will be directed into investigations that have an aim and that produce results in the way of increase of knowledge' (Dewey 1933: 40).

Dewey emphasized that, before providing students with learning experiences, teachers must carefully consider the consequences of those experiences (Langton

2007). Although students' diverse backgrounds mean that an infinite range of past experiences need to be considered, the teacher should attempt to organize individualized learning experiences by selecting appropriate material and weaving that into the students' previous practice. The challenge lies in continually adapting subject matter to the growing databank of individual experiences. Education should emphasize both the individual and the teaching of subject matter that enables pupils to understand their social world. Educational methods should aim at developing the child's capacities and interests, and educators need to be provided with the requisite resources to perform their tasks. In return, a community should demand that its educational system be a primary agent of social progress.

Democracy, community, and citizenship

For Dewey, his self-corrective method of inquiry formed the basis both for sound educational theory and practice and for use as a primary tool for the development of democratic institutions. Experiencing and learning take place in socio-cultural and political contexts (Berding 1997: 29) and inquiry was not only to be used as a pedagogical method in schools, it was also the means by which citizens became informed, communicated interests, created public opinion, and made decisions. The concept of democracy, in which the welfare of the majority was paramount, underpinned all of his thinking since he saw it as a way of creating more effective and harmonious social environments (Dewey 1916). In order to develop his democratic ideal, individuals must be taught to develop new tools for discovery and learning that would enable them to work together with other societal members to identify and realize common goals. Dewey's naturalism is reflected in his rejection of the view that education is merely preparation for some future occupation or that it should be solely concerned with the absorption of accumulated knowledge or the unfolding of dormant capacities. Education is central to democratic practice since it equips individuals for full participation in social life through promoting social interaction.

From his commitment to democracy, Dewey developed his notion of community, the collective within which the individual is situated, his belief in the possibility of citizenship as a mutual enterprise that addresses social ills, and his belief in the school as the potential model of democracy. Community, which linked school and society, was important as a basic human drive and remained at the core of Dewey's social philosophy. Communal association developed the moral (i.e. how one should behave), intellectual (i.e. the ability to think and reason), and emotional (i.e. the expression of feelings) aspects of life, as well as the foundation of democracy, so it is no surprise that Dewey argued for organizing the school along the lines of a 'miniature community' (Dewey 1916: 418). One reason to democratize the schools was to have students experience the mutuality of social life through collaboration. Where schoolwork consists in simply learning lessons, mutual assistance, a natural form of cooperation and association is not encouraged. Where active work is taking place, helping others becomes central to the process (Dewey 1900).

Dewey's modern-day critics claim that he has been responsible for the under-mining of the kinds of instruction that could lead to the development of character and the strengthening of the will, and that his educational philosophy has had a disastrous influence on moral behaviour (White 2015). However, Dewey never advocated the kinds of character-eroding pedagogy he is accused of promoting (White 2015). 'Character' and the role of the will always occupied a prominent position in his thinking and he consistently urged teachers to provide mature guidance, while insisting on the moral foundation and responsibilities of democracy (Dewey 1946: 234). For Dewey, because knowledge that does not affect conduct is of little or no value, education is a training of character and training for citizenship, which is one means of expressing character. Character is developed as an individual comes to understand and appreciate the consequences of his or her conduct, and the school acts as a laboratory in which relations and connections can be explored. Dewey also argued that a principal aim of education is the development of critical tools that a student can employ to help them distinguish between what is 'valued' and what may prove to be 'valuable'. What is 'valued' remains private and personal, subject to the vagaries of personal interpretation, while what is 'valuable' is that which has proven to be of value within a democratic community of inquiry.

John Dewey: applications to sports coaching

Experience, reflection, and pragmatic inquiry

If learning about coaching or developing the skills required by athletes involves the synthesis of all their capacities, then coaching and coach education programmes based on the principle of learning through doing are essential. In enabling coaches and athletes to question their habits and think creatively they need to be introduced to a range of activities, not just those that are sport specific, to act as problem-solving exemplars because the skills developed through that process are fundamental to the notion of knowledge and provide tools for further discovery and learning. Coach education programmes need to appreciate, therefore, that a carefully structured learning environment that values all sources of experience is critical, since coaches learn from experiences and their reflection on those experiences. Any coaching educator, especially when leading courses at the early levels of the certification system, would be well advised, for example, to become quickly acquainted with the backgrounds of those attending the programme, some of whom will have sport-specific experiences to draw on while others bring different, but equally valuable, life experiences with them. By sharing and broadening their personal experiences under the facilitative hand of the coach educator, nascent coaches can then be provided with tools and scenarios that inform and underpin the five-step inquiry process, especially if the course also incorporates sufficient space for reflection. At the same time, it is also important to ensure that coaches actively engage in domain-related practice if they are to achieve the intended outcomes from their learning.

Coach education and the development of athletes at all levels is a 'continuing reconstruction of experience', the rethinking and re-examining of concepts and experiences in order to deal with the demands of the present, and, in that respect, athletes and coaches are active participants in their learning, operating in a cyclical, transactional manner with their sporting environments. Rational and purposeful reflection, an ongoing reconsideration of beliefs and knowledge, is central to this process. The purpose of any interaction in coach education programmes or during coaching sessions, therefore, would be to initiate learning from experience through reflective thinking and engagement with Dewey's scientific method.

Coaches are regularly faced with situations that test their ability to react appropriately, whether that be in dealing with a novel situation during a training session, or a threatening one that emerges during a coach education course, such as being asked to deliver a session at a moment's notice. In these situations, if Dewey is correct, coaches automatically employ a five-step experimental method of inquiry, beginning with an emotional response, which triggers a search for alternative courses of action. The coach being asked to deliver a session at short notice experiences a moment of indecision, maybe even mild panic, about how to tackle the problem before exhibiting stage two, an intellectual response in which the coach draws on experiential knowledge to select appropriate alternatives while rejecting others as irrelevant. Coaches are helped in handling this process if they have been educated into good habits of inquiry either formally through coach education programmes or informally through their coaching networks. After the problem has been intellectualized, a possible coaching template is produced, which is then considered carefully before being tested through its active implementation. If the impromptu coaching session is effective, then the coach now has the appropriate experiential tools to employ when faced with similar challenges. If the session falls short of expectations, then the coach still has further information to work with next time around.

The role of the coach

The process of inquiry and reflection needs training and guidance in its use and the role of coaches, through whom knowledge and skills are communicated and rules of conduct enforced, is critical. Not all sporting experiences are equally educational and everything depends on the quality of the experience, something that can be enhanced through the choice of activities, and by the manner in which they are structured by the coach. Following the principles suggested by Dewey, the coach should act as a facilitator in enabling athletes to solve problems, not as an instructor aiming to achieve specific, predetermined goals. However, as with the conflicting pedagogical methods witnessed by Dewey, sports coaching practices can sit anywhere on a continuum that extends from 'laissez faire' at one end to authoritarian at the other, a perspective often characterized by a focus on the rote repetition of skills and an emphasis on immediate outcomes. In this form of coaching, the central philosophy is discipline, not the active experimentation that allows athletes (or coaches on coach education courses) to discover their own talents and best techniques for learning. Advocates of this approach view coaching as a form of indoctrination and are not concerned with equipping athletes to assess the wider context of their lives.

At the other extreme, coaches consider 'fun' and not the mastery of skills, as the main goal of sports participation, and they often interpret their role as being non-interventionist. In doing so, they fail to fulfil their responsibilities to the athlete in providing guidance or cultivating and developing potential. The development of individual skills and talents requires skilful reconstruction and refinement so the coach must be active in managing the athlete, directing energies away from negative influences and focusing attention on important themes and problems. The coach needs to 'select the kind of present experiences that live fruitfully and creatively in subsequent experiences' (Dewey 1938: 25–28) and to provide the resources and environment that direct the athlete 'into investigations that have an aim and that produce results in the way of increase of knowledge' (Dewey 1933: 40). It is critical, therefore, that before designing sessions aimed at providing certain experiences, coaches carefully consider the consequences of those experiences. In doing so, of course, the coach (or coach educator) has to recognize that the diverse back-grounds of participants creates a range of experiences for the coach to consider so learning experiences need to be individualized where possible. The challenge lies in continually adapting these as the athlete develops.

Democracy, community, and citizenship

Common assumptions are often made about the value of sport as a preparation for life, a view that has its roots in the amateur ideals that underpinned the early years of sport. Adherents to the ethos of amateurism viewed sport as an arena for the development of character and the strengthening of the will, values which are still ascribed to sporting participation today. While this perspective is by no means uncontested, sport does take place in socio-cultural contexts so coaches and coach educators should at least consider Dewey's notion that they might be responsible for teaching personal and physical skills that enable athletes and coaches to understand their social world. In sport, individuals have to develop new tools for discovery and learning that enable them to work together with others to identify and realize common goals, and sports teams provide a vehicle, a 'minia-ture community' (Dewey 1916: 418), through which notions of community and citizenship, the fundamentals of democracy, can be developed. Coaches and coach educators can help in developing this concept of community by encoura-ging the importance of mutual assistance and collaboration in their practice and by actively promoting engagement with the wider social context. Coaches might, for example, develop peer involvement by devolving responsibility to athletes during coaching sessions or encourage their athletes to share their expertise with local schoolchildren and disadvantaged groups in order to raise social awareness.

John Dewey: a practitioner commentary by Jackie Newton

As a qualified teacher, with an M.A. in Coaching Studies, my lifelong involvement in athletics teaching and coaching has always raised questions in my mind about the most effective ways of delivering material to the individuals that I work with, whatever their level of ability. I am a UKA level three coach currently coaching cross-country athletes at university level and several international athletes, many of them in my role as a performance manager for a National Governing Body (NGB). I have other responsibilities as a coach educator and manager for national teams, which includes delivering coaching camps as well as accompanying athletes to international competitions. In all of these roles, I recognize the benefit of *experience* and I constantly find myself referring back to my own athletic performances at national and international level, as well as drawing on the practices and approaches adopted by the coaches who were most influential in my own development.

Many of the key concepts in this chapter resonate with me. As I have become more experienced as a coach, I have become more *reflective* and I try to make my athletes more reflective in their performance and training evaluations. The answers to questions such as 'What is working?' and 'What do we/I need to change?' are addressed continuously in the drive to improve both my coaching practice and the athlete's performance. For me, the thinking around change being the catalyst for breaking habit and creating new plans and practices is an interesting one, and stimulates consideration of the need to assess continuously the effectiveness of practice that has become *habit*. Do we become 'stuck in a rut' to some extent with our coaching practice and, as a result, in the training sessions that we give to our athletes? What change do we need to happen in order to abandon habits? A bad performance? An injury? Performances hitting a plateau? Surely, it would be better to *change* things before any of this happens, and so the key here would be to continuously *reflect*, assess, evaluate and make the changes before things go wrong.

One particular area of development of my own coaching skill that I have focused on in recent times is the use of questioning to stimulate deeper thinking and consideration from an athlete before and after training sessions and competitions. By asking an athlete how they would deal with a situation, I aim to stimulate mental rehearsal of their plans and to help them in contingency planning for when things do not go as expected. For example, 'so, you want to go out hard in this race? What will you do in the ten minutes before the gun goes to be ready for that? What will you do if there is a delay to the start?' (adjusting to *novel circumstances*). Reflecting on actions taken can also be enhanced with skilful questioning. My aim is to choose the questions that will help the athlete to understand how they may do things differently in future in order to progress. In my experience, the coaching skill here is to pick the right time to ask the questions, neither too soon nor too late after the event, and to help the athlete to objectively analyse their performance. Without the 'right' questions, the athlete sometimes 'tells the story' of their performance without considering how they may have done it differently or better (learn from the *experience*).

For me, Dewey's five-step experimental method of inquiry is useful and, although I had never thought of it as a step process before, I recognize that, when doubt creeps into an athlete's mind, this five-step approach occurs. As a coach, I feel that step one is crucial to both athlete and coach since this emotional response informs their learning. From that point, the coach should be there to guide the athlete in interpreting the data and selecting the most appropriate hypothesis. Again, this resonates as I find that much of my time is spent in this role. For some athletes, their choice of action can be irrational when they are upset as, for example, when they react to a poor performance by training more often and pushing themselves harder, when what they really need to do is to back off, recover and allow their body to rebuild.

After reading the chapter, I have been thinking more deeply around the concept of democracy, community and citizenship. As a coach (and team manager) in individual sports, I did not, at first, connect with Dewey's thinking around the creation of more harmonious, social environments. Although we strive for a supportive and harmonious training environment, once the athletes move from that training environment to the competition, they often become rivals and the competition goal may not be a common one. This is not always the case, however. There are times when team-mates will run the race tactically to get the best result for 'the team'. From my own experience, as an athlete, I experienced this most unequivocally, when I spent time training and competing in the American collegiate system. As a team, we trained together every day of the week and our common goal was to get the best result for the team with individual success a secondary aim. This cooperation and collaboration in training led to deep-rooted friendships and positive social experiences along with the learning about training and racing. This chapter has prompted me to recall this experience and to think of strategies I may put in place to create more of a team ethos in the individual sport training environment.

John Dewey: critical questions

1. If previous life experiences do play a vital role in learning, do different coaching experiences have different impacts because of individual characteristics?
2. Do successive coaching experiences lead to the development of more complex problem-solving capacities as Dewey suggests?
3. While Dewey asserts the value of experiential learning, is 'experience' enough or do coaches need a significant amount of formal training as well?
4. Although Dewey argues for the role of reflection in learning, can it be empirically demonstrated that reflection creates learning by linking experience and education?
5. Can coaching and coach education programmes be developed that model Dewey's five phases?
6. Dewey recognized that the pedagogical environment is populated by traditionalists and progressives. How should coaches strike a balance between the two extremes of the coaching continuum?

7.   For Dewey, an educational process following his principles would enhance an individual's social awareness. If that is true, can participation in coaching lead to a valuing of community?

8.   Dewey believed in encouraging cooperation and helping others in the learning environment. Can this sense of mutuality be fostered in the competitive world of sport and, if so, under what types of coaching leadership?

References

Berding, J. W. A. (1997) 'Towards a flexible curriculum: John Dewey's theory of experience and learning', *Education and Culture*, 14(1): 24–31.

Burden, R. L. (2000) 'Psychology in education and instruction', in K. and M. R. Rosenzweig (eds) *The international handbook of psychology*, London: Sage, 466–478.

Cooperstein, S. E. and Kocevar-Weidinger, E. (2004) 'Beyond active learning: A constructivist approach', *Reference Services Review*, 32(2): 141–148.

Dewey, J. (1986) *Interest in relation to training of the will*, Bloomington, IL: Public School Publishing Company.

Dewey, J. (1897) 'My pedagogic creed', *The School Journal*, 543: 77–80.

Dewey, J. (1900) *The school and society*, Chicago: University of Chicago Press.

Dewey, J. (1902) *The child and the curriculum*, Chicago: University of Chicago Press.

Dewey, J. (1909) *Moral principles in education*, Boston: Houghton Mifflin.

Dewey, J. (1916) *Democracy and education*, New York: Macmillan.

Dewey, J. (1933 [1910]) *How we think*, Boston: D. C. Heath & Co.

Dewey, J. (1938) *Experience and education*, New York: Collier.

Dewey, J. (1946) *Problems of men*, New York: Philosophical Library.

James, W. (1890) *The principles of psychology*, London: Macmillan.

Langton, T. W. (2007) 'Applying Laban's movement framework in elementary physical education', *Journal of Physical Education, Recreation and Dance*, 78(1): 17–53.

Vazir, N. (2006) 'Reflection in action: Constructive narratives of experience', *Journal of Reflective Practice*, 7(4): 445–454.

White, B. (2015) 'Scapegoat: John Dewey and the character education crisis', *Journal of Moral Education*, DOI: 10.1080/03057240.2015.1028911.

5

DONALD SCHÖN

Learning, reflection, and coaching practice

Christine Nash

Donald Schön: a short biography

Donald Alan Schön (1930–1997) was born in Boston, Massachusetts and raised in Brookline and Worcester. He graduated from Yale in 1951 where he studied philosophy, but it was his research into the development of reflective practice for which he is remembered. He was also an accomplished pianist and clarinetist, which he studied at the Sorbonne in Paris. In 1952 he married Nancy Quint, an eminent sculptor. He gained both his master's and doctorate in philosophy from Harvard and started lecturing at UCLA in 1953. After a short time in the army, Schön became director of the Institute for Applied Technology in the National Bureau of Standards at the US Department of Commerce. He then moved to direct the Organization for Social and Technological Innovation (OSTI), a non-profit social research and development firm in the Boston area. Around this time Schön published his first two books, *Displacement of Concepts* (1963) and *Technology and Change: The New Heraclitus* (1967). As a result, he became a visiting professor at the Massachusetts Institute of Technology in 1968 and became full-time in 1972 with his appointment as Ford Professor of Urban Studies and Education.

During this time he still displayed an interest in music, playing with both jazz and chamber groups. His passion for jazz and the improvisation required within some aspects of performance led to the development of his concept of 'thinking on one's feet' – the theory of improvisation. Schön believed that people and organizations should be flexible and incorporate their life experiences and lessons learned throughout their life. However, it was Schön's work on reflective practice that has had a profound impact in all professional fields and has challenged practitioners to learn from their experience to achieve excellence in the art of professional practice. He made his mark in the fields of organization theory and pedagogy by studying how innovation occurs and how individuals and organizations learn. Schön's best-known books are *Displacement of Concepts* (1963), *Beyond the Stable State*

(1973), *Theory in Practice* (with Chris Argyris, 1974), *Organizational Learning* (with Chris Argyris, 1978), *The Reflective Practitioner* (1983), *Educating the Reflective Practitioner* (1987) and *Frame Reflection* (with Martin Rein, 1994). Donald Schön died on 13 September 1997, in hospital after a seven-month illness.

Donald Schön: key concepts

Schön's interest in professional knowledge and education would lead him to develop an overall epistemology of professional practice, based on the concepts of learning processes in organizations, and subsequent practices to change them. Over the course of his long and distinguished career Schön's work covered three distinct areas:

1. The learning society
2. Professional learning and effectiveness
3. The reflective practitioner.

The learning society

Generally, Donald Schön is best known for his research around reflective practice. However, his earlier work around the nature of learning systems and the significance of learning in changing societies has changed the value and importance of learning. In the current climate of globalization, the need for lifelong learning has been reinforced, highlighting that individuals may not stay in the same job for life, necessitating the updating of existing skills and learning new skills (Spring 2009). So learning should not be viewed as specific instances, taking place at traditional sites of learning, such as schools or universities, but as a continuous, ongoing process.

Schön says that belief in the stable state 'is belief in the unchangeability, the constancy of central aspects of our lives, or belief that we can attain such a constancy' (Schön 1973: 9). This notion of stability, or performing the same function over a period of time, has diminished both in life and the workplace, meaning that society and organizations are in a state of change, or flux. Schön referred to this as '*continuous* processes of transformation' and held that society must constantly expect change to be the new natural state (Schön 1973). He urged organizations to develop the capacity to embrace change, saying that the only way for this to happen was for both individuals and organizations to become better learners.

Schön's book, *Beyond the Stable State: Public and Private Learning in a Changing Society*, which was published in 1973, provided the platform for many of his later conceptions and research into reflective practice. He had concerns around issues in professional learning and learning processes in organizations, and considered that people needed to constantly update and reinvent themselves. His thinking around notions such as 'the learning society' has become an integral part of the culture of education in the broadest sense.

Given, at the time of his writing, the influence of traditional sites of learning, for example universities and the recognition of their training for key professions (e.g.

law and medicine), there were a number of criticisms levelled at the concept of a learning society. The main criticism surrounds the very concept, with many proponents stating that this does not exist. There has been considerable debate about learning organizations, although it is very difficult to identify real-life examples. According to Naik (2011) this may be because the vision is 'too ideal' or because the organization cannot see the relevance to their core business. Many organizations do not see the longer-term benefits of investing in the social capital of the workplace, which is necessary for the learning society to flourish.

Professional learning and effectiveness

What is professional practice and how is effectiveness judged? The answer to this question on the surface may appear to be obvious – after all, how do people enter and move through the workplace, how are employees hired, promoted and fired from professions and organizations if this is not based on some objective criteria of effectiveness? There are clear links to Schön's thoughts on the learning society as there is recognition of the benefits of a stable institutional framework within organizations and the knowledge base that professionals require to exercise their skills. There are clear differences in the basis and subsequent understanding of professional practice.

Both Glazer (1974) and Schein (1974) shared an understanding of professional practice rooted in the positivist philosophy which so powerfully shaped both early practice and the modern conception of the proper relationship of theory and practice. Rigorous professional practice is frequently conceived as essentially technical. Its rigour is predicated on the use of describable, testable, replicable techniques derived from scientific research, based on knowledge that is objective, agreed by all in the profession, cumulative, and having a 'correct solution' to professional problems. This is a very linear process: A leading to B, then C; however, this approach can reduce the study of complex human situations and issues to a formulaic approach.

Schön's (1983, 1987) alternative view is opposed to this technical and rational approach, proposing instead that professional learning and knowledge is rooted in an individual's ability to actually *do the job*. Many professionals are not able to verbalize why they act in the manner that they do – they do this seemingly automatically. Schön considered that in these situations professionals used their previous experience and work-based knowledge as a frame for action which differed from the technocratic view of positivism and rationalism. Modern professional practice, Schön claimed, must function in a situation characterized by limited resources, a plurality of paradigms, multiple agents with a manifold of political and professional interests and a deconstructed and delegitimized idea of positivist science and epistemology. The implication of this is that professional practice is no longer to be understood as a mechanical application of scientifically based rules, but should instead be conceived of as the practitioner's work with unique situations in differing but equally challenging contexts.

As a result, professional education should emphasize problem solving, but apparently the most urgent and difficult issues of professional practice were those of actually recognizing what the problem was. Professionals in many different fields do sometimes find ways of coping effectively, even sensibly, with situations of complexity and uncertainty. If the element of art in professional practice is understood, known, and teachable, it does appear occasionally to be learnable, perhaps intuitively (Nash and Collins 2006). This ability to recognize issues, appreciate the underlying causes and solve problems is an indicator of effectiveness, particularly if rooted in the context of professional practice.

The reflective practitioner

Reflective practice can refer to the ability to analyse one's own practice, the incorporation of problem solving into learning by doing, or application of critical theory to the examination of professional practice. The importance of reflecting as part of the learning process has been emphasized by many investigators (Schön 1987; Argyris 2004). However, this is not a recent concept as Dewey (1933) was among the first to identify reflection as a specialized form of thinking (see Chapter 4). Schön's early work was influenced by Dewey's theory of inquiry, the subject of his doctoral dissertation. Dewey's ideas provided a basis for the concept of 'reflective practice' which gained influence with the arrival of Schön's (1983) *The Reflective Practitioner: How Professionals Think in Action*. In this seminal work, Schön identified ways in which professionals could become aware of their implicit knowledge and learn from their experience. His main concern was to facilitate the development of reflective practitioners rather than describe the process of reflection *per se*. However, one of his most important and enduring contributions was to identify two types of reflection: reflection-in-action (i.e. thinking while doing) and reflection-on-action (i.e. after-the-event thinking).

Reflection-in-action is the almost unconscious reflective process that happens instantaneously during an event when the professional is required to solve a problem. Schön (1983) postulated that professionals drew on their repertoire of skills, knowledge, and previous experiences in order to resolve the issue. Reflection-on-action takes place after the event and is seen to be a more deliberate process. It incorporates a retrospective analysis and critical review of actions and consequences.

Dewey's (1933) philosophy has influenced the development of several theories of how individuals construct knowledge through experience (for example Schön 1983; Kolb 1984). The common thread among these theories is that knowledge and learning are fundamentally embedded in the activity and context. Furthermore, knowledge construction is dependent on reflecting on problems encountered in the activity. In Schön's first book in this area, *The Reflective Practitioner* (1983), he identified the learning process distinct to professionals in a number of empirical settings. His follow-up book, *Educating the Reflective Practitioner* (1987), discusses some of the educational implications of this theory of learning.

During this time, Schön also formed a successful professional relationship with Chris Argyris, examining conscious and unconscious reasoning processes. This relates clearly to the concepts of reflection-on-action and reflection-in-action.

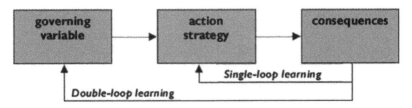

FIGURE 5.1 Argyris and Schön's (1974) conceptualization of single- and double-loop
learning

They proposed that practioners rely on concept maps to govern their actions,
referred to as theories-in-use. Theories-in-use can be explained as an individual's
worldview and how that relates to the values implied by their behaviour.

In Figure 5.1, the governing variable can be explained as the values or beliefs of
an individual, which leads to actions. All actions have consequences, intended or
otherwise, although Argyris and Schön (1974) believed that consequences could
arise as a result of not taking action or being prevented from taking the desired
action. The learning that arises from this process can also vary significantly, with
the majority of individuals only questioning their actions, thus accepting the goals
and values surrounding the actions without question. This is represented by single-
loop learning in Figure 5.1. By contrast, double-loop learning questions underlying
assumptions and values, enabling change to occur at both governing variable and
action strategy stages in Figure 5.1. Double-loop learning is viewed as the more
effective way of making informed decisions about the design and implementation
of action plans or maps (Argyris and Schön 1974).

Schön (1987) claimed that reflective practice is one of the cornerstones of a
profession. Although coaching is not currently viewed as a profession in the traditional sense, there are considerable attempts to address both initial education and
ongoing accreditation, and reflection should play an integral role in this development. Indeed reflective practice is a benchmark in many established professions, for
example teaching and law, and the ability to reflect on professional practice is one
of the traits of developing expertise (Mamede and Schmidt 2004).

Criticisms of Schön's work

While Schön's work has inspired many models of reflection and categories of
reflective practice, it has also drawn criticism. For example, Eraut (2004) considers
Schön to be more concerned with countering the technical rationality argument
subscribed to by Glazer (1974) and Schein (1974). As a result his analysis of
everyday practice is not clear and there is little recognition of how reflective processes might vary from one context to another. Boud and Walker (1998) agree that
Schön's analysis ignores critical features of the context of reflection. Moon (1999),
whose work has recently become highly cited within the context of sport coaching,
regards Schön's pivotal concept of reflection-in-action as unachievable. Ekebergh
(2009) proposed that nowadays reflection is often used as a method that has its

roots in Schön's theory of developing knowledge in action through reflection. This approach to reflection has been investigated within nursing, leading to an understanding that reflection should never be objectified or reduced to a separate process. Again phenomenologists have argued that it is not possible to create the distance from the particular context to reflect in the moment. Van Manen (1998) supports this perspective, proposing that real self-reflection can only be achieved by stepping out of the situation and reflecting retrospectively. Given this level of criticism, questions have to be raised about the widespread acceptance of Schön's work and the way it has been applied in professional practice, education, and more recently sport coaching (Usher et al. 1997; see Chapter 14). There have been calls for a more critical, reflexive exploration of the nature of reflective practice.

Donald Schön: applications to sports coaching

Schön conducted most of his work within the context of professional practice. However, in many countries sport coaching does not fulfil the necessary criteria for achieving professional status. This does not mean that many of the principles surrounding professional standing and development have not been adopted by a number of sport coaches and coaching organizations. The value attached to learning opportunities provided to sport coaches has grown significantly in the past few years (Knowles et al. 2005; Gilbert et al. 2009; Nash and Sproule 2012).

Schön's theory of reflective practice highlights the construction of domain-specific knowledge in the context of professional practice, an essential aspect in coaching, where coaches construct coaching knowledge through coaching experience. Schön's theories propose that learning occurs by experimenting with strategies used to overcome problems, which builds the individual's domain-specific knowledge necessary for professional activity. Coaching has been referred to as complex and even messy, necessitating non-standard solutions to its problems. This reinforces the need for sports coaches to consider Schön's concepts of knowing in action, being able to *do* the job and backing Schön's call for a new epistemology of practice. The practice of sports coaching would not support the technocratic approach, as coaching is not a linear process.

The roles of sport coaches have expanded beyond the preparation of athletes into administrative, managerial, and organizational responsibilities all underpinned by the coach's responsibility to develop and manage interpersonal relationships. Schön (2001) wrote about the problems arising when professions started to question themselves and their accepted practice as far back as 1972, stating:

> They were beginning to become aware of the indeterminate zones of practice – the situations of complexity and uncertainty, the unique cases that require artistry, the elusive task of problem-setting, the multiplicity of professional identities – that have since become increasingly visible and problematic.
>
> *(Schön 2001: 186)*

He attributed this growing disquiet to the rise of self-reflection within professional practice, and indeed the quote above could easily relate to the professional practice of sport coaching.

Clearly the role of the coach and the demands of coaching practice suggest that coaches would, and should, employ Schön's theories of reflection-in-action and reflection-on-action. According to Schön (1983) the use of these theories promotes professional growth – allowing the coach to develop both cognitively and behaviourally (Gilbert and Trudel 2004). As mentioned previously, reflection-in-action happens instantaneously, often tacitly, and can be likened to coaches' decision-making in practice or competition. These decisions can later be reviewed as reflection-on-action, perhaps as part of a reflective conversation. Schön suggested that there is a clear process to be followed, which when applied to coaching would entail the following: identifying the problem in the context or coaching environment; trying various solutions to solve this problem using their existing knowledge and experiences. This in turn can lead to further experimentation and reflection, leading to coaches extending their repertoire of solutions and building their experiences.

Argyris and Schön's (1974) conceptualization of double-loop learning provides an alternative notion of reflection to the simplistic single-loop form of reflection posed by the mnemonic 'Plan, Do, Review'. The popular Plan, Do, Review model refers to the steps that coaches should take when delivering sessions. Many coaches view this simplistic notion as contrived, as it does not demonstrate the level of detail, knowledge or decision-making skills that coaches must utilize on a regular basis. This approach to reflection is grounded in a positivist, linear conception of sport coaching practice. If coaches were to follow the Plan, Do, Review process then the likelihood is that they are not actually reflecting upon their practice. Indeed, in the Review stage of the reflective process, it is likely that the coach will only question their actions in the Do stage, rather than their values and beliefs (i.e. an example of single-loop learning).

For sport coaches to become reflective professional practitioners, they must question their own philosophies and underlying principles (i.e. double-loop learning). Many coaches have not formed, or find it difficult to articulate, their coaching philosophy and this correlates with limitations in their coaching behaviours and practices (Nash et al. 2008). More recently, Martindale and Collins (2015) suggest a list of questions that coaches might use as a guide to reflect upon their role and philosophy. By engaging with these deeper-level questions the sport coach can relate to the concept of double-loop learning (Argyris and Schön 1974) and challenge assumptions. In other words, sport coaches must question the decisions or actions that they make, but for true reflective practice to occur they must also question the fundamental values and motivations that influenced that decision.

Donald Schön: a practitioner commentary by a swimming coach

The practitioner in this commentary is a 38-year-old female swimming coach who has been coaching for twelve years at a national level. She currently is registered as a Head Coach with

USA Swimming, having completed the American Swim Coaches' Association Level 3 courses. As a Head Coach she has overall responsibility for the swimmers aged 6–19, but works almost exclusively with her senior swimmers, usually over twelve years old but based upon performance. She works with five assistant coaches and has a year-round programme.

As a swimming coach I have heard of reflective practice since I started coaching – it was something talked about on coach education courses as a matter of course. I always thought that I did reflect but now that I have read the information about Donald Schön and his process of reflection I would revise that statement. I now consider that I have evaluated my practice mostly as part of the 'Plan, Do, Review' process advocated as a key component of quality coaching practice. While this has been useful I feel that there was little depth or real thought about the implications for my coaching. For example, if something went wrong I would look to solve the immediate problem to ensure that it did not happen again rather than looking at the deeper, underlying issues. As a result of working together on this chapter I have undergone a thorough evaluation of my coaching, including recognizing my strengths and weaknesses and identifying reflection as a key strategy to support my future coaching practice.

One of the areas that has become a lot clearer is the actual definition of the term 'reflective practice'. Previously I had thought of it as something that you carried out after a training session, like a prescriptive list of questions that could be asked and answered relatively quickly and easily. Instead of it being this list of questions that I answer solely at the end of a training session I think of it as a process to makes sense of my experiences, not just after training sessions but also during swim meets, interactions with swimmers, parents and assistant coaches, and club meetings. I think this approach helps me to make more sense of the bigger picture, to see my coaching in a more holistic manner, which also allows me to understand how all the various aspects fit together and impact on the swimmers, swim team, and my coaching practice. I now realize the term 'reflective practice' has a number of meanings that all embrace Schön's ideal whether I am engaging in solitary intro-spection, critical dialogue with other coaches or ongoing debate with the club's committee or swimming organizations.

How I react to certain situations that arise during practice I now recognize as being reflection-in-action and by revisiting some of these situations after training I can begin to recognize patterns in my decision-making process. I still need much more practice to refine this further, but actually recognizing some of the mistakes that I continue to make on an ongoing basis has been very helpful. Once I become more used to this type of regular and structured process of reflection I think it will become easier. As I mentioned earlier, my 'reflection' was structured but now I am more interested in questioning my actions ('Why did I do that?') rather than questioning the outcomes ('Why did my swimmer do that?'). According to Schön (1983: 68)

> The practitioner allows himself to experience surprise, puzzlement, or confu-
> sion in a situation which he finds uncertain or unique. He reflects on the

phenomenon before him, and on the prior understandings which have been implicit in his behavior.

As Schön suggests, I am now realizing that situations that occur during coaching do not fulfil the 'one size fits all' criteria and I now question these situations more. For example, I realize that coaching is complex, much more complex than I initially realized, and there are no easy answers. I do feel that I react more intuitively to circumstances and actually have more belief in my reactions than I used to have. It also allows me to consider more options for solving coaching problems than I previously thought possible. My options used to be A or B but I would now see these options as opposite ends of a continuum, with many more choices in between.

I also recognize that my actions do not always reflect my thinking and I am now taking steps to address that. I always thought that I asked a lot of questions while I was coaching and gave my swimmers the opportunity to answer these. It would appear that I do not always do this – I do not ask as many questions as I thought I did and when I do ask questions I also tend to answer them as well. This is partly due to the time pressures that we are under, as we never seem to have as much water time as we need so we try to make the most of what we have. I still feel that questioning is the right approach to take but I need to balance that with the aims of the session and the available pool time. I am now taking two different approaches to questioning: first, if I want to check understanding and learning this will take more time so I have to choose the appropriate moment to use this method of questioning. Second, I am asking questions that the swimmers know the answer to, mostly as a reminder, or check and challenge to them to get them thinking, for example: 'Are you catching enough of the water at entry?'

I would say that this has been a valuable process for me and has helped me develop my coaching. It has certainly made me think but I need to consolidate my learning and allow some of this new thinking to become an integral part of my practice. The whole process needs time to become embedded but I also have valued the discussions with Christine as well as the informal mentoring that has been ongoing as part of this endeavour. I will continue to reflect, but my concern would be, who could I go to for help? Would I be able to have similar discussions with other swimming coaches? Perhaps the idea of a reflective mentor could be explored.

Donald Schön: critical questions

1. What is the relationship between the reflective sport coach and professional learning?
2. How do I question my coaching practice, using reflection-in-action and reflection-on-action?
3. Do I use single-loop or double-loop learning in my coaching? Which would be best for my practice?

4.   Do I consider novel solutions to coaching problems, using my knowledge and experience to embrace the complexities and nuances involved within sport coaching? If so, why?

References

Argyris, C. (2004) 'Reflection and beyond in research on organizational learning', *Management Learning*, 35(4): 507–509.
Argyris, C. and Schön, D. (1974) *Theory in practice: Increasing professional effectiveness*, San Francisco: Jossey-Bass.
Argyris, C. and Schön, D. (1978) *Organizational learning: A theory of action perspective*, Reading, MA: Addison-Wesley.
Boud, D. and Walker, D. (1998) 'Promoting reflection in professional courses: The challenge of context', *Studies in Higher Education*, 23(2): 191–206.
Dewey, J. (1933) *How we think*, New York: D. C. Heath.
Ekebergh, M. (2009) 'Developing a didactic method that emphasizes lifeworld as a basis for learning', *Reflective Practice*, 10(1): 51–63.
Eraut, M. (2004) 'Informal learning in the workplace', *Studies in Continuing Education*, 26(2): 247–273.
Gilbert, W., Lichtenwaldt, L., Gilbert, J., Zelezny, L. and Côté, J. (2009) 'Developmental profiles of successful high school coaches', *International Journal of Sports Science and Coaching*, 4(3): 415–431.
Gilbert, W. and Trudel, P. (2004) 'Role of the coach: How model youth team sport coaches frame their role', *The Sport Psychologist*, 18: 21–43.
Glazer, N. (1974) 'The schools of the minor professions', *Minerva*, 12(3): 346–364.
Knowles, Z., Borrie, A. and Telfer, H. (2005) 'Towards the reflective sports coach: Issues of context, education and application', *Ergonomics*, 48(11–14): 1711–1720.
Kolb, D. A. (1984) *Experiential learning: Experience as the source of learning and development*, Englewood Cliffs, NJ: Prentice Hall.
Mamede, S. and Schmidt, H. (2004) 'The structure of reflective practice in medicine', *Medical Education*, 38(12): 1302–1308.
Martindale, A. and Collins, D. (2015) 'Reflective practice', in C. Nash (ed.) *Practical sports coaching*, New York: Routledge, 223–241.
Moon, J. (1999) *Learning journals: A handbook for academics, students and professional development*, London: Kogan Page.
Naik, H. (2011) 'Social capital key to knowledge economy, for creating lasting values in learning organizations', *Asia Pacific Journal of Research in Business Management*, 2(12): 1–2.
Nash, C. and Collins, D. (2006) 'Tacit knowledge in expert coaching: Science or art?', *Quest*, 58(4): 465–477.
Nash, C. and Sproule, J. (2012) 'Coaches' perceptions of coach education experiences', *International Journal of Sport Psychology*, 43: 33–52.
Nash, C., Sproule, J. and Horton, P. (2008) 'Sport coaches' perceived role frames and philosophies', *International Journal of Sports Science and Coaching*, 3(4): 539–554.
Rein, M. and Schön, D. (1994) *Frame reflection: Toward the resolution of intractable policy controversies*, New York: Basic Books.
Schein, E. (1974) *Professional education*, New York: McGraw Hill.
Schön, D. (1963) *Displacement of concepts*, London: Tavistock.
Schön, D. (1967) *Technology and change: The new Heraclitus*, New York: Delacorte Press.
Schön, D. (1973) *Beyond the stable state*, New York: Random House.

Schön, D. (1983) *The reflective practitioner: How professionals think in action*, New York: Basic Books.

Schön, D. (1987) *Educating the reflective practitioner: Toward a new design for teaching and learning in the professions*, San Francisco: Jossey-Bass.

Schön, D. (2001) 'The crisis of professional knowledge and the pursuit of an epistemology of practice', in J. Raven and J. Stephenson (eds) *Competence in the learning society*, New York: Peter Lang, 183–207.

Spring, J. (2009) *Globalization of education: An introduction*, New York: Routledge.

Usher, R., Bryant, I. and Johnston, R. (1997) *Adult education and the postmodern challenge: Learning beyond the limits*, London: Routledge.

Van Manen, M. (1998) *Researching lived experience: Human science for an action sensitive pedagogy*, London, Ontario: Althouse Press.

SECTION 3
Humanist theorists

6

ABRAHAM MASLOW

Hierarchy of coach and athlete needs

Tristan Coulter, Megan Gilchrist and Clifford Mallett with Adam Carey

Abraham Maslow: a short biography

Abraham Harold Maslow was an American who led the humanistic psychology movement. This followed psychoanalysis and behaviourism and is thus considered the 'third force' in psychology. He was born on 1 April 1908 in Brooklyn, New York where he spent his childhood and early adulthood. Maslow was the oldest child of poor Jewish immigrants from Russia. He reported a miserable childhood. Neither parent provided much love, which resulted in his estrangement from them. Furthermore, he was raised in a non-Jewish neighbourhood and experienced anti-Semitic bullying and had few friends. The alienated Maslow spent most of his time in libraries, which spurred his love for reading and learning. This love of learning contributed to his valuing of the potential of education to improve society. He married his first cousin, Bertha Goodman, at age 20 – she was 19 – and had two daughters, Ann and Ellen.

Maslow graduated in psychology (B.A. 1930, M.A. 1931, and Ph.D. 1934) from the University of Wisconsin. He was the first doctoral student of the distinguished experimental psychologist Harry Harlow, who was famous for his separation research on rhesus monkeys. After a short stint teaching at Wisconsin he moved to Columbia University, working with the renowned Edward L. Thorndike in the area of human sexuality for a period of 18 months. During this time he also found a mentor in psychoanalyst Alfred Adler. In 1937 he transferred to Brooklyn College, during which time his life experiences and that of World War II influenced his psychological thinking. Key influences on his ideas were anthropologist Ruth Benedict, gestalt psychologist Max Werthheimer, and Henry Murray, who espoused the centrality of needs in personality development. During this period he developed the concept of the inherent drive for self-actualization (1943) from the earlier work of Kurt Goldstein (1939). The drive towards self-actualization was central to the development of his 'hierarchy of needs' (1943) within the 'third force' (i.e. humanistic psychology) that focused on human growth and potential rather than the deficit approach to understanding human development.

Maslow did not experience great health and required a two-year respite to recuperate from a heart attack in 1947. He moved to Brandeis University in Massachusetts in 1951 as Chair of Psychology, where he remained until 1969. Maslow published his theory in the book *Motivation and Personality* in 1954 and was elected as President of the American Psychological Association in 1966. Consistent with the notion of fostering human potential, Maslow studied exemplary people, from Einstein to Eleanor Roosevelt and the healthiest college students, to understand human development. He produced a second edition of *Motivation and Personality* in 1970. Maslow wrote several seminal works, including: *A Theory of Human Motivation* (1943), *Motivation and Personality* (1st edn 1954, 2nd edn 1970, 3rd edn 1987), and *Toward a Psychology of Being* ([1962] 1999). His ideas about a higher human nature pervade today and have been developed in the field of positive psychology. Sadly, in 1970 Maslow suffered a fatal heart attack at age 62 whilst jogging in Menlo Park, California.

Abraham Maslow: key concepts

Maslow's psychology of being

At the core of Maslow's beliefs about human personality is the view that people are motivated by the desire for personal growth and will often overcome many obstacles to achieve personal fulfilment. This vision of people contrasts markedly to the prevalent perspectives in psychological science of the mid-twentieth century, where psychoanalytic and behaviourist approaches, such as those espoused by B. F. Skinner, dominated (McAdams 2006; see Chapter 2). As a pioneer of humanistic psychology, alongside others such as Carl Rogers (see Chapter 7), Maslow was greatly moved by his own experiences as a child, father, and the tragic circumstances around the period of the Second World War. At first a devoted behaviourist, Maslow vowed to show that human beings were capable of achievements and dignity grander than hate and destructiveness. He also wanted to learn more about what makes people happy and the things that they do to achieve that aim, rather than devote attention to people's problematic behaviours and deficits (Phares 1984). Although he acknowledged the darker side of human nature, he believed the way to prevent psychopathology was by studying the good side of people. Rather than conceptualizing human beings according to their basic instincts (as do psychoanalysts) or as mechanically activated by conditioned stimuli or reinforces (the view of behaviourists), Maslow viewed people as striving to actualize their inner potential, to *be* the best they can be.

Maslow's interest in human potential, seeking peak experiences and improving mental health by pursuing personal growth, has had a lasting influence on the psychological field (LeUnes 2008). Among Maslow's major contributions to our understanding of human behaviour is the concept of *self-actualization*, which captures the notion of people striving to achieve a sense of personal harmony, unity, and growth (McAdams 2006). Self-actualized people are those who are fulfilled and doing all they are capable of. In self-actualization a person comes to find a meaning to life that is important to them.

To understand why Maslow emphasized self-actualization as a key component of human psychology (and healthy human functioning), one must recognize the emphasis he placed on people having a 'true self'. Having a 'true' or 'real' self implies that there is something *authentic* about people – a belief that they have an innate set of existing characteristics *inside them* waiting to be *discovered* (Schlegel et al. 2012). Maslow described this belief in authenticity as reflecting peoples' fundamental human essence – their 'biological nature' or 'own subjective biology', he called it (Maslow 1968a: 688) – whereby each person has a unique identity that he or she must search for (inside themselves) to discover their real self. The romantic idea that people have a true or real self is in contrast with the opinion that human identities are created or invented – the notion that there is no underlying true self, but, instead, identity is simply a product of choices among endless possibilities (see Fromm 1947; Sartre 1956). Maslow completely rejected this view that human beings are entirely a product of their own arbitrary choices (Maslow 1968a). Rather, he believed that people comprise deep impulses and values that are basic to their personalities and sense of self. These impulses and values mirror each person's own natural tendencies that cannot be shaped or formed by the outside world, but are an indication of one's own unique identity. Ironically, Maslow believed that the process of self-discovery, and the deep exploration and searching required to find out who one is, also helps to reveal what it means to be a human being; that is, what is common to all persons (Kluckhohn and Murray 1953), which he referred to as the specieshood or humanness essential to us all (Maslow 1968a). In contrast to behaviourist and psychodynamic perspectives of self, which Maslow argued conceive of individuals as a 'blank slate' that can be shaped, controlled, and modified in any way that somebody arbitrarily decides, he spoke of there existing 'a higher nature of man' that highlights a person's intrinsic nature and capacity to meet ultimate ends and to discover their own deepest values. For Maslow, discovering one's true self is not simply an aspect or precursor to well-being but rather the very essence of well-being and healthy functioning, whereby the goal is to experience and pursue self-actualization.

The motivation for self-actualization leads people in different directions (Kenrick et al. 2010): 'In one individual it may take the form of the desire to be an ideal mother, in another it may be expressed athletically, and in still another it may be expressed in painting pictures or in inventions' (Maslow 1943: 382–383). The growth of self-actualization refers to the need for personal growth and discovery that is present throughout a person's life. For Maslow, a person is always 'becoming' and never remains static in these terms. Self-actualization is thus a continual process of becoming rather than a perfect end state that one reaches (Hoffman 1988). However, before self-actualization can occur, the individual must satisfy a range of needs that motivate behaviour. Maslow discussed these needs in terms of a hierarchy.

Maslow's hierarchy of needs

Maslow (1970) developed a needs hierarchy that has become famous in psychology and other disciplines for explaining why people strive to reach their full potential. The earliest and most widespread version of Maslow's (1943, 1954) hierarchy included five motivational needs; however, he later expanded it (Maslow 1970) to include eight needs. According to Maslow, these needs range from those that are basic to human survival to those emphasizing intellectual and spiritual growth. The lower levels of the hierarchy, basic needs, are termed *deficiency needs* (i.e. physiological, safety, love, esteem), while the higher levels (e.g. self-actualization, self-transcendence) are called *growth needs*. Deficiency needs are essential for a person's well-being and must be satisfied before he or she is motivated to seek experiences that relate to the upper levels. After a deficiency need has been satisfied, a person's motivation to fulfil it reduces. In contrast to deficiency needs, growth needs can never be totally satisfied. While motivation for deficiency needs diminishes as each need is satisfied, as growth needs are met the individual's motivation to meet them increases; that is, the more growth needs are fulfilled, the more the person wants to pursue them. Hence, with the satisfaction of one's basic needs comes the opportunity for growth and the pull towards or desire for self-actualization. While deficit needs are shared amongst all human beings, growth needs are idiosyncratic (Maslow 1970). This is not to say that only some individuals strive to be self-actualized. Rather, self-actualization may be different depending on the individual. Overall, Maslow's theory suggests that the most basic level of needs must be met before the individual will be strongly motivated towards the higher-level needs (McAdams 2006). Each level of Maslow's hierarchy can be described as follows:

1. *Physiological needs,* such as the need for food, water, and sleep lie at the base of the hierarchy. Physiological needs are the physical requirements for human survival, which must be met for the body to function. If any of these physiological necessities is missing, people are motivated above all else to meet the missing need.
2. *Safety needs* emphasize the need for structure, security (e.g. personal, financial), order, avoidance of pain, and protection. Safety is the feeling people get when they know no harm will come to them, physically, mentally, or emotionally. Stress and anxiety often result when safety needs are not being met.
3. *Belongingness and love needs* indicate that people desire to be accepted and loved by others and want to form affiliative, loving, and intimate unions. These needs are met through satisfactory relationships (e.g. with family, friends, peers). Satisfactory relationships imply acceptance by others. Having fulfilled their physiological and security needs, people can venture out and seek relationships through which their need for love and belonging can be met.
4. *Esteem needs* concern peoples' need for self-respect and esteem from others, and the desire to be seen by others and by the self as a competent and effective person. People need to feel competent and worthy. Once individuals have satisfactorily met their need for love and belonging, they can begin to

develop positive feelings of self-worth and self-esteem, and act to foster pride in their work and in themselves as people. A failure to be accepted by the self and others leads to feelings of inferiority and incompetence.

5. *Cognitive needs* are growth needs that represent peoples' desire to gain knowledge and to understand. This motivation cannot occur until the deficiency needs have been met to the individual's satisfaction.

6. *Aesthetic needs* refer to the quality of being creatively or artistically pleasing; aesthetic needs indicate a desire to appreciate beauty, symmetry, order, and form.

7. *Self-actualization needs* reflect a person's need to become everything he or she is capable of becoming – to realize and use his or her full potential, capacities, and talents to become the best individual one can be. This need can be addressed only when the previous six have been satisfied. It is rarely met completely, although people like Ghandi have been reported as achieving self-actualization; Maslow (1968a) estimated that less than 1 per cent of adults achieve total self-actualization.

8. *Self-transcendence needs* represent the highest level in the hierarchy, and emphasize that to experience a true sense of actualization people must look beyond themselves to a higher goal (e.g. altruism, spirituality). Typifying the experience of self-transcendence is the sense of enlightenment gained by putting others' needs before oneself and supporting them in the process of self-actualization.

As a general rule, one must satisfy lower-level 'basic needs' before progressing to meet higher-level 'growth needs' (McAdams 2006). For example, a man in chronic pain will not act in accord with his needs for achievement and sense of competence (esteem needs) until he has been relieved of his distress (safety needs). Once lower needs have been reasonably satisfied, a person may be able to reach the highest levels of self-actualization. However, this does not assume that Maslow's hierarchy operates in a predictable step-by-step manner. The process of self-actualization is ongoing and dynamic and not predictable. Unexpected declines in service of fundamental needs, or changes in circumstances and contexts, can prevent the realization of psychological needs (Burton et al. 2009). Also, while every person is theoretically capable and has the desire to move up the hierarchy toward the levels of self-actualization and self-transcendence, progress is often disrupted by failure to meet the lower-level needs. As a result, not all of us will experience or will ever become self-actualizers. Self-actualization/transcendence is at the peak of the hierarchy, symbolizing that it is the weakest of all the human motives and thus can be dominated by other motives and environmental forces. For many people, in order to experience a sense of self-actualization, and to know one's 'true self', it may be very difficult to resist social demands that often offer rewards based on esteem, love, and other social needs, and for some the risks of breaking away from such demands may be too great. Nonetheless, according to Maslow (1970), self-actualization is possible, but only in an environment that has satisfied all our lower needs. Such environments afford people the opportunity for freedom of action, freedom of inquiry, and other values such as fairness, justice, and honesty. While people achieve

TABLE 6.1 Some characteristics and behaviours of self-actualizing people (adapted from Maslow 1970)

Characteristics	Behaviours
Superior perception of reality	Become totally absorbed in a task; losing oneself in a job or while interacting with others
Show greater acceptance of themselves and others	Making choices that seem right to the individual as a unique person.
Are spontaneous and natural	Being responsible toward oneself by being honest in responding to the world
Problem-focused rather than self-centred	Working hard to be the best one can be in one's field of interest
Prefer detachment and privacy	Acknowledging and accepting one's defences and what people do not like about themselves – one's faults or weaknesses
Increased autonomy and resistance to conformity	Being courageous rather than afraid to pursue what one wants
Have a fresh outlook; appreciate much of life	Experiencing life like a child, with full absorption and concentration
Higher frequency of peak experiences	Listening to one's own feelings in evaluating experiences instead of the voice of tradition, authority, or the majority
Enjoy a spirit of identity and unity with others	Trying new things instead of sticking to safe paths
Strong moral and ethical standards	Being prepared to be unpopular if one's views do not coincide with those of the majority

self-actualization in their own unique way, Maslow (1970) indicated that they tend to share certain characteristics. Some of the main characteristics, including behaviours that may lead to self-actualization, are listed in Table 6.1.

Criticisms of Maslow's hierarchy of needs

Although Maslow has been recognized as one of the pioneers of humanistic psychology, and he has provided us with an insight into personal growth and self-actualization, it is important to acknowledge some of the criticisms associated with his work; most notably, the lack of empirical support for a hierarchy of needs. Some scholars have suggested that higher order needs can be satisfied even when deficit needs – located further down the hierarchy – are not (e.g. Wahba and Bridwell 1976; Tay and Diener 2011). For example, someone who is homeless (security) may still have the respect of his or her peers (self-esteem). Maslow himself also claimed that behaviour can be motivated by a multitude of different factors, bringing into question the original notion that a needs hierarchy actually exists.

This contradiction by Maslow, and the lack of clarity with which he defines particular concepts, have made his motivational theory difficult to empirically test. Maslow's research on self-actualization has also been criticized for using highly subjective, haphazard research techniques (Wahba and Bridwell 1976; Ewen 1993). For instance, to explain self-actualization, Maslow identified individuals he thought were self-actualizers (e.g. Abraham Lincoln, Albert Einstein, and Eleanor Roosevelt) and subsequently compiled a list of common qualities and behaviours that he believed characterized them (see Table 6.1) (Phares 1984). While these individuals may have indeed been self-actualizers, some also had serious psychological issues (e.g. it was widely believed that Lincoln suffered from clinical depression) (Ellis et al. 2009). Overall, the ambiguous methods used to define and understand self-actualization have made it challenging to provide a rigorous basis for Maslow's appealing conceptual claims.

Abraham Maslow: applications to sports coaching

The application of Maslow's concepts, theories, and ideas to sports coaching become the focus of this section. How have these ideas influenced contemporary views of motivation and personality development, and specifically within the context of sport? In discussing the application of Maslow's concepts to sports coaching, we focus our attention on two key actors – athletes and coaches. In particular, we underscore the pivotal role of the coach in creating a setting in which athletes can flourish.

Maslow proposed that satisfaction of needs (basic and growth) was central to personal growth and moving towards self-actualization and self-transcendence. This notion of becoming, rather than achieving, such lofty goals suggests the importance of the pursuit and not the end in itself. Coaches and athletes alike pursue satisfaction of basic needs, such as sufficient food intake, recovery (e.g. sleep) and hydration to sustain and enhance physiological functioning. Physical and psychological safety are also essential for coaches and athletes to feel safe and secure in order to enable the pursuit of other basic needs and those for personal growth. Sport provides opportunities to belong to specific groups. This need for acceptance from others also provides the capacity to develop concern for others (empathy), intimacy and love that are foundational to adaptive relationships and higher growth needs. The multiple relations within sport (e.g. player–player; coach–player; coach–coach) can nurture satisfaction of this basic need of belonging in appropriate circumstances. The importance of feeling worthy is foundational to the successful pursuit of satisfying growth needs. The role of the coach in supporting athletes' satisfaction of this need is central to both self-determination theory and positive youth development. Coaches' and athletes' quests for increased knowledge are contingent upon other basic needs being met. Coaches' pursuits of becoming more knowledgeable enable the development of expertise in coaching others to achieve their personal goals. In terms of aesthetic needs, coaches and athletes pursue advanced skills in both technical and tactical performance. Finally, the needs for self-actualization and self-transcendence can guide a more coherent sense of meaning and purpose in the lives of coaches and athletes.

As Maslow suggested, it is likely that relatively few people experience these higher goals of altruism or spirituality. Nevertheless, this does not mean that some coaches and athletes cannot, and do not, pursue such lofty goals. Within the context of high performance sports coaching, it is challenging for coaches to pursue true self-actualization and self-transcendence when the pressures and expectations to win games to maintain status and employment is so high. Such pressures consequently have the potential to thwart satisfaction of needs for achievement, and self-esteem, and belonging. Furthermore, to what extent are coaches trying to develop self-actualized athletes? Does sport satisfy different needs for different athletes (i.e. individual variability)? For example, consider a professional athlete who earns his or her living through sport versus a weekend warrior who just wants to be part of the team: what is the coach's role in this?

Some coaches, like others in different vocations and professions, are seeking a meaningful life, and the potential to contribute to the adaptive development of others is truly an intrinsically rewarding experience. How this meaning plays out may come in several forms and degrees of importance. For some, coaching is about performance – a single-minded dedication to sport performance and improving the performance levels of athletes so as to be better and to be winners. For others, it is about discovery – discovering the art and boundaries of coaching excellence where personal reinvention and continual learning are significant behavioural drivers. Or perhaps the relational aspects of sport are what give coaching its meaning – the interdependent connection between coach and athlete (or coach and coach) in which sport performance is simply a by-product and relationships are valued above all else (Douglas and Carless 2008).

The role of the teacher

When considering how Maslow's work can be applied to sport coaching, a useful area of research to consider is education. Maslow viewed the classroom as a place that traditionally emphasized extrinsic learning (i.e. learning external to the individual, memorized responses, grades, and examination) where the predominant role of the teacher was that of a lecturer, controlling and reinforcing learning (Maslow 1971; see Chapter 2). Maslow was critical of this view, as he saw extrinsic learning having little relevance for an individual's journey toward self-actualization and transcendence. He argued that extrinsic learning undermined the 'higher nature' of peoples' characters – a process too often prioritizing associative learning and the goals of the teacher while ignoring the values and ends of the learner (Maslow 1968a). To encourage self-actualization, for Maslow the focus of learning needed to be intrinsic, with an emphasis on self-discovery and personal growth. To encourage intrinsic learning, and to help 'the person to become the best that he [sic] is able to become', Maslow (1971: 163) argued that the role of the teacher needed to be reconsidered and that a much greater emphasis in the learning process should be placed on creating experiences that have real consequences for self-development and fulfilment (Maslow 1968b).

Maslow positions the self as something that needs to be uncovered by the individual, with the process facilitated (or hindered) by those around the person. For teachers and others, such as parents and sport coaches, this humanistic goal can be achieved in several ways:

- *Know the person* (e.g. student, athlete). Encourage self-discovery by creating opportunities for people to learn about themselves. Important questions include: What kind of person are they? What do they want and value? What gives their life a sense of meaning and purpose (cf. McAdams 2006)?
- *Accept the person.* Encourage each individual to become the person that he or she fundamentally is. Focus on his or her strengths. Create awareness of personal weaknesses. Help him or her understand one's natural style and potentialities. Build upon (rather than undo/reconstruct) natural talents.
- *Encourage mastery.* Nurture a learning atmosphere that celebrates growth and development. Permit the person to express and act without fear of making mistakes. Be non-intrusive and non-controlling. Ask rather than tell. Help the person to discover what is best for him or her by getting them to decide what is best for themselves.
- *Offer feedback that encourages deep self-exploration.* Beyond coaching declarative and procedural knowledge (e.g. skills, strategies), which are forgettable to a large degree, encourage the learner to reflect on his or her personal engagement and connection with sport. What are the consequences of sport for his or her own 'human essence'? Discovering one's identity is an essential part of (sport) education. 'If education doesn't do that, it is useless' (Maslow 1968b: 171).
- *Peak experiences.* The humanistic educator and coach uses peak experiences as a reward and goal at many points in the learning process. He or she encourages learners to value and disclose moments – however small or trivial – that produce revelations, illuminations, and rapture experiences.

Abraham Maslow: practitioner commentary by Adam Carey

As a tennis coach, a key question might be: 'What is the relevance of Maslow's work to sports coaching?' More specifically, how does or can the pursuit of self-actualization and transcendence work in sports coaching? The work of Dr Maslow and his pioneering of positive psychology in the mid-twentieth century has been influential in the way we view the notion of what it is to be human. However, in what ways has his work influenced the practice of coaching?

In my view, coaches in a variety of settings for many years have (at least in rhetoric) sought to proactively contribute to the satisfaction of both basic and growth needs. However, self-reflection on the efficacy of coach contributions to self and player development is not well known. There are probably many assumptions made by others observing coaches and their claims of their altruistic actions towards athletes, but teasing out the degree of authentic altruism is more difficult. Throughout my reading of this chapter I found myself reflecting on my personal efforts towards becoming self-actualized. Self-actualization is an incredibly powerful idea for coaches to aspire to. I believe our life experiences and our personal beliefs frame the way we coach and the areas and skills we develop. In my time as a coach, I have experienced incredible personal change and growth, the catalyst of which has been my own desire for growth as a person.

For me, the greatest challenge I have as a coach aspiring to become self-actualized is to create an environment that allows the athletes themselves to become self-actualized. This involves relinquishing control and giving the athlete the time and tools to figure things out for themselves. I have learnt that the more I empower, trust, and respect my athletes, the more creative they become, the greater ownership they develop, and the deeper love they form for what they are doing. This process is time consuming and, in many senses, works against my goal as a professional coach – to get my athletes to win, and win quickly. There are times when, because of the importance of the result, I must regain control from the athlete and do what I believe is right for them in the moment to get a result. This is not my preferred way of coaching and time is spent planning and communicating with athletes and stakeholders so this type of instruction can be avoided. I also believe that this is the art of coaching – the masters among us are great because they know exactly when to push, but more importantly, when to let go.

Professional coaches are often at the mercy of societal influences, media, and a variety of stakeholders. Under their influence, effective coaching performance has come to be defined by your win/loss ratio and the number of championships you have. It is a world where the image, playing background, and reputation of a professional coach are just as important as their philosophies and competencies. Newly appointed hires have an obligation to win in a very short space of time (relative to the time requirements of self-actualization) or they will be jobless. This volatile environment provides little incentive for the professional coach to become self-actualized. While professional coaches may innately see the link between humanistic development and athlete performance, coaches living under result- and ranking-based performance criteria often lack the time, resources, and incentives necessary to identify and define what makes them tick. In many ways, the pressure for fast-track learning and performance of athletes causes many professional coaches to reject even the basic needs of themselves and the athletes they are in charge of in a desire to satisfy results-based criteria for success and job security.

Having outlined the challenges of self-actualization for coaches in professional settings, I do not believe these same factors exist in the realm of coach and junior development. While the professionalization of youth sports coaches has become a topical issue amongst all sporting codes, the ability of the coach to self-actualize and develop their identity and define their own standard of performance is still a very real attainable goal in the development space. In contrast to professional coaches, development coaches are often entrusted with the development of an athlete's entire pathway from novice to elite level. In individual sports (like tennis), the complete pathway can be entrusted to one coach. In some cases, the athlete and coach may parallel each other's journey from novice to expert, especially if their relationship is formed at the beginning of both of their 'careers'. Here is where I believe it is important for governing bodies and coach education programmes to provide opportunities for young, developing coaches to engage in education aimed at promoting their satisfaction of growth needs. These opportunities can have positive outcomes for the coaches themselves and may then allow them to create environments that allow athletes to grow and realize their full potential.

Abraham Maslow: critical questions

1. If coaches are considered as role models, is it necessary for them to become self-actualized to nurture self-actualization in others?
2. Proving a hierarchy of needs has been elusive, which might be partly due to the nature of the investigative methods. From your life experiences, what are your thoughts about whether a hierarchy of needs exists?
3. How might we shift the culture of focusing on technical and tactical aspects of coaches' work to a more humanistic focus?
4. Is self-actualization possible in high performance coaching?

References

Burton, L., Westen, D. and Kowalski, R. (2009) *Psychology* (2nd edn), Chichester: John Wiley and Sons.

Douglas, K. and Carless, D. (2008) 'Using stories in coach education', International Journal of Sports Science and Coaching, 3(1): 33-49.

Ellis, A., Abrams, M., Abrams, L., Nussbaum, A. and Frey, R. (2009) *Personality theories*, Thousand Oaks, CA: Sage.

Ewen, R. (1993) *An introduction to theories of personality* (4th edn), Mahwah, NJ: Lawrence Erlbaum Associates.

Fromm, E. (1947) *Man for himself*, Greenwich, CT: Fawcett Premier.

Goldstein, K. (1939) *The organism*. New York: American Book Company.

Hoffman, E. (1988) *The right to be human: A biography of Abraham Maslow*, New York: McGraw-Hill.

Kenrick, D., Neuberg, S., Griskevicius, V., Becker, D. and Schaller, M. (2010) 'Goal-driven cognition and functional behavior: The Fundamental-Motives Framework', *Current Directions in Psychological Science*, 19(1): 63–67.

Kluckhohn, C. and Murray, H. A. (1953) 'Personality formation: The determinants', in C. Kluckhohn, H. A. Murray and D. Schneider (eds) *Personality in nature, society, and culture*, New York: Knopf, 53–67.

LeUnes, A. (2008) *Sport psychology* (4th edn), London: Psychology Press.

Maslow, A. (1943) 'A theory of human motivation', *Psychological Review*, 50: 370–396.

Maslow, A. (1954) *Motivation and personality* (1st edn), New York: Harper and Row.

Maslow, A. (1968a) 'Some educational implications of the humanistic psychologies', *Harvard Educational Review*, 38: 685–696.

Maslow, A. (1968b) 'Music education and peak-experiences', *Music Educators Journal*, 54(72–74): 163–171.

Maslow, A. (1970) *Motivation and personality* (2nd edn), New York: Harper and Row.

Maslow, A. H. (1971) *The farther reaches of human nature*, New York: Viking.

Maslow, A. (1999) *Towards a psychology of being* (3rd edn), New York: John Wiley and Sons.

McAdams, D. (2006) *The person: A new introduction to personality psychology* (4th edn), New York: John Wiley and Sons.

Phares, E. (1984) *Introduction to personality*, Columbus, OH: C. E. Merrill.

Sartre, J.-P. (1956) *Being and nothingness*, New York: Philosophical Library.

Schlegel, R. J., Vess, M. and Arndt, J. (2012) 'To discover or to create: Metaphors and the true self', *Journal of Personality*, 80: 969–993.

Tay, L. and Diener, E. (2011) 'Needs and subjective well-being around the world', *Journal of Personality and Social Psychology*, 101(2): 354–365.

Wahba, M. and Bridwell, L. (1976) 'Maslow reconsidered: A review of research on the need hierarchy theory', *Organizational Behavior and Human Performance*, 15(2): 212–240.

7

CARL ROGERS

Person-centred learning in coaching

Chris Rowley with Callum Lester

Carl Rogers: a short biography

Carl Ransom Rogers was born on the 8 January 1902 in Chicago, USA. His fifty-nine-year career helped to establish him as arguably the most influential psychotherapist in history. Rogers initially attended the University of Wisconsin where he studied scientific agriculture. As his commitment to Christianity developed, Rogers subsequently transferred his studies to history in the belief that this would better prepare him for religious work. Following his graduation from a bachelor's degree in History at the University of Wisconsin in 1924, Rogers spent two years studying theology at Union College in New York. It was here where his burgeoning ideas surrounding education began to develop. Indeed, he and his fellow students requested the provision of additional, student-led seminars.

Alongside his commitments at Union College, Rogers studied a course in clinical psychology at the nearby Teachers College of Columbia University. He completed a master's degree at Columbia in 1927, and received his doctorate in psychotherapy from the same institution in 1931. Rogers' interest in psychology subsequently led him in 1928 to accept a post with the Child Study Department of the Rochester Society for the Prevention of Cruelty to Children, where he worked for twelve years. Following this, he was offered a full professorship at Ohio State University in 1939. In 1945 he moved to the University of Chicago to establish a 'Counseling Center'. Whilst many expected Rogers to end his career in Chicago, he instead returned to the University of Wisconsin in 1957, a position which he subsequently resigned from in 1963 following a series of professional conflicts with his colleagues surrounding his ideals on psychology and psychiatry, and the wider emphasis placed upon examinations as a means of student assessment. Freed from the 'restrictive and alienating' university system (Thorne 2003), Rogers accepted a job offer from a former student at the Western Behavioral Sciences Institute in

California. Rogers and a number of his colleagues subsequently left to form the 'Center for Studies of the Person' in 1968, this served as his professional base for the remainder of his career.

Rogers received a number of awards throughout his professional career, including the first American Psychology Association's Distinguished Scientific Contribution Award in 1956, and the APA's Distinguished Professional Contribution Award in 1972. He was also nominated for the Nobel Peace Prize in 1987. Prior to his death from a heart attack in 1987, Rogers authored sixteen books and over 200 research articles, with his work extending beyond his own fields of counselling and psychotherapy, to reach other helping professions (Rogers 1989).

Carl Rogers: key concepts

Rogers' philosophical underpinnings

In a 1978 article titled 'Do We Need "A" Reality?' Rogers suggested that a high priority in education was to help individuals acquire the learning, information, and personal growth that would enable them to deal more constructively with 'the real world'. Furthermore, Rogers stated that his own experiences and readings had gradually led him to the realization that:

> The only reality I can possibly know is the world as *I* perceive and experience it in this moment. The only reality you can possibly know is the world as *you* perceive and experience it at this moment. And the only certainty is that those perceived realities are different.
>
> *(Rogers 1989: 424)*

Rogers suggested that the way of the future was to base our lives and our education on the assumption that there are as many realities as there are people. Rogers astutely acknowledged the challenges of adopting such principles within educational settings, but in doing so, he also suggested that this basic fact of human life served as the most promising resource for learning in all the history of the world. Rogers stated that we could enrich our own lives by learning from one another through a process of open-mindedly exploring the many perceptions of reality that exist.

Whilst Rogers challenged any notion of a single reality, his therapeutic career also led him to develop views on the 'nature of man', a notion which led him to reject any suggestion that man [sic] was a 'malleable putty which can be shaped into any form' (Rogers 1989: 403). In summarizing his position, Rogers (1989) stated that he had, over time, made a number of observations as to what man is *not*, as well as what man *is*. Rogers suggested that man was not 'fundamentally hostile, anti-social, destructive, evil', and that in fact the 'basic substratum of species characteristics' that he had observed, centred upon inherent characteristics which depicted man as generally being 'positive, forward-moving, constructive, realistic, trustworthy' (Rogers 1989: 403). Rogers (1989) stated that man was a basically trustworthy member of the human species, whose *deepest* characteristics were directed towards development, differentiation, and the creation of cooperative relationships in order to preserve and enhance both oneself, and one's species in general.

Rogers (1977) viewed human life as an active process, suggesting that this actualizing tendency remained constant throughout favourable and unfavourable circumstances. Rogers defined this actualizing tendency as:

> the inherent tendency of the organism to develop all its capacities in ways which serve to maintain or enhance the organism ... It is development toward autonomy and away from heteronomy, or control by external forces.
>
> *(Rogers 1959: 196)*

Rogers (1977) viewed this as being a trustworthy function of the whole human organism, with the organism deemed to be controlled by the self and one which moved toward its own enhancement and an independence from external control. Rogers (1951) spoke of the potential benefits of mirroring the self-actualizing principles of therapeutic practice within educational settings, and his experiences of having provided the 'freedom to learn' to students served to reinforce this belief (Rogers 1977).

This very notion of 'freedom', however, was a concept that Rogers (1969) viewed as one of the deepest issues within the scientific world. Rogers acknowledged that the generally held view at that time – which included the widely received workings of the behaviourist psychologist B. F. Skinner (see Chapter 2) – suggested that human behaviour was controlled by external factors and that man could therefore not be viewed as being free. Rogers' own experiences within psychotherapy led him to challenge this view, with the capability of having the freedom to choose serving as one of the deepest elements underlying positive changes that he had observed within his clients. This freedom was viewed as existing within the individual, and as something phenomenological rather than external, which should be prized and used as an individual looks to achieve their potentialities (Rogers 1969). Rogers stated that a person who was free, who was open to experience and had a sense of their own freedom and responsible choice, was not nearly as likely to be controlled by the environment as one who did not possess such qualities. Based on this assumption, and his aforementioned approach to teaching, Rogers encouraged educators to place their trust in their learners by permitting them to become active participants in the learning process, providing an environment of freedom that attempted to minimize 'determinism' and the shaping of human behaviours. Furthermore, Rogers (1969) considered the 'sort' of person who might emerge from a programme of education that was successful in promoting personal growth and development. Rogers provided a detailed description of a 'fully-functioning person' or the person who is continually learning how to learn (Rogers 1961, 1969).

Rogers' (1961, 1969) conceptualization of the fully functioning person was one that was based upon his experiences within client-centred therapy, with person-to-person interaction being required in order to create a theoretically optimal environment for personal growth. Rogers (1961, 1969) suggested that the person who emerged from such a process of learning was one who was open to their experience, rather than being defensive when environmental stimuli were deemed to be incongruent with the structure of the self. This openness in turn allowed the individual to experience each moment as if it were new, with the self and personality emerging from experience, rather than experience being translated or twisted to fit a pre-conceived self-structure. This relinquishing of a perceived requirement for control, would also enable a person to do what 'feels right' and allowed for maximum levels of adaptability, rather than to rely upon guiding principles such as codes of action laid down by groups or institutions, or by past behaviours in similar circumstances (Rogers 1961). Creativity was also central to this characterization, as he believed it was a trait that enabled man to adapt and survive under changing environmental conditions and be free to behave in a self-directed manner, whilst maintaining an awareness of how the existential situation served to determine one's behaviour. In making such propositions, Rogers (1969) stated that the person who he described was one who did not exist, serving instead as the theoretical goal, or the 'end-point' of personal growth. However, he stated that his best career experiences within therapy, and person-centred education, allowed him to witness individuals moving 'in this direction' (Rogers 1969: 295).

The goal of democratic education: the facilitation of learning

Within his 1951 text *Client-Centered Therapy*, Rogers acknowledged that education which embodied therapeutic principles held relevance only for one type of educational goal, with traditional, authoritarian principles needing to be discarded in order for a revolutionary, person-centred approach to education to be adopted instead. Accordingly, Rogers (1969) rejected a conceptualization of teaching as meaning solely 'to instruct', with his belief being that such a definition could only ever serve as logical within an unchanging and constant environment. In contrast to this, he claimed that 'the only man who is educated is the man who has learned how to learn; the man who has learned how to adapt and change' (Rogers 1969: 104). Indeed, Rogers proposed that because 'modern man' lives in an environment which is continually changing, the goal of education should be the 'facilitation of change and learning', a concept which encouraged a reliance on process rather than upon static knowledge (Rogers 1969: 104). Central to this notion of 'changingness', was the belief that such an approach could allow learners to develop constructive, tentative, changing, process answers to some of the deepest perplexities which confronted individuals within professional practice (Rogers 1969). Here, Rogers (1969) provided guidelines for educators wishing to become facilitators of learning, suggesting that facilitators demonstrate the following capacities:

1. The facilitator has much to do with setting the initial mood or climate of the group or class experience.
2. The facilitator helps to elicit and clarify the purposes of the individuals in the class as well as the more general purpose of the group.

3. He [sic] relies on the desire of each student to implement those purposes which have meaning for him, as the motivational force behind significant learning.
4. He endeavours to organize and make easily available the widest possible range of resources for learning.
5. He regards himself as a flexible resource to be utilized by the group.
6. In response to expressions in the classroom group, he accepts both the intellectual content and the emotionalized attitudes, endeavouring to give each aspect the approximate degree of emphasis which it has for the individual or the group.
7. As the acceptant classroom climate becomes established, the facilitator is able increasingly to become a participant learner, a member of the group, expressing his views as those of one individual only.
8. He takes the initiative in sharing himself with the group, his feelings as well as his thoughts, in ways which do not demand nor impose but represent simply a personal sharing which students may take or leave.
9. Throughout the classroom experience, he remains alert to the expressions indicative of deep or strong feelings.
10. In his functioning as a facilitator of learning, the leader endeavours to recognize and accept his own limitations.

If educators were able to successfully adopt these facilitative guidelines, Rogers suggested, significant, meaningful, or experiential learning could occur. For Rogers (1969), such learning was characterized by 'a quality of personal involvement', with self-initiation and self-evaluation on the learners' part being viewed as critical requirements for 'pervasive' learning to occur. However, Rogers (1989) went on to discuss the politics of power within education, and the manner in which his student-centred approach served to challenge traditional assumptions regarding educational authority.

The 'politics of power' within education

In an article titled 'The Politics of Education', Rogers (1989) suggested that traditional education and the person-centred approach which he advocated represented opposite ends of a continuum of teaching and learning. Rogers (1989) stated that traditional education was characterized by a number of basic assumptions, including the beliefs that (a) the teacher is the possessor of knowledge and the student the expected recipient; and (b) the teacher is the possessor of power in relation to rule making, the goal of curricula, and other policy-related discussions. Rogers (1989) argued that trust was at a minimum, and that democracy and its values were largely ignored and scorned in practice, when 'authoritarian rule' was adopted within learning. Alternatively, Rogers (1989) stated that the person-centred mode of education differed in terms of philosophy, methods, and politics, resting upon the precondition that the 'leader' or authority figure has an essential trust in the capacity of others to think and learn for themselves. Within such settings, Rogers (1989) stated that the responsibility for learning was shared, suggesting that if such an environment could be created, and if self-determination on the learner's part was present, then a deeper, more pervasive learning could occur.

In making these recommendations, Rogers (1980, 1989) also acknowledged the challenges and political struggles associated with adopting such a strategy, considering the threat that person-centred learning held for students, teachers, and administrators of education. Rogers (1980) recognized that the person-centred approach posed a political threat to existing orthodoxy, acknowledging a shift of power and control from the teacher to the whole group of learners, which included the teacher, functioning as a learner-facilitator. Rogers (1980) also recognized that for many students, taking responsible control of themselves and their own learning could be equally as frightening, stating that:

> Nothing in their background has prepared them to make choices, to make mistakes and live with the consequences, to endure the chaos of uncertainty as they try to select directions in which they wish to move.
>
> *(Rogers 1980: 305)*

Critiques of Rogers' philosophizing and theorizing

Whilst Rogers' philosophical views and his theorizing on education offer a potentially useful lens through which to critically reflect on existing practices in coaching and coach education, it is important to recognize some critiques of his work. Thorne (2003: 79) stated that many of the criticisms levelled at Rogers' work centred on what researchers perceived as being a 'grossly inflated trust in and regard for the individual', suggesting that Rogers' position provided an overly optimistic portrayal of human nature. Furthermore, Rogers was seen to underrate forces of the unconscious and of evil, as theorized and popularized by Sigmund Freud around that time (Thorne 2003). Rogers' aforementioned contrast with the theorizing of Skinner was seen to be representative of a wider critique aimed at Rogers' work and his apparent disregard for environmental influences and behavioural reinforcements. Thorne (2003) observed that Rogers' notion of an internalized locus of evaluation serving as a trustworthy guide for behaviour was seen by many as being 'unconvincing and unpersuasive' (Thorne 2003: 79). Thorne (2003) also provided an overview of some of the main criticisms directed at Rogers' educational theorizing, stating that many of these were similarly rooted in Rogers' beliefs about the significance of self-discovered learning. Thorne (2003) acknowledged that Rogers' educational theorizing served to threaten the careers of those whose professional identities were closely bound up with the importance of knowledge and the role of the 'expert', a notion which holds clear implications when considering the applicability of his work within sports coaching and coach education.

Carl Rogers: applications to sports coaching

Implications for sports coaching and coach education

Rogers' (1951) conceptualization of the goal of democratic education highlights the critical role that learners should play in shaping their own development at a fundamental level, with self-evaluation on the learners' part also serving as one of the key features of significant, experiential learning (Rogers 1969). This would suggest that coaches should work to involve their athletes in all stages of the developmental process rather than being the sole arbiter of training programmes, scheduling, and the assessment of performance (Nelson et al. 2014). However, Rogers (1969) recognized that imposing this critical involvement on learners can be just as rigid and oppressive as more authoritarian approaches, and could arguably lead to an 'ideology of person-centeredness'. Consequently, Rogers (1969) also suggested that 'there should also be provision for those who do not wish or desire this freedom and prefer to be instructed or guided' (Rogers 1969: 34), a suggestion which places considerable focus on the relationship between a coach and their athlete(s), and their ability to identify who may benefit from self- or coach-directed pedagogy.

Rogers' (1969) conceptualization of facilitation, and his guidelines for individuals wishing to become facilitators of learning, provides a further opportunity to focus on certain qualities which may be sought within a coach–athlete relationship. Rogers proposed that effective facilitators should be flexible in terms of their approach, willing to utilize a wide range of resources, and also eager to increasingly become a participant learner within the group itself, all of which contributes to the creation of a growth-promoting climate. Such discussion possesses very practical implications for coaching pedagogy and stresses the importance of openness and shared responsibility in coach–athlete partnerships. However, competence in sports coaching is traditionally measured by predetermined parameters that focus largely on the 'technical' or 'procedural' aspects, rather than the particular needs of athletes or athlete learning (Cushion 2010). With this in mind, coaches are encouraged – and have been found to want – to 'take charge' and control of the coaching process and environment over which they preside (Jones and Wallace 2005). Similarly, Nelson et al. (2014) acknowledge that the implementation of a Rogers-inspired 'person-centred' approach to coaching would require individuals to struggle against the existing dominant discourse of sports coaching practice.

Alternatively, it could be argued that for coaches to provide facilitative, athlete-centred support within their own practice, they first need to be introduced to and recognize the applicability of such approaches within their own coach education programmes. Nelson et al. (2014) state that traditional approaches to coach education are aimed at developing a 'standardized' knowledge base, along with a range of strategies developed to overcome what are perceived as 'typical' coaching dilemmas. Recently, however, this depiction of coaching as a controllable, sequential process has left practitioners dissatisfied and disillusioned with much coach education, which they perceive as being 'fine in theory' but unconnected to reality (Jones and

Wallace 2005; Potrac and Jones 2009). Instead, researchers have argued that coach education programmes need to acknowledge and appreciate the social nature of coaching, as well as the functional complexity that lies behind and between coaching's principal relationships (Cushion and Jones 2006; Potrac and Jones 2009; Nelson et al. 2014). The application of these guidelines would certainly challenge existing practices, encouraging coach educators to refrain from teaching and instead become facilitators of learning. For example, rather than delivering and assessing a prescribed curriculum, coach educators would work with learners to identify aspects that would assist their ongoing learning and development. Furthermore, learners would identify the pedagogical approaches to best aid their development and furthermore consider how they should evaluate their learning and learning objectives on coach education programmes (Nelson et al. 2013). Therefore, it becomes increasingly important that consideration is given to the environmental conditions within which Rogers proposed facilitative learning could take place. Rogers' own work in psychotherapy led him to acknowledge the existence of three core attitudinal conditions which he believed helped to promote whole-person learning, namely: 'realness'; prizing, acceptance, trust; and empathetic understanding (Rogers 1959, 1969, 1980). It was Rogers' (1980) belief that these conditions were as applicable to the classroom as they were to the therapist's office.

Facilitating learning: core conditions

Rogers (1959, 1969, 1980) repeatedly suggested that the most basic of these three essential attitudes was that of *realness* and *genuineness*. Rogers (1959, 1969, 1980) stated that when the facilitator is a real person – entering into a relationship with a learner without presenting a front or a facade – then they are much more likely to be successful in achieving their goals. Whilst Rogers himself openly acknowledged that being 'real' in practice was not always easy, he argued that it represented a fundamental requirement for becoming an effective facilitator of learning, mirroring the emphasis that he also placed on the importance of congruence throughout his wider work within psychotherapy. Rogers' conceptualization of *realness* should not, however, be understood as suggesting that coaches and coach educators should act upon every emotion. Instead, coaches and coach educators would live their feelings and, where appropriate, choose to share these feelings if they believed they might benefit learning (Nelson et al. 2014).

Additionally, Rogers discussed the importance of *unconditional positive regard*, based on his belief that effective facilitators of learning are those who strive to prize, accept, and trust their learners (Rogers 1969). In expanding upon this, Rogers (1980) proposed that prizing and acceptance represented a non-possessive, caring attitude to learners, as well as a basic trust and belief that the other individual is fundamentally 'trustworthy'. Rogers (1980) stated that a facilitator who displays a considerable degree of this attitude can fully accept students' fear and hesitation as they approach new problems, as well as accepting their satisfaction in achievement. Such a condition allows educators to 'accept the students' occasional apathy' and 'personal feelings that both disturb and promote learning' (Rogers 1980: 272).

Finally, Rogers (1980) stated that a further element in establishing a climate for self-initiated, experiential learning, was that of *empathic understanding*. Rogers commended the ability of facilitators to stand in their students' shoes and view the world through their eyes in an attempt to be sensitive to how the process of education and learning appears to them. Rogers (1969, 1980) suggested that when an educator can display such awareness, this in turn increases the likelihood of significant learning taking place. Interestingly, Rogers (1980) also stated that empathic understanding differed sharply from the usual evaluative understanding, which followed a pattern of 'I understand what is wrong with you' (Rogers 1980: 272).

Upon considering these three core conditions for facilitative learning within coaching contexts, it can be argued that contemporary 'athlete-centred' literature can already be seen to mirror some of the fundamental practices encouraged throughout Rogers' work. An example of this can be found in the recent body of literature focusing on the importance of 'empathic accuracy' in sports coaching (cf. Lorimer et al. 2011; Lorimer 2013), or from recent work by Lyle (2002) in which guidelines are offered as to how coaches can adopt a humanistic, interpersonal approach to their practice. However, it can be argued that the work of Carl Rogers deserves greater critical scrutiny than has been evidenced in the coaching literature thus far (Nelson et al. 2010).

Carl Rogers: a practitioner commentary by Callum Lester

I am currently working for the (English) Football Association (the FA) as a coach mentor and educator, I hold the UEFA A License (Level 4), and over the past ten years I have worked at a number of elite-level clubs in several different countries including England, Canada, Croatia, and the United States of America. After completing my BSc (Hons) degree in Sport Development and Coaching, I opted for a career change and took an M.B.A. degree from California State University Stanislaus, to gain further insight into how the organizations I was working for operated. Becoming involved with the writing of this chapter challenged my thinking, and directly related to a number of my professional roles. I now run a coaching business, and part of my role is to support and educate the coaching staff, as well as deliver accredited courses for different levels of aspiring coaches.

Having delivered many coaching courses, I am in agreement with Rogers' discussion around the facilitation of learning and, accordingly, I have drawn a number of conclusions linked to how I use this both in my own coaching and in a coach education environment. In my sessions I use the four-corner model, which is a large part of the FA Youth Module courses and encourages players to assess their own learning, as well as allowing me to see what they have or have not understood. In a coach education setting, however, this is very difficult to implement given that coaches are assessed against predetermined criteria. Through my time spent in the United States of America and working with the NSCAA (National

Soccer Coaches Association of America), however, I believe they may have achieved something of a compromise in relation to coach education, by allowing the prospective coach to be peer-assessed and to feed back their own thoughts and reflections on an assessed session. This information in turn contributed to the overall review provided by the assessor and ultimately allows trainee coaches to have an opinion on their grade through the means of self-assessment. In my view, this approach allows not only the students within the group to gain more from the course, but also the coach educator by considering the learner's current level of understanding, and also taking into account their previous experiences. This is the environment I like to create, especially when conducting a continuing professional development session, where the sharing of experiences and reflecting upon practical aspects are vital components of learning and development. However, because most coaching qualifications require trainee coaches to achieve specified criteria, there are instances where the coach educator has to be very specific on the content delivered, not allowing for as much input and creative control on the participant's part. In essence part of this has replicated Rogers' observations about the traditional model of education.

Rogers also discusses three core conditions: *realness* and *genuineness, unconditional positive regard*, and *empathic understanding*. On reading this chapter I reflected on whether they are evident within my own practice, and their potential value. In my current practice, I certainly believe that I maintain '*realness* and *genuineness*' as it allows me to connect with the prospective coach more easily. This is especially important in small group scenarios, as some coaches will not respond positively if you enter the setting with bravado, something that I have learnt from past mistakes. *Unconditional positive regard* is another of Rogers' concepts that I believe features in my practice as a coach and coach educator. I believe that if the facilitator is accepting of others and allows individuals to express themselves in a way that can benefit their learning, the environment created is more suitable to enhancing learning. Hopefully, this will promote greater learning, as the coaches appreciate an educational relationship that is based on trust, and where no stigma, blame, or embarrassment is attached to the making of mistakes. *Empathic understanding* is the core condition I can relate to the most from Rogers' work, and one which is a regular theme in the courses I deliver (i.e. the need to see through the eyes of your students). As an educator, you have to display an understanding and awareness that the coach may experience difficulties in certain learning environments. Therefore, from my perspective, it is the adoption of an interpersonal approach where you can understand what they are experiencing that helps learning to occur.

Carl Rogers: critical questions

1. What challenges do Rogers' conceptualization of the actualizing tendency, and his belief in the human need for autonomy, pose for traditional coaching methods?
2. To what extent can Rogers' guidelines for the facilitation of learning be applied to sports coaching and coach education contexts?

3.   What implications does Rogers' theorizing surrounding freedom and determinism hold for 'coach–athlete' and 'coach educator–coach learner' relationships? Why?

4.   Should the preparation of coaches focus on delivering and assessing a prescribed curriculum, or can coach educators work with learners to identify aspects that would assist their ongoing development?

5.   What qualities do you think coaches and coach educators need to develop in order to be effective? Are these reflective of the three core conditions proposed by Rogers?

References

Cushion, C. J. (2010) 'Coach behaviour', in J. Lyle and C. J. Cushion (eds) *Sports coaching professionalization and practice*, London: Elsevier, 43–62.

Cushion, C. J. and Jones, R. L. (2006) 'Power, discourse, and symbolic violence in professional youth soccer: The case of Albion Football Club', *Sociology of Sport Journal*, 23(2): 142–161.

Jones, R. L. and Wallace, M. (2005) 'Another bad day at the training ground: Coping with ambiguity in the coaching context', *Sport, Education and Society*, 10(1): 119–134.

Lorimer, R. (2013) 'The development of empathic accuracy in sports coaches', *Journal of Sport Psychology in Action*, 4(1): 26–33.

Lorimer, R., Jowett, S., Philippe, R. and Huguet, S. (2011) 'Empathic accuracy, shared cognitive focus, and the assumptions of similarity made by coaches and athletes', *International Journal of Sport Psychology*, 42(1): 40–54.

Lyle, J. (2002) *Sports coaching concepts: A framework for coaches' behaviour*, Abingdon: Psychology Press.

Nelson, L., Cushion, C. and Potrac, P. (2013) 'Enhancing the provision of coach education: The recommendations of UK coaching practitioners', *Physical Education and Sport Pedagogy*, 18(2): 204–218.

Nelson, L., Cushion, C. J., Potrac, P. and Groom, R. (2014). 'Carl Rogers, learning and educational practice: Critical considerations and applications in sports coaching', *Sport, Education and Society*, 19(5): 513–531.

Nelson, L., Potrac, P. and Marshall, P. (2010) 'Holism in sports coaching: Beyond humanistic psychology. A commentary', *International Journal of Sports Science and Coaching*, 5(4): 465–469.

Potrac, P. and Jones, R. (2009) 'Power, conflict, and cooperation: Toward a micropolitics of coaching', *Quest*, 61(2): 223–236.

Rogers, C. R. (1951) *Client-centered therapy*, London: Constable.

Rogers, C. R. (1959) 'A theory of therapy, personality, and interpersonal relationships, as developed in the client-centered framework', in S. Koch (ed.) *Psychology: A study of a science, volume 3: Formulations of the person and the social context*, New York: McGraw-Hill, 184–256.

Rogers, C. R. (1961) *On becoming a person*, New York: Houghton Mifflin.

Rogers, C. R. (1969) *Freedom to learn*, Columbus, OH: Charles E. Merrill.

Rogers, C. R. (1977) *Carl Rogers on personal power: Inner strength and its revolutionary impact*, London: Constable.

Rogers, C. R. (1978) 'Do we need "a" reality?' *Dawnpoint*, 1(2), 6–9.

Rogers, C. R. (1980) *A way of being*, New York: Houghton Mifflin Harcourt.

Rogers, C. R. (1989) *The Carl Rogers reader*, London: Constable.

Thorne, B. (2003) *Carl Rogers*, London: Sage.

SECTION 4
Constructivist theorists

8

JEAN PIAGET

Learning and the stages of athlete development

John Toner and Aidan Moran with Laura Gale

Jean Piaget: a short biography

Jean Piaget was born in Neuchâtel, Switzerland in 1896. A precocious child, he published his first scientific article (a one-page paper on a rare albino sparrow) at the age of 10. In 1917, he obtained his *licence* in natural sciences from the University of Neuchâtel, and in 1918 was awarded a doctorate in biology from the same university for a thesis on molluscs. At this stage, Piaget made a 'psychological turn' (Archives Piaget) and having visited Eugen Bleuler's laboratory in Zurich, spent two years studying psychology and philosophy at the Sorbonne University in Paris. By chance he met Theodore Simon, who had pioneered the development of intelligence tests at Alfred Binet's Paris laboratory. Somewhat reluctantly, Piaget initially worked on the standardization of Binet's reasoning tests for children. Soon, however, he became fascinated by the 'conversations' he had with these children about the thought processes that lay behind their reasoning – especially for incorrect answers on the intelligence tests. The subsequent publication of three papers based on this research at Binet's laboratory led to his return to Geneva in 1921, where he became director of the Rousseau Institute. In 1925, he gained his first chair at the University of Neuchâtel. In 1929, Piaget became the director of the International Bureau of Education in Geneva, and he remained in this position until 1968. He was admitted to membership of sixteen learned societies and was awarded twelve international prizes and thirty-one honorary doctorates throughout his distinguished career. Among these prizes were the Distinguished Scientific Contribution Award (American Psychological Association 1969) for his research on 'the nature of human knowledge and biological intelligence'; the Erasmus prize (1972) for his contributions to social science, and the Balzan prize (1978) for social and political sciences. Piaget died in Geneva on 16 September 1980, at the age of 84.

Piaget spent most of his life searching for the mechanisms of human knowledge and biological intelligence. An extraordinarily prolific scholar, he wrote more than sixty books and hundreds of articles on these subjects. Unfortunately, it is beyond the scope of this chapter to consider all of his scholarly work. Instead, we draw on what contemporary scholars consider to be his most influential works, which include *The Moral Judgement of the Child* (1932), *The Psychology of Intelligence* (1950), *The Language and Thought of the Child* (1959) and *Play, Dreams and Imitation in Childhood* (1962).

Jean Piaget: key concepts

Epistemology

During his formative years Piaget developed a keen interest in epistemology (i.e. the branch of philosophy concerned with the origins of knowledge) and, having completed his doctoral studies, decided that the study of psychology would enable him to integrate his love of zoology and epistemology. He drew on these two subjects to develop a new science of the 'genesis' (development) of knowledge which he termed 'genetic epistemology' (or the experimental study of how knowledge develops in humans). Arguing that knowledge is a *process* rather than a state, he claimed that children come to know or understand something by *acting* on it – either physically or mentally. So, children 'construct' knowledge.

Piaget's epistemological beliefs were shaped significantly by Arnold Reymond (a philosopher at Neuchâtel) who had taught him that logic could provide key insights into the evolution of human thinking. Furthermore, while in Paris, Piaget had attended Brunschvig's lectures, which led him to believe that teachers could promote intellectual development by encouraging cooperative exchanges with students. Central to Piaget's epistemological approach was the use of 'naturalistic observations' (i.e. a method in which researchers observe behaviour as it occurs in its natural environment) to study intellectual growth. This approach was influenced both by Binet's method of observing children in their natural setting and by Bleuler's clinical observation techniques.

Piaget's view on intelligence

Piaget defined intelligence as a *basic life function* that helps an organism adapt to its environment. According to Piaget (1950), it is 'a form of *equilibrium* toward which all the structures arising out of perception, habit and elementary sensori-motor mechanisms tend' (Piaget 1950: 6). He argued that we engage in intellectual activity with the goal to produce a balanced relationship between our thought processes and our environment. This balanced state of affairs is known as *cognitive equilibrium*, and the process by which one may achieve it is called *equilibration*. Through his naturalistic observations, Piaget discovered that children are challenged by, and actively seek to understand, the many novel stimuli and events that they encounter in their environment. These challenges typically cause *cognitive disequilibria* or imbalances between the child's modes of thinking and environmental events (Shaffer and Kipp 2010). However, being challenged in this manner is helpful as it prompts children to make mental adjustments to deal with these puzzling experiences in an effort to restore cognitive equilibrium. Piaget's view of intelligence represents an 'interactionist' perspective because he believed that intellectual growth is promoted by the desire to restore the 'mismatch' between one's internal *schemas* (see next section) and the external environment.

How children construct knowledge: cognitive schemas and cognitive processes

Piaget argued that cognition develops through the refinement and transformation of mental structures known as 'schemas' – the building blocks of knowledge. A *schema* is a pattern of thought or action that is used by children to interpret their world and organize experience. Schemas evolve and change from one stage of development to the next. Before outlining Piaget's stages of cognitive development, however, we need to consider his concept of the 'invariant' (i.e. unchanging) aspects of thought, the broad characteristics of intelligent activity that remain constant at all ages. These characteristics include the *organization* of schemas and their *adaptation* through *assimilation* and *accommodation*.

Organization allows children to compile existing schemas into more complex intellectual schemas. Consider, for example, infants who use gazing, reaching, and grasping reflexes but soon assimilate these unrelated schemas into a more complex structure which enables them to visually guide their reach. By acquiring this new schema children can reach out and discover the extraordinary number of novel objects and stimuli that they encounter in their environment. The goal of organization is *adaptation* – the process by which the organism strives for balance (or equilibrium) with its environment and which occurs through the complementary processes of *assimilation* and *accommodation*. *Assimilation* allows children to 'take in' a new experience and incorporate it within an existing schema. For example, imagine a child learning the words 'cat' and 'car'. For a while, this child will refer to all animals as 'cats' (i.e. different animals will be incorporated into the child's schema and related to their understanding of cat), and to all four-wheeled vehicles as 'cars'. Importantly, through *accommodation*, the child modifies existing schemas to account for new experiences. So, when a child sees a horse for the first time she may try to assimilate it into one of her existing schemas for four-legged animals and think of this creature as a cat. However, the young child in question will soon notice that this animal she has labelled 'cat' is quite large and has an unusual purr! Having sought a better understanding of these observations, she is likely to modify or accommodate her schemas for four-legged animals to include a new category of experience – horses. Accordingly, the child begins to understand that horses can be distinguished from cats or that cars can be distinguished from tractors. Piaget argued that assimilation and accommodation work in concert to promote cognitive growth and help achieve a state of equilibrium. However, equilibrium is not a permanent state. Inevitably, the cognitive balance will be upset as the child assimilates new experiences or seeks to accommodate existing schemas by incorporating new ideas. Adaptation is the ultimate goal, whereby one achieves a balance between one's cognitive structures and the environment.

Stages of cognitive development

Perhaps the boldest of Piaget's claims is the proposition that cognitive development proceeds through a series of stages – or periods of time in which children's thinking and behaviour tends to reflect a particular type of mental structure (Miller 2002). Specifically, Piaget proposed four major stages of intellectual/cognitive development: the *sensorimotor stage* (from birth to about 2 years), the *pre-operational stage* (from about 2 to 7 years), the stage of *concrete operations* (from about 7 to 11 years), and the stage of *formal operations* (from about 11 years and onwards; see Table 8.1). These stages represent an *invariant developmental sequence* – that is, all children progress through these stages in the same order. No stage can be skipped, as each successive stage builds on the knowledge acquired during the previous stage. Although the stages are fixed, Piaget recognized that there are significant differences in the ages at which a child might enter or emerge from any stage. Indeed, because cultural

TABLE 8.1 The stages of intellectual development according to Piaget

Stage	Approximate age (years)	Characteristics
Sensorimotor	0–2	Infants acquire knowledge of their world through actions and sensory information. This stage involves a transition from a *reflexive* to a *reflective* being. Children develop object permanence and the capacity to form internal mental operations.
Pre-operational	2–7	Children begin thinking at the *symbolic level* (i.e. the ability to use images and words) to represent objects and experiences. However, thinking is characterized by egocentrism and children are not yet using *cognitive operations* (an internal mental activity that allows children to manipulate images and symbols to reach a logical conclusion).
Concrete operational	7–11	Children can now understand conservation of length, weight and volume, and can more easily take another person's perspective. However, they can apply mental operations only to objects, situations, or events that are real or imaginable. That is, thinking is tied to the factual or the observable.
Formal operational	11 and beyond	Children can now engage in deductive reasoning, can manipulate ideas, and formulate and test hypotheses.

factors or environmental influences (e.g. children who have limited interactions with their environment will have fewer opportunities to develop and reorganize their cognitive structures) are likely to hasten or hinder a child's rate of intellectual growth, Piaget recognized that the age norms assigned to each developmental stage should be seen as rough approximations at best.

First, let us consider the characteristics associated with the *sensorimotor stage* (birth to 2 years). The infant's cognitive advancement occurs at such a rapid rate that Piaget divided the sensorimotor period into six substages (see Shaffer and Kipp 2010 for a more detailed account). An important aspect of sensorimotor development is the growth of *object permanence* (i.e. the idea that objects continue to exist when they are no longer visible or detectable through the other senses). At 18–24 months infants understand that objects have 'permanence' about them and are capable of *mentally representing* displacements (i.e. when an item is hidden or moved out of view) and using these mental inferences to guide their search for objects that have disappeared. In addition, over the first two years, sensorimotor development occurs as infants change from being reflexive creatures (where they accommodate new objects into reflexive schemas, for example sucking on various objects such as toys), who possess little knowledge, into problem solvers who have begun to learn a great deal about themselves and their environment. Perhaps the most significant achievement of the sensorimotor stage occurs when infants are capable of symbolic problem solving (18–24 months). At this stage, infants are able to construct mental symbols (or images) to guide future behaviour.

The *pre-operational* stage (2–7 years) is characterized by *symbolic function* – the ability to use symbols (e.g. images and words) to represent objects and experiences. Language represents the most obvious form of symbolism used by children. During this period, children will begin to move from egocentric speech (i.e. loud self-talk which is inconsequential in nature) to socialized speech which is used to modify the behaviour of others or to inform them of something. Another hallmark of this period is the emergence of *pretend* (or symbolic) play. Piaget argued that pretend play served a semiotic function – that is, it allows a child to separate a memory from its context, or an idea from its referent, so that they can 'entertain and elaborate on mental content that is separate from the physical present reality' (Lillard et al. 2013: 3). Although the earliest episodes of pretend play (involving simple activities such as eating or sleeping) can be seen at 11–13 months of age, it is between the ages of 2 and 5 that this behaviour becomes increasingly social and complex. During this stage children are capable of using *pretence* as a means of cooperating with each other when *planning* their pretend activities. So, children might assign roles to one another and even suggest play scripts that they wish to enact. Children who engage in a great deal of pretend play have been found to perform better in tests of Piagetian cognitive development, language skills, and tests of creativity than their counterparts who 'pretend' less often.

Piaget called this period 'pre-operational' because he believed that children had yet to acquire the operational schemas that would enable them to think logically. He believed that the most striking deficiency in children's pre-operational reasoning is their *egocentrism*. This refers to their tendency to view the world from their own perspective and their inability to adopt another person's point of view. Piaget and Inhelder (1956) demonstrated this deficiency in the 'three-mountain problem' (where children are presented with a model of a mountainous landscape) where pre-operational children state that another child viewing the mountain from a different vantage point sees exactly what they see from their own position. This deficiency arises as during this period of development children's thinking is intuitive because their understanding of objects and events is still *centred* on the way things appear to be rather than on any logical or rational thought processes.

The *concrete operational* period (7–11 years) represents Piaget's third stage of cognitive development and is characterized by the acquisition of cognitive operations that enable children to think logically about real objects and experiences. The emergence of cognitive operations allows children to move beyond centred thinking and helps them to solve *conservation problems* (tests of logical thinking ability). A popular example of a conservation problem involves presenting children with two identical balls of playdough. At this point the child agrees that both balls have equal amounts of clay. Next, the experimenter rolls one ball into the shape of a sausage. Here, the pre-operational child will claim that the sausage shaped ball contains greater mass than the dough shaped ball while the concrete operational child can use two important cognitive operations: (1) *reversibility* (the ability to undo the shaping process and imagine the ball in its original form) and (2) *decentration* (the knowledge that increases in the length of an object is compensated by decreases in its height to preserve its absolute amount) to reach the correct solution. Concrete operators are also capable of *mental seriation* – an operation that allows them to mentally order items along a quantifiable dimension such as height or weight.

In the concrete operational stage children can reason in terms of objects when those objects are present. However, the *formal-operational* stage (11–12 years and beyond) involves a notable transition as children are now capable of *hypothetico-deductive reasoning*. This form of reasoning means that the child is no longer dependent on the 'concrete' existence of objects in their immediate environment but can reason by considering the logical relation among several possibilities and by taking hypothetical propositions and using them to reach logical conclusions. For example in the pendulum problem (see Inhelder and Piaget 1958) the child is presented with a string, which can be lengthened or shortened, and a set of weights. Next, she is asked is consider which factor (i.e. the length of the string, the weight at the end of the string, the height of the release point and the force of the push) has the greatest influence on the speed of the pendulum's swing. Although the materials are 'concretely' in front of the child, successful reasoning requires formal operations. That is, operations might include a methodical consideration of various possibilities, the construction of various hypotheses (e.g. 'what would happen if I tried a longer string?') and logical conclusions resulting from trials of different combinations of materials.

An evaluation of Piaget's theory

Piaget's work is widely recognized to have made a hugely significant contribution to our understanding of children's thinking. However, as with any influential theory it has also been subject to extensive critical evaluation and critics have pointed to a number of its shortcomings (e.g. Bryant 1982). For example, investigators have suggested that children are much slower to acquire *formal operations* than Piaget had thought. Indeed, Neimark (1979) suggested that a significant percentage of the American adult population rarely reason at the formal level and cross-cultural research suggests that in some cultures *no one* solves Piaget's formal-operational problems. However, it seems plausible that the failure of adolescents and adults to solve these tasks may simply represent a lack of interest or lack of experience with the subject matter (e.g. lack of exposure to schooling that addresses logic, mathematics, or science) rather than an inability to reason at the formal level (Shaffer and Kipp 2010). Perhaps the greatest criticism levelled against his work is that he underestimated the intellectual capacities of infants, preschoolers, and grade-school children (for example, see Wellman and Gelman 1998). Unfortunately, it would appear that many of the problem-solving tasks he set were too complex to allow children to demonstrate what they actually knew. For example, even though they were being asked to think about familiar concepts Piaget required young children to verbally explicate their answers and to provide rationales that these relatively inarticulate preschoolers often struggled to supply. In fact, more recent research has shown that Piaget's participants may have been perfectly capable of demonstrating certain knowledge if presented with more familiar tasks, were asked different questions or given nonverbal tests of the same concepts.

Furthermore, Piaget has been criticized for overemphasizing the self-directed nature of cognitive growth, as if children explore their world and make important discoveries almost entirely of their own volition. Today, our knowledge of cognitive development is heavily influenced by the work of certain theorists (e.g. Lev Vygotsky's sociocultural perspective – see Chapter 9) who believed that human cognition is an inherently sociocultural activity involving the transmission of a culture's values, beliefs, and problem-solving strategies through collaborative dialogues with more knowledgeable members of that society. As a result, scholars have tended to portray Vygotsky as a *social constructivist* and Piaget as a *cognitive constructivist*. However, criticisms levelled against Piaget for ignoring social and cultural processes seem to be somewhat misplaced. Indeed, a close inspection of his work reveals that he did recognize the important role the social environment played in children's intellectual adaptation (see DeVries 1997 for a detailed discussion).

Jean Piaget: applications to sports coaching

Like a number of other researchers (e.g. Cassidy et al. 2009), we believe it is helpful for coaches to view what they do as a pedagogical enterprise. Adopting this perspective enables coaches to consider the holistic nature of their practice, since pedagogues are expected to develop the cognitive, affective, moral, and psychomotor domains of their students. So, Piaget's 'social theory', and the importance it places on teachers creating an interactive classroom (which encourages exchanges of a *cooperative* type) in order to promote social, moral, and intellectual development, may be of particular interest to coaches seeking to encourage holistic development. In fact, such an approach mirrors recent attempts to reconceptualize coaching as an educational relationship which aims to facilitate the rounded development of athletes. Let us start by considering how a coach might contribute to a child's 'socio-moral' development.

Piaget (1932) believed that socio-moral development (i.e. an understanding of the moral rules and regulations of society) involved a transition from *heteronomy* (i.e. unilateral respect for parents or other authorities and the rules they prescribe) to *autonomy* (i.e. respect for the rules that guide the interaction of equals). He argued that there are two types of morality relating to two categories of adult–child relationships. The first type is a morality of obedience and what Piaget referred to as *'heteronomous'* morality. Here, the individual who is heteronomously moral follows rules out of obedience to an authority, who has coercive power (DeVries 1997). By contrast, *autonomous* morality involves following rules that are self-constructed or self-regulated. In a heteronomous adult–child relationship children are likely to be extremely submissive and exhibit a mindless conformity in *moral* and *intellectual* life. Alternatively, we might encounter rebellion (owing to the lack of opportunity to develop personal feeling about the necessity of moral rules) or a tendency to follow rules only when under adult surveillance. Unfortunately, some educators seek to reinforce children's natural heteronomy through the use of rewards and punishments. Such coercive socialization is unlikely to promote the kind of reflection necessary if one is to commit to autonomous regulation of moral judgement.

Instead of using punishments, Piaget advocated *sanctions by reciprocity* (e.g. temporarily excluding a child from a group activity but allowing them to determine the point at which he or she can behave well enough to return) to encourage children to construct rules of conduct through the assimilation of various viewpoints. Adopting such an approach might help coaches to develop autonomous relationships which are characterized by mutual respect and cooperation. By encouraging children to regulate their behaviour voluntarily, adults pave the way for children to become independent and creative thinkers who are capable of developing moral rules that consider the best interests of all parties.

If coaches wish to facilitate such socio-moral development, they must strive to create pedagogical environments which encourage *cooperative* behaviour and the fostering of social exchanges. Pedagogists facilitate autonomy by considering the child's point of view, as well as encouraging children to consider the point of view of others. For example, the cooperative community coach might encourage *concrete operational* children (between 7 and 11 years old) to make rules that, when conserved, become the norms or values that govern behaviour and interactions with their peers in that setting. Here, the community coach could ask children what rules might be set that would ensure that all participants are treated with respect and consideration. In doing so, they might ask children to consider some of their peers' behaviours (e.g. being shouted at or receiving expressions of disapproval) that they find upsetting. Having discussed these issues children might decide that these behaviours are unacceptable and agree that anyone behaving in this manner is likely to face exclusion from the session. If children are involved in setting these rules they are more likely to follow them than if the rules are dictated to them by the coach. For example, research has found that sporting performance is more likely to be enhanced when athletes set goals themselves rather than having them imposed from the outside (see Moran 2004). Of course, we are not suggesting that children should make *all* of the decisions in these environments (autonomy is not the same as complete freedom) but there is no reason why they cannot be encouraged to make decisions about issues that are meaningful to them.

At what developmental stage should these rules be introduced? *Pre-operational* children in preschool settings are likely to prefer parallel play (i.e. playing next to, but not necessarily with their peers) and associative play (playing in a group but without group direction or interaction). However, towards the end of the pre-operational stage (approximately 5–7 years old) children typically become less interested in 'make believe' and more interested in 'real' games that are more structured and rule-bound. Group games provide children of this age with an excellent opportunity to interact under a set of agreed upon rules. Importantly, games challenge children to make mutual agreements, to develop a sense of obligation that they must abide by the rules and learn to accept the consequences of rules that are broken.

The preceding section considered some of Piaget's recommendations relating to the promotion of *moral autonomy* in children, but he also believed that a principal aim of education was to develop *intellectual autonomy*. Piaget felt that traditional education could be deeply conformist in nature and rarely encouraged children to think autonomously. In these environments, teachers may use sanctions to persuade children to give 'correct' answers. However, Piaget believed that children can only develop intellectual autonomy when all of their ideas (including wrong ones) are respected. The implication is that in cooperative settings (like group games), coaches should initially accept children's 'wrong' ideas but encourage them to defend their perspectives until they themselves discover that their opinions were incorrect. By doing so, children learn to construct knowledge by modifying old ideas (or schemas), not by accumulating new ones. Encouraging debate in these settings allows children to consider (or assimilate) a number of different ideas and to modify (or accommodate) old ideas autonomously when they are convinced of the efficacy of a new idea. Moreover these types of encounters provide the opportunity for what Piaget termed conflict resolution. When conflicts arise, children are challenged by the *disequilibrium* in an interaction and must seek ways of re-establishing reciprocity. To do so, children must make an effort to *decentre* and to consider their peers' point of view. Coaches can play an important role here by encouraging pre-operational children (between 5 and 7 years of age) to develop appropriate negotiation strategies. Additionally, they can help children move out of the *egocentric* phase by encouraging discussion which requires participants to listen to the opinions of others, places them in a position where their own views are challenged and helps them see (through the reactions of others) the illogicality of certain concepts/beliefs. At this stage, coaches might start to look for signals that children are moving out of the egocentric phase. For example, responding to tag games may indicate that children are beginning to play with others and consider others during play.

Jean Piaget: a practitioner commentary by Laura Gale

I am currently employed by a local council as a swimming coach. Here I fulfil a number of coaching roles on their disability provision. Reading Piaget's work has been a very interesting experience, as it has led me to reflect upon my own pedagogical practice and to consider the various ways in which I seek to promote intellectual and moral development in the children I work with. This self-analysis was guided by the following question: 'Do I create or provide an environment, schemes of work, materials, and instruction that are suitable for the swimmers in terms of their physical and cognitive abilities and their social and emotional needs?' I believe that I generally achieve the latter aim but Piaget's work prompted me to consider whether my practice allows children to construct knowledge through the refinement and transformation of 'schemas'.

In my experience, when children are in a state of *equilibrium* they are calm, relatively unfazed, engaged, and confident due to being familiar with their environment (i.e. being submerged in the water with other swimmers). However, when they are presented with new/unfamiliar information (e.g. a new skill such as 'breaststroke legs') which challenges their current schemas they can quickly become nervous and experience a state of *disequilibrium*. Although this might sound like a negative state, I've found that it is actually an important source of motivation for learning because children are eager to make sense of a new sensory experience (i.e. legs lifting off the floor, horizontal movement through the water, using new buoyancy aids, or deeper water). To help them refine their schema for this new action I set goals that are appropriate for their current skill level (i.e. I ask them to perform as much of the movement as possible). I also encourage self-evaluations, for example I ask the learners 'How do you think it went?', 'What did you accomplish?', 'Would you try it again with less support from me?'

By providing them with appropriate help and guidance I find that children can develop the ability to deal with and respond to these new objects, movements, and skills. That is, they assimilate and accommodate these new ideas and eventually achieve adaptation. To help them through this process I might supply them with specific learning aids for the water or use demonstrations and key instructions that help support the learners to acquire these new movements/skills. Overall, analysis of this process has made me more aware of how I already seek to facilitate the adaptation of new schemas, and the internal cognitive steps needed by a child to work towards a greater complexity of thought and knowledge of their environment.

Furthermore, as I predominantly coach *pre-operational* (2–7 years) children, I find that I regularly encounter egocentric behaviour. For example, children in this developmental stage are often unable to infer what I am feeling (i.e. that I am clearly frustrated that they are ignoring my instructions) or seeing (i.e. that I am observing them misbehave, push boundaries, and break rules and yet they persist). Instead, they continue to break rules and ignore fair play, as they seem to have little concept of how their actions affect others. However, I try to employ a number of strategies in seeking to help children move out of the egocentric phase. For example, I ask questions which encourage children to consider their peers' perspective and I provide them with clear information on boundaries and the consequences of rule breaking. Here, I utilize what we refer to as a 'rules board' which includes a diagrammatic presentation highlighting prohibited behaviours. I try to avoid coercive instruction by inviting the learners to discuss their views on these rules, and asking them 'Do you think these rules are correct and should we follow them?' I believe that this approach encourages cooperative behaviour and I find that children are more likely to adhere to these rules having played a role in setting them. Accordingly, I feel this approach encourages the development of 'autonomous' morality as the children play an important role in constructing and regulating the rules. I also believe that this approach challenges learners' perceptions of water safety and allows for different ideas and multiple vantage points. From my experiences, a child does begin to realize there are other viewpoints, and after enough exposure to *concrete experiences* (e.g. rule setting activities and opportunities to play in 'rule-bound' games) they begin to move beyond self-centred thinking.

I believe Piaget's work holds particular relevance for coaches interested in the intellectual and moral development of children. More specifically, his work can help community coaches understand how they must consider a child's current level of cognitive functioning when designing learning opportunities. Coaches can make a special effort to arrange session activities for individuals and small groups of children as well as for the total class group. In addition, because individual differences are expected, assessment of children's educational progress should be made in terms of each child's own previous course of development, not in terms of normative standards provided by the performances of same-age peers.

Jean Piaget: critical questions

1. Why is it important to encourage cooperative activity in a coaching setting?
2. How can coaches help children move out of the egocentric phase, and how might they help advance logical reasoning or the acquisition of other key cognitive operations?
3. How can coaches promote autonomous intellectual activity and help children construct regulations, operations, and co-operations?
4. What role does cooperative behaviour play in socio-moral development?
5. Why is it important for coaches to avoid coercive instruction?

References

Bryant, P. E. (ed.) (1982) *Piaget: Issues and experiments*, Leicester: British Psychological Society.

Cassidy, T., Jones, R. L. and Potrac, P. (2009) *Understanding sports coaching: The social, cultural and pedagogical foundations of coaching practice* (2nd edn), London: Routledge.

DeVries, R. (1997) 'Piaget's social theory', *Educational Researcher*, 26(2): 4–17.

Inhelder, B. and Piaget, J. (1958) *The growth of logical thinking from childhood to adolescence*, London: Routledge and Kegan Paul.

Lillard, A. S., Lerner, M. D., Hopkins, E. J., Dore, R. S., Smith, E. D. and Palmquist, C. M. (2013) 'The impact of pretend play on children's development: A review of the evidence', *Psychological Bulletin*, 139(1): 1–34.

Miller, P. H. (2002) *Theories of developmental psychology* (4th edn), New York: Worth.

Moran, A. P. (2004) *Sport and exercise psychology: A critical introduction*, London: Psychology Press and Routledge.

Neimark, E. D. (1979) 'Current status of formal operations research', *Human Development*, 22(1): 60–67.

Piaget, J. (1932) *The moral judgement of the child*, New York: Harcourt Brace.

Piaget, J. (1947) *La psychologie de l'intelligence* [*The psychology of intelligence*], Paris: Armand Colin.

Piaget, J. (1950) *The psychology of intelligence*, London: Routledge and Kegan Paul.

Piaget, J. (1959) *The language and thought of the child* (3rd edn), London: Routledge and Kegan Paul.

Piaget, J. (1962) *Play, dreams and imitation in childhood*, London: Routledge and Kegan Paul.

Piaget, J. and Inhelder, B. (1956) *The child's conception of space*, London: Routledge and Kegan Paul.

Shaffer, D. R. and Kipp, K. (2010) *Developmental psychology: Childhood and adolescence* (8th edn), Berkeley, CA: Cengage Learning.

Wellman, H. M. and Gelman, S. A. (1998) 'Knowledge acquisition in foundational domains', in D. Kuhn and R. Siegler (eds) *Handbook of child psychology, vol. 2: Cognition, perception and language* (5th edn), New York: Wiley, 523–573.

9

LEV VYGOTSKY

Learning through social interaction in coaching

Paul Potrac, Lee Nelson and Ryan Groom with Kenny Greenough

Lev Vygotsky: a short biography

Lev Vygotsky was born in Orsha, which is now part of modern-day Belarus, in 1896. One of eight siblings, he began his life in pre-revolutionary Russia. At that time, anti-Semitism was widespread and his family's educated background offered no immunity from the consequences of such discrimination. Despite growing up in these troubled circumstances, Vygotsky was considered by his teachers to possess considerable intellectual ability. Indeed, alongside demonstrating excellence in his studies, especially in mathematics and philology, he was noted for the maturity and seriousness that he attached to his academic work (Smidt 2009). Following the completion of his schooling, Vygotsky successfully applied to study medicine at Moscow University. However, he decided against studying medicine and then law at this institution, and subsequently transferred to Moscow's Shanavsky University. Here, Vygotsky enjoyed a stimulating and productive period of student life, which saw him develop his interest in psychology. Indeed, his thesis, 'The Psychology of Art', which was his first piece of published scientific research, explored the issues of interpersonal relationships, power, and madness in Shakespeare's play *Hamlet*.

Following his graduation from Shanavsky University in 1917, Vygotsky returned to his family, who now lived in Gomel. This was a particularly challenging time for Vygotsky, as it included the town's occupation by the invading German army, his mother suffering from a serious bout of tuberculosis, and two of his brothers dying from typhoid fever. However, following the communist-inspired October Revolution in 1918, Vygotsky was presented with new opportunities. While he did not agree with all aspects of Marxism, Vygotsky was able to take up various teaching and leadership posts at a vocational school and a teacher training college, and at the town council in Gomel. His work in these posts allowed him to concentrate on his passion for education and culture (Smidt 2009).

Later, Vygotsky decided to turn his attention to research and it was this decision that led him to meet, and ultimately collaborate with, Alexander Luria and Alexi Leontiev. He obtained a post at the Institute of Psychology at Moscow State University, and his research there addressed the education of deaf and mute children. He soon received plaudits for the quality of his work. Despite suffering from tuberculosis he continued his investigative work, and his writing, in which he explored the education of children, aroused considerable interest across Russia. Sadly, Vygotsky succumbed to a further bout of tuberculosis when he was only 37 years of age. He left behind a number of books and research articles, which were not translated into English until the 1960s. However, the richness and quality of his academic insights are perhaps best illustrated by the considerable debate, application, and discussion his work continues to attract today (Smidt 2009). Indeed, Vygotsky has been referred to by some as the 'Mozart of psychology' (Toulmin 1978).

Lev Vygotsky: key concepts

At the core of Vygotsky's work in education is the premise that all learning is social, historical, and cultural in nature. Importantly, his approach to learning rejected the various beliefs and ideas that have underpinned nativist and behaviourist theories of learning. For example, he did not consider learning and development to be based upon heredity, or, indeed, conditioning (Kozulin et al. 2003; Karpov 2014). Instead, he argued that the ideas and concepts that an individual learns are mediated (or facilitated) by, and cannot be separated from, his or her social interactions and relationships with more experienced individuals, be they teachers, parents, or more advanced peers (Werstch 1991; Smidt 2009; Vygotsky 2012; Moll 2014). In his own words:

> It is through the mediation of others, through the mediation of the adult that the child undertakes activities. Absolutely everything in the behaviour of the child is merged and rooted in social relations. Thus, the child's relations with reality are from the start social relations.
>
> *(Vygotsky 1932 cited in Ivic 1994: 473)*

Indeed, Vygotsky's scholarly work emphasised the importance of language, inter-personal communication, and relationships in the learning process. For example, in illustrating the importance of language and mediation in supporting the mental development of children, Vygotsky noted:

> Just as a mould gives shape to a substance, words can shape an activity into a structure. However, that structure may be changed or reshaped when children learn to use language in ways that allow them to go beyond previous experiences when planning future action ... once children learn how to use the planning function of their language effectively, their psychological field changes

radically. A view of the future is now an integral part of their approaches to their surroundings.

(Vygotsky 1978: 28)

Learning from a Vygotskian perspective is, then, something that occurs in a social context (i.e. something that is shared and negotiated with others), entails building upon an individual's existing level of understanding, and principally takes place through the application of cultural and psychological tools (i.e. the objects, signs and systems developed by human beings to assist thinking in particular communities) (Kozulin et al. 2003; Smidt 2009; Moll 2014). The latter include language, symbols, music, art, and other forms of representation and semiology. Unlike Piaget (see Chapter 8), who believed that development preceded learning, Vygotsky (1978: 90) considered learning to be 'a necessary and universal aspect of the process of developing culturally organized, specifically human psychological functions'. More simply put, Vygotsky argued that social learning tends to precede an individual's cognitive development (Kozulin et al. 2003; Smidt 2009; Moll 2014).

In his now classic works, Vygotsky (1978, 1981, 1997) outlined how young children's development entails a shift from being dominated by natural processes (e. g. sleep, food, and warmth) to a stage in which more complex and instrumental psychological processes begin to develop as a result of their relations with adults. Indeed, it is during their interactions with adults, who primarily mediate a child's contact with the social and physical world, he argued, that children begin to develop their higher order mental functions. These include, but are not limited to, the ability to classify, order, generalise, and compare, as well as to make purposeful movements. Interestingly, Vygotsky made a distinction between lower order mental functions such as elementary perception, memory, attention, and intelligence, and higher order mental functioning. Specifically, he considered the former to be psychobiological in nature and related to more concrete forms of thinking, while the latter is conscious and abstract in form and is concerned with logical reasoning, selective attention, and verbal thinking (Daniels 2001; Smidt 2009; Moll 2014).

Vygotsky highlighted how the development of higher order mental functions is embedded in social contexts and relationships. Specifically, he noted:

> Every function in the child's development appears twice: first, on the social level, and later on the individual level; first between people, and then inside the child. This applies equally to voluntary attention, to logical memory, and the formation of concepts. All the higher-level functions originate as actual relations between human individuals.

(Vygotsky 1978: 57)

Vygotsky's above words illustrate how the process of learning is initially inter-psychological in nature, as it occurs between child and adult. Later, however, the learning occurs on an intra-psychological level. Importantly, this entails the child internalising a particular idea or notion so that they are able to apply it independently in their efforts to address particular problems and challenges (Daniels 2001; Moll 2014). The process of internalisation includes the development of the learner's language and inner speech, which collectively provide the basis for future learning, reflection, and problem solving. The inter-related notions of the joint construction of knowledge and understanding and its internalisation by the learner are perhaps well captured in the scenario presented below:

> When the school child solves a problem at home on the basis of a model that has been shown in class, he continues to act in collaboration, though at the moment the teacher is not standing near him [sic]. From a psychological perspective, the solution of the second problem is similar to this solution of a problem at home. It is a solution accomplished with the teacher's help. This help – this aspect of collaboration – is invisibly present. It is contained in what looks from the outside like the child's independent solution of the problem.
>
> *(Vygotsky 1987: 216)*

In his work, Vygotsky (2012) also differentiated children's learning in relation to everyday or spontaneous concepts (or understandings) and scientific concepts. The former are concepts that a child is likely to encounter in their everyday home and community life. These might, for example, relate to eating, sickness, or going to school (Smidt 2009). Importantly, these concepts are learned through interaction and mediated speech and are largely experienced first hand by the child. In contrast, scientific concepts are those that a child develops through some form of instruction in a formal knowledge system, are abstract in nature (e.g. dark and light, long and short), and are largely reliant on a child's memory (Smidt 2009). Furthermore, Vygotsky (1987: 216) noted that 'the fundamental difference between the problem which involves everyday concepts and that which involves scientific concepts is that the child solves the latter with the teacher's help'.

Vygotsky suggested that the development of a child's higher mental functions takes place within what he termed the 'zone of proximal development', which he defined as:

> The distance between the actual development as determined by individual problem solving and the level of potential development as determined through problem solving under adult guidance or in collaboration with more capable peers.
>
> *(Vygotsky 1978: 86)*

In simple terms, the zone of proximal development can be understood to be the space or gap that exists between what a child (or learner) is capable of achieving alone and what they are able to achieve with the assistance of a person who has more knowledge or expertise in a particular topic area: someone Vygotsky termed a more capable other (Smidt 2009; Moll 2014). The zone of proximal development is then an area where the child can participate in social and cultural practices slightly above their existing capabilities. In some ways the zone of proximal development can be thought of as comprising three inter-related phases. These are (a) assistance by others, (b) transition from other assistance to self-assistance, and (c) assistance by the self. These phases could pictorially be represented as a staircase, where the 'learner's independent development of achievement can be conceived as the stair upon which the learner is standing, having successfully climbed the other stairs' (Cassidy et al. 2004: 74). For Vygotsky, the learning that takes place within the zone of proximal development 'awakens a variety of developmental processes that are able to operate only when the child is interacting with people in his environment and in collaboration with his peers' (Vygotsky 1978: 90). Of course, it is important to note that the zone of proximal development is not a clearly demarcated space that exists separately from the process of joint activity. Instead, it is created in the course of collaboration, sharing, and negotiation between learners and more capable others (Smidt 2009).

In further illustrating the importance of the social and collaborative essence of the zone of proximal development, Vygotsky discussed the importance of play for children, especially fantasy forms of play that entail children being able to understand and engage with particular social roles and rules in order to successfully play out particular scenes and events. For example, he noted:

> Play creates a zone of proximal development in the child. In play, the child always behaves beyond his average age, above his daily behavior; in play it is as though he were a head taller than himself. As in the focus of a magnifying glass, play contains all developmental tendencies in a condensed form and is itself a major source of development.
>
> *(Vygotsky 1978: 102)*

For Vygotsky (1987: 209), 'the zone of proximal development has more significance for the dynamics of intellectual development and for the success of instruction than does the actual level of development'. Indeed, his own experiments challenged the ways that schools had traditionally measured intelligence. In this regard, he described some of the potential shortcomings of categorising children's mental development according to their chronological age or mental age and not considering what they can achieve when working with others. In his own words:

> Most of the psychological investigations concerned with school learning measured the level of mental development of the child by making him solve certain standardised problems. The problems he [sic] was able to solve by himself were supposed to indicate the level of his mental development at the particular time … We tried a different approach. Having found the mental age of two children was, let us say, eight, we gave each of them harder problems to that he could manage on his own and provided some slight assistance: The first step in a solution, a leading question, or some other form of help. We discovered that one child could, in co-operation, solve problems designed for twelve-year-olds, while the other could not go beyond problems intended for nine-year-olds.

The discrepancy between a child's actual mental age and the level he reaches in solving problems with assistance indicates the zone of his proximal development; in our example, this zone is four for the first child and one for the second. Can we truly say that their mental development is the same? Experience has shown the child with the larger zone of proximal development will do much better in school.

(Vygotsky 1986: 186–187)

Vygotsky, of course, recognised that a child's potential for learning and development is not an unlimited capacity. Indeed, he argued that a child's learning and development would ultimately be influenced by their capacity for intellectual advancement. In his own words:

We said that in collaboration the child can always do more than he can independently. We must add the stipulation that he [sic] cannot do infinitely more. What collaboration contributes to a child's performance is restricted to the limits which are determined by the state of his development and his intellectual potential.

(Vygotsky 1987: 209)

In considering how to facilitate the learning and development of children, Vygotsky argued that educators should consider their practice to be effective only when it 'moves ahead of an individual's development' (Vygotsky 1987: 212). He believed that when a learning encounter is structured and delivered in this way, it is more likely to awaken 'a whole series of functions that are in a stage of maturation lying in the zone of proximal development' (Vygotsky 1987: 212). As such, for Vygotsky (1987) instruction that does not contribute to assisting the development of the learner is unnecessary. In a related vein, Vygotsky was similarly critical of educational practices that were based solely on didactic instruction and rote learning. In this regard he believed such approaches to teaching and learning produced little more than the repetition of words without understanding on the learner's behalf. In his own words:

Pedagogical experience demonstrates that direct instruction in concepts is impossible. It is pedagogically fruitless. The teacher who attempts to use this approach achieves nothing but mindless learning of words, and empty verbalism that stimulates or initiates the presence of concepts in the child. Under these conditions, the child learns not the concepts but the word, and this word is taken by the child through memory rather than thought. Such knowledge turns out to be inadequate in any meaningful application. This mode of instruction is the basic defect of the purely scholastic verbal modes of teaching which have been universally condemned. It substitutes the learning of the dead and empty verbal schemes for the mastery of the living knowledge.

(Vygotsky 1987: 170)

Given his reservations outlined above, it is perhaps unsurprising that Vygotsky advocated a co-operative and collaborative approach to teaching and learning that emphasised the learner's understanding and application of particular scientific concepts. In his own words:

> The development of the ... scientific concept, a phenomenon that occurs as part of the educational process, constitutes a unique form of systematic co-operation between the teacher and child. The maturation of the child's higher mental functions occurs in this co-operative process, that is, it occurs through the adult's assistance and participation. In the domain of interest to us, this is expressed in the growth of the relativeness of casual thinking and in the development of a certain degree of voluntary control in scientific thinking. This element of voluntary control is a product of the instructional process itself ... In a problem involving scientific concepts, he [sic] must be able to do in collaboration with the teacher something that he has never done sponta-neously ... we know that the child can do more in collaboration than he [sic] can independently.
>
> *(Vygotsky 1987 cited in Daniels 2001: 55)*

Like all theories of learning, Vygotsky's work is not without its critics. For example, it has been suggested that Vygotsky's conceptualisation of learning may not be appropriate or applicable to all cultures and all types of learning (Rogoff 1990). Equally, others have claimed that his work is not social enough (Lave and Wenger 1991). A further complication related to the assessment of Vygotsky's theorising is that, unlike scholars such as Piaget (see Chapter 8) and Rogers (see Chapter 7), he did not provide many specific and testable hypotheses. As a result, the confirmation or refu-tation of his work is difficult. Finally, it should be noted that our access to Vygotsky's work is also influenced by logistical and linguistic considerations. These include a lack of certainty regarding the availability of all his work in Russian, disagreements as to the origins of some texts, and the contested translations and interpretations of his original work (Daniels 2001; Smidt 2009; Karpov 2014; Moll 2014).

Lev Vygotsky: applications to sports coaching

Having briefly considered above some of the key ideas and concepts from Vygotsky's theorising about learning, this section explores some of the ways in which his work could be utilised to underpin and guide a coach's pedagogical practices. At this stage, it is important to note that Vygotsky never provided a detailed list of the pedagogical methods or the forms of social assistance that educators should or ought to utilise with learners (Potrac and Cassidy 2006; Moll 2014). Indeed, while his work outlined some ideas regarding the importance of collabora-tion and direction – providing demonstrations, asking leading and open questions, and introducing the initial elements of a task's solution – he did not specify beyond these general prescriptions. As a result, the following should be understood as an interpretation of some of the ways in which Vygotsky's ideas might be utilised to support athlete learning (Potrac and Cassidy 2006).

In framing our discussion in this section, we have primarily drawn upon Smidt's (2009) Vygotskian-inspired work in education, as we believe it has considerable utility and transferability in terms of stimulating our thoughts about coaching practice. Importantly, she urges educators to recognise that learning is an undeniably social activity and that we should not ignore the role of others in the learning process. We should, however, also recognise that the notion of social refers to more than learning taking place in the presence of, and relationship with, others (e.g. coaches, more experienced athletes, and peers). It also refers to the established understandings and experiences of the learner and their use of socially and culturally constructed tools (such as language). As such, it is perhaps important that coaches seek to ensure not only that there are meaningful opportunities for interaction between athletes and coaches, as well as athletes and athletes, but also that these opportunities are planned for and exploited (Smidt 2009; Karpov 2014). When planning for such pedagogical interactions, coaches may benefit from considering the experiences and cultural tools that athletes have at their disposal and that, wherever feasible, they should have an opportunity to access and utilise these tools as part of the learning process (Smidt 2009; Karpov 2014). A further factor for coaches to consider in their planning is how the zone of proximal development is operationalised and produced in practice. Essentially, this entails the coach reflecting upon how an individual or individuals might be assisted in making the transition from dependence to independence in relation to specific scientific concepts (Smidt 2009).

From a Vygotskian perspective, coaches are encouraged not to adopt a prescriptive pedagogy where athletes are told when and how they should perform specific skills, movements, or strategies. Arguably, the adoption of such an approach might lead to athletes feeling undervalued and bored, and adopting a robotic approach to their performances, and, importantly, to reducing their opportunities to develop their ability to solve problems and make informed decisions. Equally, the adoption of a Vygotskian philosophy does not mean giving athletes total ownership of their learning (Potrac and Cassidy 2006). Indeed, Butler (1997: 42) noted that although an athlete's understanding may develop through their active engagement in a problem solving activity, the failure to check and assist their learning could see them 'go from one level of being wrong to another'. Instead, Potrac and Cassidy (2006: 43) suggested that the role of coaches is to assist athletes not only to 'explore how and why they address the sporting problems that they encounter in the ways that they do', but also to help them to variously construct and deconstruct their understanding of the various features of their sporting performances.

In seeking to scaffold (or take carefully measured steps that support) individual and collective learning, Smidt (2009) believes that educators should provide learning opportunities that are not only grounded in experience, but which also seek to actively engage the learner. In the context of coaching, this arguably entails coaches planning and resourcing sessions and activities that are accessible and relevant to athletes, that address relevant scientific concepts (e.g. various team strategies and individual and group tactics), and that allow athletes to create and develop symbols that will, hopefully, enable or enhance their ability to think abstractly and act purposely with regard to particular aspects of their individual and collective sporting performances (Karpov 2014).

Here, Smidt (2009) also noted that there are many modes or ways of learning that ought to be considered. For example, Vygotskian-inspired coaching sessions might combine the use of play, problem solving, and game-like situations with the use of questioning and discussion as the basis for promoting athlete learning and development. However, it is also important to recognise that there may be other ways that a coach could seek to motivate athletes and gain their focused attention, provide them with cognitive challenges, and allow them to build upon their existing knowledge through their deep involvement in a particular activity or set of activities. For example, coaches may wish to include reciprocal coaching, constructing resources (e.g. a team or individual playing handbook), analysing techniques and strategies on video, or discussions of experiences, thoughts, and feelings associated with training sessions and competitive performances in their respective coaching programmes and repertoires. At the heart of all such activity, however, should be the opportunity for athletes to ask and respond to questions. Through their engagement in such tasks and the accompanying questioning, athletes and coaches might come to better understand what aspects of their individual and collective learning and performance they find difficult, avoid doing, or simply do not do, as well as the reasons why this might be the case (Potrac and Cassidy 2006; Smidt 2009).

Finally, Smidt (2009) argued that the success or impact of such learning activities could be affected by the quality of the interpersonal relationships that exist between those participating in a particular learning environment. She therefore encourages educators to reflect upon how they attempt to create learning environments where individuals value sustained, shared attention, are supportive of one another, and collaborate to develop, use, and respect shared cultural tools, and where questioning, experimentation, and seeking answers are embedded. In a sporting context, Smidt's (2009) suggestions might include coaches considering the nature of the relationships that exist between them and athletes, and between athletes and athletes, as well as between a variety of significant others (e.g. assistant coaches, support staff, and parents) in their quest to create a culture of learners and learning. Indeed, a coach may wish to consider the following questions in relation to not only their own personal beliefs and practices, but also those of other individuals (e.g. assistant coaches and performance analysts) that they might work collectively with:

a   How is a physically and emotionally safe environment for learners and learning facilitated?
b   What types of task and activities are athletes encouraged to participate in? How are they planned for and resourced, and how is their relevance communicated? How are athletes' understandings of particular tasks and activities supported and examined?

c   When and how is feedback provided to athletes? Who provides feedback? How specific is it? How does the feedback provided recognise achievement and progress, and positively promote further learning and engagement? How are learners' understandings of feedback judged or explored?

d   What opportunities are there for athletes (and assistant coaches and other support staff) to ask questions and explore topics and issues with the coach and other knowledgeable individuals? How might such opportunities for interaction be included in the coaching programme or schedule?

Lev Vygotsky: a practitioner commentary by Kenny Greenough

In my work as a football coach, I have sought to assist the learning of players, both young and old, in professional, semi-professional, and amateur settings. While I am a Union of European Football Associations (UEFA) qualified coach, it has been the educational theorising that I encountered whilst studying for a master's degree in Education that has probably had the greatest impact on my thinking, choices, and actions as a coach. Indeed, my exposure to the work of Vygotsky as part of my studies has had a lasting impact on the ways that I think about the *learning* and *understandings* of the players with whom I engage.

The main focus of my current coaching duties is on the strategic and tactical aspects of performance. Here I seek to help players, both individually and collectively, to appreciate a variety of abstract (*scientific*) *concepts* regarding time, space, movement, and functional inter-relationships between individual team members (in attack, whilst defending, and in the transition between attacking and defending). In order to facilitate players understandings with what can be new or complex intricacies of individual and collective performance, I attach great emphasis to the nature of the *learning environment* that I seek to facilitate and maintain. In particular, I strive to create an atmosphere that promotes *problem solving, questioning, and interaction*, and caters to the development of individuals and groups of players over time. Normally, I will spend up to three years with a particular player or group of players.

Within my coaching programme and individual sessions, I structure my interactions, as well as the tasks that players are invited to participate in ways that promote the development of their *higher mental functions* regarding the use of specific playing formations, game plans, and strategies. As part of this process, I strive to understand and build upon their existing knowledge and levels of understanding. As such, my interactions with individuals and groups can vary according to my understanding of particular tactics and strategies. These forms of *mediation* and *scaffolding* primarily include *questioning* and *problem solving* in game-related activities on the training field, and often involve the exploration of particular football-specific *ideas, language,* and trigger or cue words that were initially unknown or poorly understood by the players. My efforts to assist player learning also include the use of various coaching tools such as tactic boards, iPads, and animation systems such as Globall. Importantly, in my practice, I strive to actively involve the players in the learning process. For example, the players may move pieces or draw lines on the tactic board, make physical runs on the training pitch and, importantly, ask questions and interact with me and each other in our shared quest to enhance their understanding of the game and their subsequent on-field problem solving.

This pedagogical approach is not just limited to training sessions but is also a feature of match-days for the teams that I coach. Questions are posed, explored and engaged with before games, at half-time, and in our post-match analysis and debrief sessions, with the aim being to help them read the dynamics of a particular match or period of a match and make informed choices and decisions about how best to deal with the problems that the opposition present to us or, sometimes, that we present to ourselves. Ultimately, I don't want to be in a situation where they always look to me to solve particular tactical challenges. Sure, I could set practical sessions and have players follow specific patterns of play, but from my perspective at least, a successful team needs players who can analyse and respond to the particular challenges that they encounter in competitive matches.

Of course, players will not all learn at the same rate. As such, I have to modify or simplify some challenges so that I feel that they fall within a particular player's or group of players' respective *zones of proximal development*. This might mean differences in the tasks set, questions asked, the amount of a particular answer that I reveal, and can also include partnering less knowledgeable players with players who I would consider to be *more capable others*. It also entails detailed planning and can be time consuming. For example, whilst some players may well demonstrate an improved understanding of particular attacking and defending ideas over six weeks, for others it may sometimes take up to six months. Ultimately though, I find that most, but certainly not all, players appreciate the thought and care that is put into helping them to understand the tactical aspects of performance.

However, my approach meets with resistance on occasions. This can be especially so with new players who have been training and playing in an environment where the coach tells them what to do, when, and how. These players often want and expect me to do the same. Trying to change their thinking about learning and development is just another everyday feature of my coaching work, and is a challenge that I do not shy away from. However, the trials and tribulations of working with players are, for me at least, always offset by the rewards. It feels great when a player grasps the distinction between rote learning and repetition, and a genuine understanding of a particular dimension of play. Equally, I feel encouraged when players want to seek assistance from myself and other players to explore particular topics or issues that they are encountering. For me, it is on these occasions when the 'stair-climbing' analogy discussed earlier in the chapter seems to ring true and it all seems so worthwhile.

Lev Vygotsky: critical questions

1.   How, from Vygotsky's perspective, is learning a *mediated* activity? What role do *language* and *social interaction* play in the process of learning?
2.   What are *cultural* and *psychological tools*? How do these relate to the learning of athletes and its facilitation?

3. What is the *zone of proximal development*? How and why might this concept be used to underpin and support a coach's pedagogical choices and practices?
4. What do you understand by the notion of a *more capable other*? How might this concept influence how you view and enact the role as a coach? Why might you choose not to engage in exclusively didactic or completely athlete-led forms of learning?
5. What are *scientific concepts*? What scientific concepts might athletes benefit from learning and understanding within your chosen sport? How and why might you *scaffold* or facilitate the learning of such concepts or understandings?

References

Butler, J. (1997) 'How would Socrates teach games? A constructivist approach', *Journal of Physical Education, Recreation, and Dance*, 68(9): 42–47.

Cassidy, T., Jones, R. and Potrac, P. (2004) *Understanding sports coaching: The social, cultural, and pedagogical foundations of coaching practice*, London: Routledge.

Daniels, H. (2001) *Vygotsky and pedagogy*, London: Routledge Falmer.

Ivic, I. (1994) 'Lev S. Vygotsky', *Prospects*, 24(3/4): 471–485.

Karpov, Y. (2014) *Vygotsky for educators*, Cambridge: Cambridge University Press.

Kozulin, A., Gindis, B., Ageyev, V. and Miller, S. (2003) *Vygotsky's educational theory in cultural context*, Cambridge: Cambridge University Press.

Lave, J. and Wenger, E. (1991) *Situated learning: Legitimate peripheral participation*, Cambridge: Cambridge University Press.

Moll, L. (2014) *L. S. Vygotsky and education*, London: Routledge.

Potrac, P. and Cassidy, T. (2006) 'The coach as a "more capable other"', in R. Jones (ed.) *The sports coach as educator: Reconceptualising sports coaching*, London: Routledge, 39–50.

Rogoff, B. (1990) *Apprenticeship in thinking: Cognitive development in social context*, Oxford: Oxford University Press.

Smidt, S. (2009) *Introducing Vygotsky*, London: Routledge.

Toulmin, S. (1978) 'The Mozart of psychology', *New York Review of Books*, 28: 51–57.

Vygotsky, L. S. (1978) *Mind and society*, Cambridge, MA: MIT Press.

Vygotsky, L. S. (1981) 'The genesis of higher mental functions', in J. V. Wertsch (ed.) *The concept of activity in Soviety psychology*, Armonk, NY: M. E. Sharpe, 134–143.

Vygotsky, L. S. (1986) *Thought and language*, edited and translated by A. Kozulin, Cambridge, MA: MIT Press.

Vygotsky, L. S. (1987) 'Thinking and speech', in R. W. Rieber and A. S. Carton (eds) *The collected works of L. S. Vygotsky, vol 1: Problems of general psychology*, New York: Plenum.

Vygotsky, L. S. (1997) 'Analysis of higher mental functions', in R. W. Reiber (ed.) *The collected works of L. S. Vygotsky, vol 4: The history of the development of higher mental functions*, New York: Plenum.

Vygotsky, L. S. (2012) *Thought and language*, edited and translated by E. Hanfmann, G. Vakar and A. Kozulin, Cambridge, MA: MIT Press.

Wertsch, J. (1991) *Voices of the mind*, Cambridge, MA: Harvard University Press.

10

YRJÖ ENGESTRÖM

Coaching and activity theory

Robyn L. Jones, Gethin L. Thomas, Irineu A. Tuim Viotto Filho, Tatiane da Silva Pires Felix and Christian Edwards

Yrjö Engeström: a short biography

Yrjö Engeström completed his Ph.D. in education at the University of Helsinki in 1987. From 1989 to 2005 he was a Professor of Communication at the University of California, San Diego, holding the position of Director of the Laboratory of Comparative Human Cognition from 1990 to1995. From 1995 to 2000 he was also a Professor of the Academy of Finland. Engeström is currently a Professor of Adult Education, and the Director of the Centre for Research on Activity Development and Learning (CRADLE), at the University of Helsinki, Finland, whilst remaining a Professor Emeritus at the University of California, and a Visiting Professor at the University of Oslo. In addition, he holds numerous other visiting academic positions worldwide. He is perhaps best known both for his theory of expansive learning, which can be considered a methodology aimed at social change, and for his progressive interpretation and development of activity theory (AT). The basic premise of his work involves the redesign and re-creation of activity systems by practitioners; in essence, the construction of new patterns of cultural activity. Although Engeström's work was initially applied to large-scale transformations often spanning several years, in recent years his ideas have been directed at much smaller phases and cycles implying an increased focus on radical change at the local level.

Yrjö Engeström: key concepts

> People and organizations are all the time learning something that is not stable, not even defined or understood ahead of time. In important transformations of our personal lives and organizational practices, we must learn new forms of activity which are not yet there. They are literally learned as they are being created. There is no competent teacher. Standard learning theories have little to offer if one wants to understand these processes.
>
> *(Engeström 2001: 137–138)*

Engeström's writings build on the so-called cultural-historical or activity-theoretical approach (CHAT) to learning and mental development; something initiated in the Soviet Union in the 1920s and 1930s by the educational psychologist Lev Vygotsky (see Chapter 9). In order to delineate the central concepts of Engeström's work, it is important to locate them within the confines of related theoretical development; and in particular that of activity theory (AT) itself. AT is commonly associated with Vygotsky's (1978) concept of mediated action and Leont'ev's (1978) hierarchical or graded structure of human activity. According to Vygotsky, all social action is mediated, in that it occurs with or through a mediational means (i.e. a cultural tool or lens). Consequently, action is never considered to occur in a social vacuum. In addition to being culturally mediated, activity is also deemed to be hierarchical, with some goals becoming functionally subordinate to others (i.e. some things or skills have to be learned or performed before others). AT, then, provides an ecological perspective, that is, an holistic, culturally bound outlook, from which to understand the inseparable connection between human mind and activity (Nardi 1996). In doing so, it undertakes analysis in many and varied ways. For example, 'moving up and outward, it tackles learning in fields of interconnected activity systems with their partially shared and often contested objects. [Similarly], moving down and inward, it tackles issues of subjectivity, experiencing, personal sense, emotion, embodiment, identity, and moral commitment' (Engeström and Sannino 2010). Indeed, it is here that Engeström's thinking deviates from many other learning theorists whom he accuses of primarily depicting learning as a one-way conservative progression from incompetence to competence, with little serious analysis of horizontal movement. Alternatively, Engeström's theorization embraces the radical notions of partial rejection of the old, transformation and the creation of culture.

As recently outlined by three of us (Jones et al. 2014), activity theory (AT) or cultural-historical activity theory (CHAT) was instigated by Vygotsky and based on the premise that, because all action is mediated, humans are not passive participants in relation to it (see Chapter 9). Rather, they are considered as agents operating within a social environment where interactions instigate meaning-making processes, enabling them to engage in shared activity (Jones et al. 2014). Hence, explanations of complex phenomena such as learning and/or cognition lie not in their reduction to single elements, but in their inclusion and integration into a rich net of essential relations. An investigation into any aspect of AT, therefore, necessitates a recognition or engagement with numerous others. When the theory first appeared, the insertion of culture into human action was revolutionary in that 'it overcame the split between the Cartesian individual and the untouchable societal structure' (Engeström 2001: 134). It meant that the individual could no longer be understood without recourse to culture. Although ground breaking, Vygotsky's theorization was criticized for remaining at the individual level of analysis. In response, Alexei Leont'ev (1978) and others developed a framework to illustrate how cognitive change happens within a collective or mutual context (Blin and Munro 2008). Subsequently, they became considered second-generation activity theorists.

To illustrate his idea of collectivity, and the individual's role within it, Leont'ev (1981) described a 'primeval collective hunt':

> a beater, for example, taking part in a primeval collective hunt was stimulated by a need for food, or perhaps, a need for clothing, which the skin of the dead animal would meet for him. At what, however, was his activity directly aimed? It may have been directed, for example, at frightening a herd of animals and sending them towards other hunters, hiding in ambush. That, properly speaking, is what should be the result of the activity of this man. And the activity of this individual member of the hunt ends with that. The rest is completed by other members. This result, i.e. frightening of the game, etc., understandably does not in itself, and may not, lead to satisfaction of the beater's need for food, or the skin of the animal. What the processes of his activity were directed to did not, consequently, coincide with what stimulated them, i.e., did not coincide with the motive of his activity; the two were divided from one another in this instance. Processes, the object and motive of which do not coincide with one another, we shall call 'actions'. We can say, for example, that the beater's activity is the hunt, the frightening of the game the action.
>
> *(Leont'ev 1981: 210–213)*

What Leont'ev was at pains to emphasize here was the importance of social relationships, arguing that a subject (i.e. a particular person's behaviour) can only be understood in relation to the world around it. Hence, he drew a distinction between individual action and collective activity, with the former only forming part of the latter. Individual action then (like the beater's behaviour above), was considered a part, and the result, of a system of social endeavours, as opposed to the isolated or unrelated cognitive functions of a human agent (Nardi 1996).

When researchers from the West began to become interested in AT in the 1970s and 1980s, questions emerged in relation to diversity and dialogue between different traditions and perspectives. This gave rise to the work of Yrjö Engström among others (e.g. Michael Cole 1988), who became known as the third generation of activity theorists. Here, the basic model of activity theory was expanded to include, as the basis for analysis, at least two interacting activity systems (Engström 2001). In moving still further away from Vygotsky's person-centred considerations of AT, Engström (1987) addressed both the individual and the social through the concept of activity systems analysis. Five basic principles underpinned his amended theorization of AT.

The first of these key concepts was that of the *basic unit of analysis*; that is, the interaction a collective 'artefact-mediated and object-orientated activity system' experiences in its network relations with other such systems (Engström 2001: 136); that is, how a system or network of actors, be they sportspeople, teachers or lawyers, comprehends itself. Here, goal-directed activity is only understandable when interpreted against a wider contextual backdrop. The second principle is the *multi-voicedness* of activity systems. This alludes to such systems' omnipresent community of multiple viewpoints and interests, which necessitates disputation and negotiation. Here, a division of labour creates different positions and interests; something particularly evident in the contested arena of sports performance. The third principle is *historicity*, which recognizes that systems evolve and take shape over considerable periods of time. It is subsequently argued that the issues both individuals and systems face can only be understood in relation to their histories. History in this instance needs to be examined both at a local, context-specific level, and in relation to more general ideas about what the activity 'should look like'. Any coaching act then, can only be grasped in terms of what preceded it. The fourth principle relates to the *centrality of contradictions* as a source of change and development. Although they generate disturbances, such contradictions are perceived as opportunities for innovation and progressive practice. The fifth and final principle is to do with the *possibility of expansive learning or transformations* within activity systems. This occurs when movement is generated as a result of progressive aggravation of the aforementioned contradictions leading to both questions and deviations from established norms. An example, here, could involve the adoption of an amended coaching philosophy or approach from a growing interrogation of practice.

Engeström (2001) drew a direct parallel between this final principle and Gregory Bateson's (1972) earlier hypothesis of learning. The ultimate phase of both theorizations was considered to be where a person or group begins to radically question the meaning of context and to consequently construct an alternative one. The purpose of expansive learning then, as viewed by Engeström, was to produce new cultural patterns of activity; in terms of the current chapter, perhaps an alternative way of coaching. Echoing the quote with which we began this section, such new patterns are not inherently stable or well understood ahead of time. On the contrary, they are 'learned as they are being created', making learning an unfolding journey into the relatively unknown. In expansive learning then, learners learn something that is not yet there. In other words, they construct and implement new knowledge in and through practice. Relatedly, the idea of a 'competent' teacher imparting prearranged knowledge is given considerably less credence than in other theorizations of learning. Taken as such, an AT standpoint, of which expansive learning is the latest incarnation, provides an ecological perspective from which to understand the accord connecting awareness and what people actually do (Nardi 1996; Jones et al. 2014).

Engeström's interpretation of AT also conceptualized human activity as resulting from the interaction of six inseparable and mutually constitutive elements: *subject(s), tools, object(s) and outcomes, rules, a community*, and *a division of labour*. In short, the system under study is referred to as a *community* or a group who share a common *object* and who use *tools* (or mediating artefacts) to transform it. In terms of coaching, the object (defined by Engeström as the 'raw material' or 'problem space' at which the activity is directed) can refer to the goal that both coach and athlete(s) are working towards (e.g. improving the latter's sprint technique). This can be considered as the primary focus of the activity system, and gives the activity its 'structured' or shared meaning (Kaptelenin 2005). In turn, this object is transformed into outcomes with the assistance of a variety of mediating instruments, which can be deemed the 'tools' used by a coach. These tools are considered to mediate thought between the coach (who can be considered the subject of the activity) and context, and can be either physical (i.e. material) or, 'perhaps more obviously in relation to coaching, to do with language and discourse' (Jones et al. 2014: 7). Material tools could, for example, be the cones, bibs or tactical boards used by coaches of invasion games. Similarly, they could also include the use of metaphor or verbal means of explanation taken from different perspectives in efforts to generate athlete learning. The rules, meanwhile, refer to the norms of the gym or sports field, which both enable and constrain the coach's (i.e. the subject's) actions. According to Jones et al.:

> rules can be [further] divided into those that concern the instructional context, and those that involve the social order. The first include evaluative rules towards the goal at hand, while the latter refers to the social rules that govern [contextual] interaction and organization.
>
> *(Jones et al. 2014: 7)*

Finally, as stated, those that comprise coaching (usually athletes and coaches) do so as members of an active community, a community who work towards a shared object. Additionally, like the beaters in Leont'ev's earlier cited example, within the community a given division of labour exists, with responsibilities, tasks and power being constantly (re)negotiated (Cole and Engström 1993).

Of course, Engeström's work is not without its critiques. A principal one is the assumption that contradictions (at the systemic level) are the motor or engine of progress and development. Here, Engeström presupposed that 'people confront themselves with specific contradictions, and that they gain the motivation to address and solve them' (Langemeyer 2006). In doing so, he has been accused of underestimating the probability that people only comply with and accommodate themselves to such tensions, not to generate some form of transformation, but conversely, to *avoid* any conflict; in essence, that people go along with change to avoid further discord and dispute, not because they feel liberated by it. Hence, lacking motivation to engage with such conflict or internalized constraints does not appear as a possible obstruction to learning (Langemeyer 2006). In some ways, this mirrors Avis's (2007) explicitly political critique that expansive learning, although accepting contradiction as a central tenet, essentially sidelines notions of concrete social antagonism, exploitation and oppression, leading to a conservative 'marginalization of radicalized and politicized agendas' (Avis 2007: 165). For Avis (2007: 169) then, the concept of expansive learning is far too functionally orientated and defined, it being little 'more than a consultancy aiming to improve work practices'.

Additionally, Young (2001) criticized expansive learning as a model seemingly directed at enhancing incidental learning. Hence, he queried 'to what extent can it be used in a context where learning is the explicit goal?' Similarly, he also asked 'how does the expansive learning cycle enable learners to access knowledge that does not emerge directly out of practice – for example, medical knowledge about new treatments and organizational knowledge about health policies' (Young 2001: 160). Finally, in this respect, Engeström's relatively weak integration of power into his writings has also drawn a degree of derision and critique (e.g. Blackler and McDonald 2000). Although Engeström and others (e.g. Engeström and Sannino 2010) have taken pains to respond to and rebuff such accusations, questions and criticisms of expansive learning and its relation to AT remain. Despite such scepticism, Engeström's work continues to provoke thought and reflection at theoretical and empirical levels.

Yrjö Engeström: application to sports coaching and a practitioner commentary by Christian Edwards

As stated in the introduction, in a slight departure from other chapters, we thought it pertinent to amalgamate the final two sections; that is, (1) an outline of the utility of Engeström's work to coaching, and (2) a practitioner commentary in relation to 'How does it actually work?' This was because almost all of us are either former or currently practising coaches, whilst three of us have actively attempted (and continue to attempt) to implement notions associated with AT in our coaching work. The following section then, is presented as a case-study illustrative of efforts to change the culture or 'social geography' of a semi-professional football club through the integration of (activity) theory to practice. It is written from one of our individual (Christian's) perspectives in a further attempt to ground such thinking in personal practice.

Yrjö Engeström: a coach's commentary, a view from the field: Christian's story

When I became the Director of Football in 2009, the *object* ('problem space') revolved around establishing a new culture and dynamic at the university-based football club where I worked. From the outset, I understood that the main learning challenge was organizational and could not be resolved simply by 'better' personal coaching. It needed more than another 'badge' and innovative drills. I also realized that the challenge was unique to the context; that there was no individual expert, specific model or functional system that would provide me with a linear solution. It was this realization that drew me to reading about AT and Engeström's interpretation of it. Although not the easiest to initially understand, on deeper reading the ideas increasingly resonated.

Within my context then, I came to see the *basic unit of analysis* as consisting of three separate but interconnected systems: that of the club, that of the student footballers, and that of the university. Within each, there existed multiple voices (*multi-voicedness*). These included myself as the Director of Football, the current squad of players, and club staff members, all of whom had conflicting opinions and interests regarding the club's culture and direction. The *historicity* of each of the three activity systems provided a background from which to analyse how these contradictions emerged within this active *community*. At the start of the new millennium, the club had enjoyed some successful years in the Welsh League's top tier and had reached the quarter-final of the Welsh Cup (2003–04). Since that period, however, performances had declined, resulting in relegation to the second division in 2007. When I was appointed, the club was a blank canvas; there was no longer a clear identity, while a culture caring of standards both on and off the field did not exist.

It was within this context that the student football activity system existed. When I arrived, it was evident that the players who formed the first team squad had established a 'social club' as opposed to a 'football club'. Here, the *rules* (norms, interactions and social conventions) were firmly focused on the social experience. The order had created a community of players who attached a greater importance to off-field activities than to playing performances. The existing *division of labour* reflected a hierarchy of player seniority, often regardless of ability. Here, the senior players put themselves before the club, and made arbitrary decisions in terms of training and game selection. There was a lack of respect for the game and for the club, and a high level of ignorance about the commitment, effort and ability required to achieve high-standard performances.

The culture was also reflected in the attitude of the university, whose overall expectations for the football club were low. Although the public rhetoric emphasized the existence of an elite performance structure, this was not reflected in practice, as little support existed for the club with regard to recruitment, facilities, equipment and rehabilitation. In some ways, this was not surprising as the club had also damaged its relationship with the university (and in particular the student union [SU]), principally by failing to honour financial commitments and not supporting key events.

I could see that instability existed in the connections between the club, players and university. I believed these differences could be reconciled by introducing a new pattern/activity based on my own experiences as a professional footballer, and my developing resonance with AT. This would allow for complementarity between the systems and the establishment of a new culture at the football club. To work towards this shared *object*, I began by instilling principles about maintaining and respecting high standards in everything. I was also constantly listening and analysing how other similar sports clubs had formed through their own historical contexts. I wanted to shape the football club; first and foremost based on how I was brought up as young professional apprentice, through establishing and respecting new *rules* and boundaries related to firm yet fair practice. My players then had to appreciate and value everything they were given and not take anything for granted. Additionally, I vowed not treat the players as I had been treated at another (later) club. I wanted a strong relationship with players, and to treat them justly and reasonably. There was no specific model or framework to work from, just some principles born from experience and some ideas guided by theory. Although I knew what I wanted, and tried to think through how the objective(s) would be achieved, implementing the process was not an uncontested, unproblematic or linear procedure. It was a journey into the relative unknown, where the learning patterns were not stable or clearly understood beforehand. Consequently, although I could articulate them, the practical uses of the 'new' standards were literally developed 'on the hoof' by myself, the players, and the management of the SU (i.e. the university). For the first two seasons I was in charge things were very difficult; a rollercoaster of emotions. Constructing an alternative culture did not happen overnight; the old patterns constantly struggled and fought against the new. There was an ongoing power struggle characterized by seemingly ever-present conflict, resistance and frustration, resulting in a dynamic, evolving and realigned *division of labour*. Through action, however, we all came to better understand the growth and shape of the evolving *rules*. From my own perspective, this meant mediating through language, discourse and modelling, to produce the desired change.

From the outset, I used these and other such *tools* to construct new cultural patterns of activity, often through constant critical questioning of the meaning of the existing club context. I was (and still am) always at training sessions, meetings and matches on time. The practice pitch and drills were laid out in advance. Actions and words were used to reaffirm expected standards. Once these boundaries (*rules*) were set, the consequences of contravening them were made clear. Players had to commit fully to the club and not miss matches as and when they pleased. The correct kit had to be worn both on and off the field; the excessive drinking culture was curbed. These principles not only challenged the players but also conflicted with the standard of support given by the university, where inadequate maintenance of resources and facilities had become normal practice. Throughout the first two seasons, these contradictions between the systems triggered numerous daily conflicts. Many questioned and fought against the new direction in varied ways.

Although I acted with conscientiousness and motivation, with hindsight I can see that I orchestrated several situations in-action to produce *outcomes* that allowed crucial steps in establishing the new culture. These included openly challenging egos in the dressing room, and within the (university) SU management, which often led to unforeseen consequences. Allies emerged from least expected places. Re-establishing supportive links with the university was crucial. I started by building relationships with key individuals, and meeting expected funding targets. The players had to earn the right to be supported, and they soon realized the benefit of this. By the end of the second season, the new patterns were becoming embedded. Although some tension continued to exist, I could now work better with new players, developing an understanding of what we wanted on and off the field. Additionally, players who had seen things change started to support the new culture and further standards. Even when inevitable disagreements occurred, players complied with the new social rules of the dressing room and generally resolved these issues themselves. There was initial evidence of transformation and a shift in the *division of labour*.

When Robyn joined the coaching team in the third season, there was another change of perspective. As coaches, we began to engage more explicitly with theory, linking it to all areas of practice; a process that continues to this day. We began orchestrating the application of developed principles through a more strategic approach as opposed to being overly reactive. To achieve these *outcomes*, we changed the mediating language-in-use (*tools*). Now, we increasingly talked to the players through suggestions and ideas, and less in terms of firm instructions. This was both challenging (to all involved) and rewarding. Sometimes we would use many cones to construct and configure a drill, but more than often, not. We wanted the knowledge internalized as soon as possible. Likewise, the challenges at the 'executive' level altered in nature. The club was growing faster than its management would easily allow, so our talk and negotiations with the university also developed. Although changed, the contest was nevertheless ongoing.

As we began to win (usually but not always) on the field, the respect gained from a variety of sources within the wider *community* grew. Greater investment and support was sought and, to a large extent, given. These included a dramatic improvement in our infrastructure and a bespoke stadium inclusive of a 3G artificial playing pitch; while our successful bid for promotion eligibility, which required further ground criteria development, was fully supported by the university management. Although positive, these changes have created new tensions and disturbances in the three systems, and it is likely that hostility towards the football club will always exist in certain areas. The cycle of expansion is not complete, and in all probability never will be.

It has been a long journey; never did I think it would pan out the way it did. At the start, it was just about giving credibility to the club and myself within the organization. The social rules of the club have never been written, but the norms and conventions have been accepted by the players and the coaches, and have become a part of the club's DNA. Over the six years, we have not stuck rigidly to these rules, as a degree of flexibility exists in their application. They are things we discuss and contest daily as coaches, through constantly debating the priority of values, beliefs and morals against performance. A high degree of interconnectedness now exists between the three activity systems of club, players and university. Still, the culture of the club (i.e. *the object* of the exercise) is constantly evolving and will never be inherently stable; the contestation and expansion goes on.

Yrjö Engström: critical questions

1. What are the five basic principles which underpin Engström's developed theorization of Activity Theory?
2. What are the six inseparable and mutually constitutive elements which, according to Engström, comprise human activity?
3. What are some of the criticisms of Engström's work?
4. What are some of the 'rules' evident in your coaching context? (or a coaching context you are familiar with).
5. Try to conceptualize your coaching context as a *basic unit of analysis*. What are the artefacts most prominent within it? What are its principal objectives?
6. How does such a unit (or contextual system) currently relate to other competing units or networks it is in contact with?

References

Avis, J. (2007) 'Engeström's version of activity theory: A conservative praxis?' *Journal of Education and Work*, 20(3): 161–177.

Bateson, G. (1972) *Steps to an ecology of mind*, New York: Ballantine Books.

Blackler, F. and McDonald, S. (2000) 'Power, mastery and organizational learning', *Journal of Management Studies*, 37: 833–852.

Blin, F. and Munro, M. (2008) 'Why hasn't technology disrupted academics' teaching practices? Understanding resistance to change through the lens of activity theory', *Computers and Education*, 50(2): 475–490.

Cole, M. (1988) 'Cross cultural research in the socio-historical tradition', *Human Development*, 31(3): 137–151.

Cole, M. and Engström, Y. (1993) 'A cultural-historical approach to distributed cognition', in G. Saloman (ed.) *Distributed cognition: Psychological and educational considerations*, Cambridge: Cambridge University Press, 3–17.

Engeström, Y. (1987) *Learning by expanding an activity: Theoretical approach to developmental research*, Helsinki: Orienta-Konsultit Oy.

Engeström, Y. (2001) 'Expansive learning at work: Toward an activity theoretical reconceptualization', *Journal of Education and Work*, 14(1): 133–156.

Engeström, Y. and Sannino, A. (2010) 'Studies of expansive learning: Foundations, findings and future challenges', *Educational Research Review*, DOI: 10.1016/j.edurev.2009.12.002.

Jones, R. L., Edwards, C. and Viotto Filho, I. A. T. (2014) 'Activity theory, complexity and sports coaching: An epistemology for a discipline', *Sport, Education and Society*, DOI: 10.1080/13573322.2014.895713.

Kaptelenin, V. (2005) 'The object of activity: Making sense of the sense-maker', *Mind, Culture and Activity*, 12(1): 4–18.

Langemeyer, I. (2006) 'Contradictions in expansive learning: Towards a critical analysis of self-dependent forms of learning in relation to contemporary socio-technological change', *Forum: Qualitative Social Research*, 7(1): Accessed from www.qualitative-research.net/index.php/fqs/article/view/76/155

Leont'ev, A. (1978) *Activity, consciousness and personality*, Englewood Cliffs, NJ: Prentice-Hall.

Leont'ev, A. N. (1981) *Problems of the development of the mind*, Moscow: Progress.

Nardi, B. (1996) *Context and consciousness: Activity theory and human–computer interaction*, Cambridge, MA: MIT Press.

Vygotsky, L. (1978) *Mind and society*, Cambridge, MA: MIT Press.

Young, M. (2001) 'Contextualising a new approach to learning: Some comments on Yrjö Engeström's theory of expansive learning', *Journal of Education and Work*, 14(1): 157–161.

11

IVOR GOODSON

Narrative coach learning and pedagogy

Jennifer McMahon and Brett Smith

Ivor Goodson: a short biography

From a childhood up in the outer suburbs of Reading in England, Ivor Goodson has come to be known as one of the world's leading academics in education. Goodson's father was a gas fitter, while his mother was a factory worker and then a dinner lady. During his adolescence he found school increasingly difficult and failed eight out of nine O-level exams. As a result, at 15 years of age, Goodson left school and obtained employment in a crisp factory. Some time later, with the encouragement of one teacher, Goodson returned to school. Even though he still found it difficult to identify with subject matter, he engaged in rote learning which subsequently resulted in him passing his examinations.

Goodson then went on to gain a degree in Economic History from the University of London. After completion of his degree, he conducted doctoral research on Irish immigrants in Victorian England. When Goodson completed his doctorate, he immediately gained employment as a lecturer at the University of Kingston from 1966 to 1969. It was during this time that Goodson found himself drawn to education, in particular the new comprehensive schools developed as a result of a scheme implemented by the Labour government. As a result, in 1969, his strong interest in education inspired him to go back and train as a teacher. Shortly after completing his teacher training he replaced university teaching with school teaching, starting work at a comprehensive school in Leicestershire.

For the last 30 years Goodson has dedicated his life to researching, thinking and writing about various issues in education such as curriculum history and the history of school subjects; change management and reform; teachers' lives and careers; professional and learning identities; narrative and educational policy and life politics. According to his website, Goodson has contributed to over 50 books and 600 journal articles, and has worked at numerous universities in England, Canada and the USA.

Most recently, Goodson conducted a large scale research project on people's life histories. In particular, the 'Learning Lives' project funded by the Economic and Social Research Council (ESRC) studied people's learning experiences across the life course and resulted in the book *Narrative Learning*, a key concept covered in this chapter. The theoretical insights generated by this project, as well as the 'Professional Knowledge' project funded by the European Union, led to an additional book entitled *Developing Narrative Theory*.

It may come as no surprise that Ivor Goodson has won numerous awards, with two of the most recent being elected Life Fellow of the Royal Society of Arts, and included in *Who's Who in the World*, both in 2009. Goodson is currently Professor of Learning Theory at the Education Research Centre at the University of Brighton in the United Kingdom.

Ivor Goodson: key concepts

Narrative learning theory

According to Goodson (2013), *narrative learning theory* emphasizes the role of narrative (i.e. the story of a lived experience or encounter) and narration (i.e. the action or process of telling a story) as an individual learning encounter where a particular understanding of how one acts in the world is established. In this respect, the process of recalling and transcribing or telling a story does not just provide us with a sense of who we are (i.e. identity), but the narratives we use to detail our lives can play an important role in the ways in which we learn from our lives and in the ongoing construction of our life story. In this way, narrative can be viewed as a site for learning to occur with action potential.

Goodson's epistemology in relation to narrative learning theory highlights two distinct educative encounters where learning occurs. The first learning encounter occurs through the knowledge that is acquired from the narratives (stories) we tell about our lives and ourselves. The second learning encounter occurs through the 'internal conversations' we have (Goodson 2013) through the process of the narration (either telling or transcribing) where the 'new' is incorporated into the existing narrative (Goodson et al. 2010). Goodson et al. (2010) says that such an internal conversation centres on the different voices one has within oneself. Each of these voices holds a different authority over the individual. These two distinct learning encounters central to narrative learning theory highlight why Goodson (Goodson et al. (2010) believes learning to occur *in* and *through* the act of narration.

Goodson's thinking and theorizing of narrative learning theory

Goodson's thinking and theorizing of narrative learning theory was born of a number of detailed case-studies where he conducted longitudinal interviews over a four-year period with participants who engaged with telling a life story.[1] Through this process, Goodson and colleagues realized that people spend a significant amount of time rehearsing and recounting their life story, which becomes a strong influence on their actions and agency, and an important site of learning in itself (Goodson et al. 2010). Further, this research revealed that narrative learning was not only evidenced in the substance of the narrative but also in the act of narration (Goodson et al. 2010). Goodson et al. (2010: 3) state that narrative learning is 'not solely learning *from the narrative*; it is also the learning that goes on *in the act of narration*.' As such, narrative resources can be seen as a kind of 'narrative capital' and the narrative 'repertoire' assists people to navigate change and transition in their lives (Goodson et al. 2010). It was during the Learning Lives project that Goodson and colleagues analysed the life stories collected and realized that the stories people tell about their lives could be likened to tools. Specifically, these tools varied in their characteristics (i.e. quality) and in the way that people made use of them to learn from their lives. Through this process, some interesting analytic categories relating to narrative quality and efficacy were found. Specifically, Biesta et al. (2011) identified five dimensions of narrative quality:

- narrative intensity (more or less elaborative);
- descriptive-analytical-evaluative;
- plot-emplotment;
- chronological-thematic; and
- theorized-vernacular.

In relation to learning potential, two key areas were highlighted:

- learning potential (i.e. the ways and extent to which certain narratives enable learning), and
- action potential (i.e. the ways and extent to which learning results in action) (Biesta et al. 2011).

These categories helped Biesta, Goodson and colleagues to analyse how narrative quality influences learning and how learning (if at all) translates into action.

The case studies provided by Goodson et al. (2010) reveal ample evidence of reflection on storying about and re-storying of the self. A person's sense of self is heavily embedded in the narrative construction. To be a person is not only to be connected to the narrative, but more importantly, it is to be connected to how a person lives their life in relation to that narrative which is central to an individual's learning and understanding of how to act in the world, thus providing insight and understanding of their life (Goodson et al. 2010). Narratives are, then, a fundamental form of meaning-making, with the potential to enhance lives, giving them coherence and meaning, and making them a significant site for individual learning. Narrative learning theory highlights the importance of both the narratives and narration process as important tools and sites for learning, and with the opportunity for possible action to result (Goodson et al. 2010). Further, narrative learning theory reveals how learning does not just have to be restricted to a formal educational setting, but can occur anywhere and at any time.

Critical discussion of narrative learning theory

While there is no disputing the potential of narrative learning theory as evidenced through the numerous studies that Goodson and colleagues have conducted, narrative learning theory still ultimately falls under the constructivist umbrella, because it is a requisite for the narrator to actively participate in the learning process. Specifically, the following cognitive learning process must be undertaken for learning to occur. First, the lived experience or encounter occurs in a pre-linguistic context. Then, the lived experience needs to be 'languaged', or 'storified' and it is only through the process of languaging or storifying the experience that meaning can be ascribed and subsequent learning can result. As Goodson et al. (2010) revealed, everyone has differing abilities to storify their lives and consequently, such differing abilities can affect subsequent learning and resultant action. Further, it is also essential to recognize that this process is primarily dependent on intrinsic motivation and that without this, narrative learning will not result.

It could also be assumed that individuals have varying abilities to reflect on the encounters they are transcribing. Narrative learning theory is dependent on a certain degree of reflexivity, as the encounter that is central to the narrative would need to be viewed from multiple perspectives or through a variety of lenses, otherwise the learning that could occur is somewhat limited to a singular or insular perspective. Through the process of narration, the narrator would need to consider whose voice the narrative is being told by and which other voices or alternative perspectives could be offered. Consideration of other perspectives and voices would in turn present different insights in the narrative. Additionally, in the act of narration, the narrator needs to also consider emotions and subconscious knowledge which have been embodied to ensure full understanding of the experience and the learning that occurs. Despite the learning that is believed to occur in and through the narrative process (as outlined above), not all learning that transpires from this process translates into action or transformation. Goodson et al. (2010: 4) assert that the 'narrative resources that people have available differ widely in their characteristics – their narrative quality – and in their efficacy.' Because of this, Goodson et al. (2010: 128) highlight that

> the presence of an elaborate, analytical and emplotted narrative is not, in itself, evidence of *ongoing* learning. It is here that the distinction between the narrative as the outcome of learning and the narration as a process of ongoing learning is important in theorising narrative learning – and we can characterise this as a distinction between more 'closed' and more 'open' narratives. But what our cases also show is that more 'open' narratives – narratives 'under construction,' so to say, narratives where there appears to be ongoing narrative learning – are not in themselves a guarantee for 'translation' into action.

Narrative pedagogy

Narrative pedagogy consists of narratives, reciprocation and pedagogic encounters (Goodson and Gill 2011). When we construct our narratives and swap them with each other, a pedagogic encounter takes place. Goodson and Gill's (2011) notion of narrative pedagogy suggests that educational endeavours are dependent on facilitating dialogue and deep personal engagement through narrative exchange. Specifically, they define narrative pedagogy as the 'facilitation of an educative journey through which learning takes place in profound encounters, and by engaging in meaning-making and deep dialogue and exchange' (Goodson and Gill 2011: 123).

The narrative pedagogy process does not have to be just restricted to text narratives but can also include verbal accounts and conversations. Relationships are fundamental to narrative pedagogy and for optimal learning to occur, as this requires an interplay of giving and taking (Hayden 1980). Witherell (1995: 40–41) further brings forth the importance of relationships in narrative pedagogy, saying how it

> allows us to enter empathically into another's life and being – to join a living conversation. In this sense, it serves as a means of inclusion, inviting the reader, listener, writer, or teller as a companion along on another's journey. In the process we may find ourselves wiser, more receptive, more understanding, nurtured, and sometimes healed.

Through such giving and sharing, the narrative exchanges mutually enrich each other's humanity (Hayden 1995) and pedagogic encounters take place.

Goodson's thinking and theorizing of narrative pedagogy

Goodson and Gill's (2011) thinking and theorizing about narrative pedagogy stemmed from the idea that narrative is not only a rich and profound way for humans to make sense of their lives, but also a process of pedagogical encounter, learning and transformation. They not only saw the potential of narrative as a phenomenon, but also as a methodology and pedagogy. However, unlike narrative learning theory outlined above, narrative pedagogy is not an individual learning encounter. Rather it requires individuals to reflect, revisit and collaborate with meaningful others in order to generate new understandings or an alternative way of knowing. In this respect, narrative pedagogy involves a reciprocation of narrative encounters between a person and another, and is deeply social. Fundamentally reflecting and examining the narratives of each other's lives in the process of learning is what is central to narrative pedagogy.

Through extensive research, Goodson and Gill (2011) found that through the construction of the narrative and then swapping of the narrative with another, pedagogic encounters arose (Goodson and Gill 2011). Subsequently, those individuals involved in the narrative pedagogy process take on the role of both learner and pedagogue as they embark on a narrative journey of inquiry, questioning, facilitating and learning in a reciprocal arrangement. This is central to narrative pedagogy. Narrative pedagogy has the ability to redefine the personal and professional identities of those involved in the process, as well as provide meaning to past lived experiences through the lens of present historical reality (Goodson and Gill 2011). Our capacity as humans to reconstruct our personal narrative through a reciprocation with another (i.e. teacher and student) allows us to gain a more critical and interpretive perspective on our life and thereafter our actions and ways of being in the world (Goodson and Gill 2011). Narrative pedagogy can thus lead to meaningful change and development for individuals and groups within a learning environment and in life learning.

Critical discussion of narrative pedagogy

Narrative pedagogy is based mostly on a theory of social constructivism wherein knowledge is constructed with another through a sharing of stories, artefacts and meanings. However, for this process to be successful, both parties who take part in the process need to agree to undertake an exchange of their narratives of lived experience. Moreover, this exchange is also dependent on a deep and trusting relationship. If one party is not as invested or is apprehensive about sharing deep personal insights, the learning outcome will be affected. Additionally, power relationships may affect one's ability to effectively engage in a meaningful exchange with someone who is older, more experienced, a mentor, etc. For instance, outside of the education context and in the coaching context, those with more perceived expertise hold a privileged position in terms of education (Johns and Johns 2000) and their ability to open themselves up to learning from someone not as experienced has been found to be limited (Zehntner and McMahon 2013).

Ivor Goodson: applications to sports coaching

Preparation of coaches and coach educators

Goodson's work raises key ideas that are essential to coaches' ongoing development and education. Two key points that emerge from Goodson's work (Goodson et al. 2010; Goodson and Gill 2011) in the educational context is the learning potential associated with narrative learning theory and narrative pedagogy. In particular, *efficacy* and the ways in which, as well as the extent to which, certain narratives allow for *learning* and *action potential* and the ways in which and the extent to which such learning may translate into action (Goodson et al. 2010; Goodson and Gill 2011). As Douglas and Carless (2008: 35) showed in their work with elite golf coaches, narratives (stories) stimulate 'new ways of seeing the world', thus Goodson's two key ideas outlined in this chapter have the potential to provide space for coaches to share, learn and reflect on their practice through narrative.

These revelations highlight the potential of narrative learning theory and narrative pedagogy in coach education. In some ways, which we outline below, Goodson's concepts have already been incorporated by a few coaching scholars unknowingly in coach education and coach development. However, this has occurred more through research investigations rather than through official coach education courses. Numerous coaching researchers have revealed how coach education often consists of a standardized curriculum with a focus on technocracy by providing coaches with tools to achieve competitive performance (Abraham and Collins 1998; Cushion et al. 2003; Nelson et al. 2006; Cushion and Nelson 2013). Specifically, in Australian swimming (the context which the coach practitioner below practises), to become an accredited coach, one needs to complete a general principles coaching course that includes a sport-specific practical component (12.5 hours total) with a bio-scientific focus and 30 hours supervised coaching practice (Australian Sports Commission, n.d.), where they obtain the knowledge and skills to deliver complex training programmes. No emphasis is placed on the sharing of stories and experiences or understanding one's own lived encounters using narrative as a tool.

While coaches constructing narratives and sharing them with others does not specifically occur in the coach education context, a handful of coaching scholars (Douglas and Carless 2008; McMahon 2013; Zehntner and McMahon 2013; Zehntner and McMahon, 2015) recently made use of narrative in various ways in relation to coach development and coach learning. In particular, narrative was used to initiate reflexivity and alternative ways of knowing. Bolton (2006) highlighted how critical reflection associated with personal narratives can assist the coach practitioner to understand the complexity associated with social and cultural aspects of coaching. Goodson revealed how in the process of narrative learning theory, the process of recalling and transcribing or telling a story, provides us with a sense of who we are (i.e. identity), and plays an important role in the ways in which we learn from our lives and in the ongoing construction of our life story. The work of Zehntner and McMahon (2015) has revealed how, for one coach (Zehntner), the narrative process assisted him as a coach practitioner to clarify whose themes/ideas he wanted to adopt in and through his coaching practice (Cassidy et al. 2009), and further recognize the forces (i.e. mentor coaches; cultural ideologies) that shaped him. Goodson et al. (2010: 3) state that narrative learning is 'not solely learning *from the narrative*; it is also the learning that goes on *in the act of narration*'. In and through the narrative process, Zehntner developed a sustainable, personally appropriate coach identity. Zehntner's learning (Zehntner and McMahon, 2015) subsequently was not unlike the experience of Kitrina Douglas (Carless and Douglas 2011), another coaching scholar who reflected on coaching events that occurred fleetingly, via the development of narratives and with positive results. Narrative learning and narrative pedagogy thus seek to shift the focus of learning from the prescriptiveness of a rigid curriculum to accommodate preferred narrative styles (Goodson et al. 2010). Goodson and Adair (2007), and Goodson and Gill (2011), acknowledge that a person's interior conversation, storying of a personally constructed encounter, is striking: 'It is striking in the sense that such a personal story becomes a "commanding voice" as people live their lives and take decisions and actions' (Goodson and Adair 2007: 2). It also can then be a crucial lens for viewing the interaction of identity, agency and learning, as realized in the work of Zehntner and McMahon (2013). The construction and analysis of personal narratives – the root of Goodson's narrative learning theory and narrative pedagogy – are fundamentally important to the development of a sustainable coaching identity, as they allow critical reflection on practice and on the cultural biases and dominant discourses influencing coaching practice (McLeod 2006).

Coaching literature reveals that a number of researchers have made use of aspects of Goodson's process of narrative pedagogy in coach education and coach development with positive results. However, as we outline the work of these coaching scholars below, it must be acknowledged that while narratives were presented to coaches, there was no reciprocation or opportunity to have an ongoing conversation with the narrator – a key aspect of narrative pedagogy as outlined by Goodson and Gill (2011). McMahon (2013) and Douglas and Carless (2008) presented athletes' stories to coaches in order to discover whether it would initiate a response or possible action. For these researchers, the athletes' narratives provided coaches with the opportunity to enter the mind of the athlete – to hear their stories of experience, feeling their emotions and personal dilemmas. For Douglas and Carless (2008) this was done with professional golf coaches, while McMahon (2013) worked with swimming coaches with various levels of expertise. Douglas and Carless (2008) found that coaches responded to the athletes' stories in three ways. The first included 'questioning' in the form of the action of challenging, seeking further information and reflective practice. The second response included 'summarizing' and active listening that led to coaches drawing their own conclusions. Finally, the coaches responded to the stories through 'incorporating' (i.e. incorporation of the athlete's story into their own experience, as well as displaying emotional reactions, such as empathy, to stories).

McMahon (2013) adopted a similar approach to that of Douglas and Carless (2008) with coaches in the sport of swimming. Various coaches with ranging levels of experience engaged with swimmers' lived experiences (in narrative text form). Like Douglas and Carless (2008), positive results were revealed as this narrative process initiated a method of self-discovery and knowing for the coaches. As such, the swimmers' narratives were an effective tool in allowing coaches space to cast a beam of consciousness over their own practice/pedagogy. As a result, self-reflection was initiated, in conjunction with increased empathy, and a more holistic and athlete-centred approach to coaching. While all the coaches reported that engaging with the athletes' narratives had some impact on their pedagogy, like the approach of Douglas and Carless (2008), this educative process was not a reciprocal arrangement of the giving and taking of narratives between coach and athlete. Indeed, Goodson and Gill (2011) and Hayden (1980) showed that for optimal learning to occur and subsequent pedagogic encounters to arise, the relational aspect of narrative pedagogy is essential to the process, with an interplay of giving and taking (Hayden 1980). This reciprocation or interplay did not occur in the research outlined above, and thus the learning and results that arose are limited in terms of what actually could be achieved when undergoing the process as outlined by Goodson and Gill (2011).

In coach education, it has been shown that technical competencies are often well catered for through a standardized curriculum with particular emphasis on bio-scientific content (Abraham and Collins 1998; Cushion et al. 2003; Nelson et al. 2006; Cushion and Nelson 2013). However, while the emphasis on coach education remains focused on technocratic ideologies, the concepts of narrative pedagogy and narrative learning theory outlined by Goodson et al. (2010) and Goodson and Gill (2011) could not only be easily integrated into coach education courses, but also made further use of by coaches as an ongoing reflective tool.

Ivor Goodson: a practitioner commentary by a swimming coach

The coach practitioner's voice included in this section has over 20 years' coaching experience in the sport of swimming. He has coached numerous athletes, from the beginner swimmer through to swimmers vying for national representation, as well as dabbling with the master swimmer. Goodson's concepts of narrative learning theory and narrative pedagogy were shared with the coach and his responses are below. Minor grammatical edits were made to his account and his identity remains confidential due to his wishes.

Narrative learning theory

I often find myself retelling or reliving an incident from the pool in a storied form. This may happen verbally as I share it with someone else (my wife or another coach) or it might be the process of me storying it internally and then reflecting upon it. I find this a valuable process – a process that assists me to gain clarity into what has occurred and how I might do something differently next time. Coaching for me is a process of constant reflection and reliving of incidents, encounters, conversations and performances. It needs to be, because the swimmers' performance is dependent on it. I think that any change is started by me and it usually involves a bit of detective work where I feel like I have to interpret different scenarios and figure out the why's and what's. In terms of the technical side of swimming, I have to consider a particular performance and think about how I can make a change for a better result. While I already undergo this sort of process, the concept of narrative learning theory has helped me realize how my learning actually occurs in and through the stories I tell and retell to myself.

Narrative pedagogy

As a coach, I see myself as the teacher of swimming and the athlete (swimmer) as the person who will get the benefit from the instruction. I see myself and my athlete or protégé in something like a teacher–student relationship. I bring a lot of experience and I often work with swimmers with limited experience and results in terms of performance. I know that I am always thinking about how I can prepare my swimmers better. I reflect on the things that I have control over but I also try to consider things that are out of my control. I know that it is the right thing to say that I can learn from the athlete as much as they learn from me. I do feel a little uncomfortable saying this but the only really helpful stuff that I get from athletes is how their personal lives affect their training. Sometimes you can tell that they are not right but physically they are OK. They are recovering OK but they just do not seem to be coping. It usually ends up being more about something in their personal lives. In terms of learning about or improving my coaching practice I cannot see the direct effect from the athlete.

I think that swimmers understand this approach and you can see it when they move between coaches as they are looking to tap into other, different or better knowledge. In that way, they too look at it as a teacher–student relationship. When I think about the theory by Goodson and Gill where there is a reciprocal learning agreement, I can see that on some levels this may be the case, such as the peripheral stuff that affects their performance, but the most important technical aspects are more from me. I definitely think that there needs to be agreement with the direction of the programme; if you are not both on the same page then that can cause conflict. I just think that my approach is not as balanced as this theory suggests that it should be.

Coaches are a competitive bunch so the stories told to each other often feel like they are just trying to outdo each other. The amount of times that I have heard stories about this swimmer or that swimmer and the amazing workload or mental toughness that they have. That sort of story is not really useful in terms of education. I'm always using stories with kids if I am trying to inspire them or warn them about what could happen to them if they stray from the path so to speak. In that way I use it like an educative tool, but I think narratives are most helpful to me when I share them with people who are not directly involved or can be directly affected. This is when my telling of a story changes me and what I do (coaching) the most. I find this a valuable process – a process that assists me to gain clarity into what has occurred and see how I might do something differently next time.

Ivor Goodson: critical questions

1. Using narrative learning theory, what process would a coach undergo for subsequent learning and possible action to occur?
2. Does narrative learning result in action for a coach?
3. According to Goodson, what role does the lived experience of a coach play in narrative pedagogy?
4. In a coaching context, why is it important for narrative pedagogy not to be an individual encounter?

Note

1 Goodson and Sikes (2001) use the term 'life story' to mean a person's view and account of their life, specifically the story they tell about their life.

References

Abraham, A. and Collins, D. (1998) 'Examining and extending research in coach development', *Quest*, 50: 59–79.

Australian Sports Commission (n.d.) 'Minimum course requirements', table, available at: www.coachingaus.org/levels.htm

Biesta, G., Field, J., Hodkinson, P., Macleod, F. and Goodson, I. (2011) *Improving learning through the life course*, Abingdon: Routledge.

Bolton, G. (2006) 'Narrative writing: Reflective enquiry into professional practice', *Educational Action Research*, 14(2): 203–218.

Carless, D. and Douglas, K. (2011) 'Stories as personal coaching philosophy', *International Journal of Sports Science and Coaching*, 6(1): 1–12.

Cassidy, T., Jones, R. and Potrac, P. (2009) *Understanding sports coaching: The social, cultural and pedagogical foundations of sports practice* (2nd edn), London: Routledge.

Cushion, C. J., Armour, K. M. and Jones, R. L. (2003) 'Coach education and continuing professional development: experience and learning to coach', *Quest*, 55: 215–230.

Cushion, C. J. and Nelson, L. (2013) 'Coach education and learning: Developing the field', in P. Potrac, W. Gilbert and J. Denison (eds) *The Routledge handbook of sports coaching*, London: Routledge, 359–374.

Douglas, K. and Carless, D. (2008) 'Using stories in coach education', *International Journal of Sports Science and Coaching*, 3: 33–49.

Goodson, I. (2013) *Developing narrative theory*, London: Routledge.

Goodson, I. F. and Adair, N. (2007) 'Combining methodologies to study learning in the life course: Insights from the learning lives project', European Conference on Educational Research (ECER), 19–21 September, Ghent, Belgium.

Goodson, I. F., Biesta, G., Tedder, M. and Adair, N. (2010) *Narrative learning*, London: Routledge.

Goodson, I. and Gill, S. (2011) *Narrative pedagogy: Life history and learning*, New York: Peter Lang.

Goodson, I. F. and Sikes, P. (2001) *Life history research in educational settings: Learning from lives*, Buckingham: Open University.

Hayden, T. (1980) *One child*, New York: Avon.

Hayden, T. (1995) *Tiger's child*, New York: Avon.

Johns, D. P. and Johns, J. S. (2000) 'Surveillance, subjectivism and technologies of power: An analysis of the discursive practice of high-performance sport', *International Review for the Sociology of Sport*, 35(2): 219–234.

McLeod, J. (2006) 'Narrative thinking and the emergence of postpsychological therapies', *Narrative Inquiry*, 16(1): 201–210.

McMahon, J. (2013) 'The potentiality of using narrative in coach education: A tool that affects short and long term practice?', *Sports Coaching Review*. DOI: 10.1080/21640629.2013.836922.

Nelson, L. J., Cushion, C. J. and Potrac, P. (2006) 'Formal, nonformal and informal coach learning: A holistic conceptualisation', *International Journal of Sports Science and Coaching*, 1(3): 247–259.

Witherell, C. (1995) 'Narrative landscapes and the moral education: Taking the story to heart', in H. McEwan and K. Egan (eds) *Narrative in teaching, learning, and research*, New York: Teachers College Press, 39–49.

Zehntner, C. and McMahon, J. A. (2013) 'Mentoring in coaching: The means of correct training? An autoethnographic exploration of one Australian swimming coach's experiences', *Qualitative Research in Sport, Exercise and Health*, 6(4): 596–616.

Zehntner, C. and McMahon, J. (2015). "The impact of a coaching/sporting culture on one coach's identity: how narrative became a useful tool in reconstructing coaching ideologies", Sports Coaching Review (OnlineFirst) pp. 1–17. doi:10.1080/21640629.2015.1051883 ISSN 2164-0629 (2015).

Critical and post-structural theorists

12

PAULO FREIRE

Problem-posing coach education

Lee Nelson, Paul Potrac and Ryan Groom with Claire Maskrey

Paulo Freire: a short biography

Paulo Freire was born on 19 September 1921 in Recife, Brazil. Educated at the University of Recife, Freire graduated from the School of Law in 1947 and received his Ph.D. from the University's Faculty of Philosophy, Science, and Letters in 1959. He was awarded the certificate of 'Livre-Docente' in History and Philosophy Education in 1961 and subsequently appointed as an academic member of staff. In 1963, Freire became director of Brazil's National Literacy Program, a position in which he sought to reduce the high level of illiteracy in Brazil at that time. The Brazilian coup d'état in 1964 brought Freire's work to halt, as his adult literacy programme was seen as subversive by the new regime. Indeed, during this time, Freire was twice placed under house arrest. He left Brazil, travelling first to Bolivia and eventually to Chile, where he remained in exile for the next five years. While in Chile, Freire secured a post at the University of Santiago. Following this, Freire spent some months in the USA at Harvard University before moving to Geneva to work for the World Council of Churches in Switzerland. In the 1980s Freire returned to Brazil and resumed university teaching duties in São Paulo, where he was later appointed Secretary of Education for the municipality of São Paulo.

Like many of the theorists discussed in this book, Freire's work is extensive. He was a prolific writer, and new books continue to be published posthumously. While Freire is perhaps best known for his classic and most widely read book, *Pedagogy of the Oppressed* (1970), he published a number of other important texts, including *A Pedagogy for Liberation: Dialogues on Transforming Education* (Shor and Freire 1987), *Pedagogy of Freedom: Ethics, Democracy, and Civic Courage* (1998), and *Teachers as Cultural Workers: Letters to Those Who Dare Teach* (2005).

Through these and other works Freire developed a critical, dialogical, and transformative pedagogical approach that strives to resist and reverse oppression by promoting humanization through liberation. These theoretical and practical insights resulted from his practical work and his reading of literature from an array of intellectual traditions, including liberalism, Marxism, critical theory, existentialism, phenomenology, and radical Catholicism. While Freire was of the belief that his theorizing could be applied to both the First World and the Third World, care should be taken when interpreting and applying Freirean ideas to Western settings, as, ultimately, the roots of Freire's pedagogy 'are deeply embedded in his experiences in Brazil, Chile, and other Third World countries' (Roberts 2000: 6). Freire received numerous awards. These included honorary doctorates, the King Balduin Prize for International Development in 1980, the Prize for Outstanding Christian Educators in 1985, and the UNESCO 1986 Prize for Education for Peace. Paulo Freire died of a heart attack in Rio de Janeiro on 2 May 1997, aged 75.

Paulo Freire: key concepts

Freire's moral philosophy

To better appreciate his educational propositions, it is important to develop an understanding of Freire's philosophizing about ontology (i.e. the nature of reality), epistemology (i.e. the nature of knowledge), and ethics (i.e. how people should act) (see Roberts 2000 for a detailed overview). Ontology is a branch of philosophy that deals with the nature of being and existence. There are many contrasting positions in this area of philosophy, and debates surrounding ontology are often very complex and highly contested. Of particular relevance to this chapter, Freire adopted a *dialectical ontology*. To understand this stance it is useful to consider how it differs from other ontological positions. For example, Freire eschewed mechanical objectivism; that is, he rejected the belief that human actions are directly caused by material and environmental influences. He did not see the world as a static and sequential set of 'cause and effect' relationships between people and their surroundings. Freire also rejected solipsistic idealism, which posits that there is no external world outside of our conscious minds. Contrary to these positions, Freire's dialectical ontology proposes that reality is a complex, unfinished, and evolving process involving interactions between human beings and the world. It is a position that holds there is an external world as well as our conscious understanding of it, and that both exist in a dynamic relationship.

Whereas ontology is a branch of philosophy that contemplates reality, epistemology is concerned with the nature of knowledge. In many ways, Freire's epistemology is a natural extension of his ontology. Again, in an attempt to understand Freire's epistemology it is useful to consider it in light of other belief systems. For example, Freire was not an epistemological relativist (Roberts 2000). He rejected the idea that there are no truths. Freire was of the opinion that some beliefs and ways of being are superior and morally preferable to others. Equally, however, it would seem incorrect to label Freire an absolutist, as he did not believe that there are static truths that transcend space and time. Rather, Freire held that knowledge is actively constructed within particular social relations and is, as a result, reflective of particular ideological and political formations (Roberts 2000). Knowledge, according to Freire, is constantly evolving and is constructed through dynamic encounters with the world and others.

Finally, it is important to give some thought to Freire's philosophizing about ethics. Central to Freire's writing on this topic was his exploration of the dialectic between *humanization* and *dehumanization*. Humanization in Freire's work refers to a process of becoming more fully human as a social, historical, communicating, transformative, and creative person (Salazar 2015). Importantly, Freire considered humanization to be an *ontological vocation*. That is, he believed that humanization was an undeniable feature of being human. In contrast, dehumanization was, for Freire, the thwarting of humanization. While Freire considered humanization to be an ontological vocation, he acknowledged that a person might experience humanization and/or dehumanization. Analytically speaking, however, Freire considered dehumanization to be a distortion of this ontological vocation.

Banking vs problem-posing education

Freire's most widely cited contribution continues to be his contrasting of *banking* and *problem-posing* forms of education in his internationally acclaimed book *Pedagogy of the Oppressed*. It was here that Freire famously claimed that education is suffering from 'narration sickness' (Freire 1970/1993: 52). His argument followed that the teacher–student relationship tends to comprise a narrating subject (i.e. the teacher) and a listening object (i.e. the student) that is expected to passively receive, memorize, and repeat the narrated content. Teachers, according to Freire's analysis, 'deposit' information into students who are waiting to be filled with the intellectual wisdom of their knowledgeable teachers (Freire 1970/1993: 53). Knowledge, therefore, is seen as a 'gift' bestowed by teachers on their passive and ignorant students (Freire 1970/1993: 53).

Freire termed this the 'banking concept of education' (Freire 1970/1993: 53). He was highly critical of such teaching practices, as he believed that banking education inhibits the development of critical thought and creativity by turning students into 'automatons', who come to accept the teacher's dominant but often 'fragmented view of reality' (Freire 1970/1993: 54). Freire also considered such teaching practices to be oppressive, as they promote ideologies of the oppressors 'who care neither to have the world revealed nor to see it transformed' (Freire 1970/1993: 54). From a Freirean perspective, banking education is thoroughly dehumanizing as it goes against a student's 'ontological vocation to be more fully human' (Freire 1970/1993: 55). Here it is clear how Freire's underpinning philosophical assumptions about ontology, epistemology, and ethics shaped his analysis of educational practices.

It was in light of his critique of banking forms of education that Freire (1970/1993) went on to propose *problem-posing* (or 'authentic' or 'liberating') education. Freire contrasted his problem-posing education with his analysis of banking education. Presented as an educational ideal, Freire's vision of problem-posing education

abandoned the goal of knowledge transfer ('depositing') and embraces instead a relational and dialogical understanding of practice. For Freire, this stance had significant
implications for resolving, what was for him, the teacher–student contradiction:

> Through dialogue, the teacher-of-the-students and the students-of-the-teacher
> cease to exist and a new term emerges: teacher-student with student-teachers.
> The teacher is no longer merely the-one-who-teaches, but one who is himself
> [or herself] taught in dialogue with the students, who in turn while being
> taught also teach. They become jointly responsible for a process in which they
> grow ... Here, no one teaches another, nor is anyone self-taught. People teach
> each other ...
>
> *(Freire 1970/1993: 61)*

In problem-posing education, the student is not considered to be a 'docile listener'
but rather a 'critical co-investigator' who engages in interactive inquiry with others
(Freire 1970/1993: 62). Dialogue is central to this pedagogical process. Rather than
issuing communiqués, the teacher-student communicates *with* the student-teacher,
and in so doing (re)learns with them (Roberts 2000).

Unlike banking education's goal of depositing static knowledge, Freire's problem-
posing education seeks to promote learning through the posing of problems that
the participants experience in and with their worlds. Such an approach, Freire
argued, helps to support the 'unveiling of reality' and the emergence of critical
thought, reflection, and creativity (Freire 1970/1993: 62). Through dialogue participants begin better to understand their world in ways previously unconsidered.
Central to Freire's discussion of problem-posing education, then, is a desire to help
those involved to 'perceive critically *the way they exist* in the world *with which* and *in
which* they find themselves' and to learn 'to see the world not as a static reality, but
a reality in process, in transformation' (Freire 1970/1993: 64). Problem-posing
education affirms that humans are not part of a predetermined historicity, but are
instead always in the process of becoming, and can transform themselves and the
world in which they live. Indeed, by entering into dialogical relations with others, it is
hoped that participants will 'begin to sense that dominant ideas can be challenged and
oppressive social formations transformed' (Roberts 2000: 55). By openly supporting
efforts to resist oppression, Freire's problem-posing education is a radical, critical,
and liberating pedagogy. It is an approach to education that aligns with Freire's
underpinning philosophical assumptions about ontology, epistemology, and ethics.

The widespread interest in Freire's work following the publication of *Pedagogy of
the Oppressed* was accompanied by numerous misinterpretations. In *A Pedagogy for
Liberation*, Freire endeavoured to address many of these misconceptions while elabor-
ating on his earlier thinking. One such misconception was that problem-posing
education, with its emphasis on dialogue, opposed the use of lectures. Freire corrected
this belief by explaining that lecturing is not necessarily incongruent with a liberating educational approach, as lectures can be used to illuminate reality and make it
less opaque. Freire was also keen to point out that democratic teaching should

never become laissez-faire (Shor and Freire 1987). Unlike student-centred pedagogies that seek to gradually withdraw the teacher from the learning process, democratic educators, for Freire, 'can never stop being an authority or having authority', as he believed, somewhat paradoxically, that authority permits the opportunity to become free (Shor and Freire 1987: 91). Of importance to Freire was not the giving up of authority, but, rather, teachers refraining from transforming 'authority into authoritarianism' (Shor and Freire 1987: 91).

In *A Pedagogy for Liberation*, Freire also sought to further clarify his beliefs about the teacher–student relationship. While stressing the importance that he placed on teachers working democratically with their students, importantly Freire acknowledged that in problem-posing education the teacher and student are not, in reality, entirely equal. Rather, Freire stressed that liberating teachers play a directive, albeit non-commanding, role:

> The teacher is unavoidably responsible for initiating the process and directing the study. Choosing goals makes neutrality impossible. By directing a course of study, by choosing certain books and by asking certain questions, and by the social relations of discourse in the class, every teacher expresses his or her political choices.
>
> *(Shor and Freire 1987: 157)*

Critiques of Freire's work

Of course, Freire's work is not without its critics and it has been subjected to a number of criticisms. In their summary of these various critiques, Roberts and Freeman-Moir (2013) highlight that Freire was accused of making education too political, employing an overly abstract writing style in his earlier work, failing to give adequate attention to class, gender, and ethnicity, and, despite being sympathetic to postmodernist thinking, seldom referring to the work of the writers in this area and employing terms and a dialectical understanding that many postmodernists had abandoned. In addition to this, Roberts and Freeman-Moir (2013) also discuss how the eminent sociologist Peter Berger attacked Freire's work for creating an epistemological dichotomy between the 'masses' and an intellectual vanguard, whereby educators are seen to possess the higher level of consciousness required to help students rise from their relative ignorance.

Paulo Freire: applications to sports coaching

The preparation of coaches and coach educators

It is our belief that Freire's work raises critical questions about the preparation and ongoing development of coaches, as well as the practice of coach education. For example, in *Pedagogy of Freedom* Freire wrote that 'teacher preparation should never be reduced to a form of training', and went on to contend that it 'should go beyond the technical preparation of teachers and be rooted in the ethical formation both of selves and of history' (Freire 1998: 23). Freire spoke of the need to promote within teacher education a *universal human ethic* that challenges elitists' exploitations of labour and those practices that promote racial, sexual, and class discrimination. For Freire (1998), it is essential that teachers be taught to deconstruct the dominant 'immobilizing ideology of fatalism, with its flighty postmodern pragmatism, which insists that we can do nothing to change the march of social-historical and cultural reality because that is how the world is anyway' (Freire 1998: 27). In other words, teacher preparation needs to take the form of problem-posing rather than a banking education.

Freire's recommendations for the professional preparation of teachers would appear to be at odds with existing coach education practices. Coaching scholars have, for example, questioned the 'education' in 'coach education', arguing that its provision might be more appropriately conceived as 'training' or even 'indoctrination' (Nelson et al. 2006; Chesterfield et al. 2010; Cushion et al. 2010; Cushion and Nelson 2013). The coaching literature suggests that coach education often comprises a standardized curriculum that privileges technocratic rationality through a 'tool box' of professional knowledge and a 'gold standard' of coaching (Abraham and Collins 1998; Cushion et al. 2003; Nelson et al. 2006; Cushion and Nelson 2013). The content of these courses tends to favour the bio-scientific disciplines (i.e. physiology, psychology, and biomechanics) and the technical and tactical features of sporting performance (Jones 2000). Thought is rarely given to the social, cultural, and historical aspects of coaching and the investigation of such features (Cassidy et al. 2009). Rather, the delivery of coach education often conforms to a 'methods-and-materials orientation' (Lawson 1993: 155), presenting coaching as a mechanistic process that can be learned and implemented in a standardized manner (Nelson et al. 2006; Cushion and Nelson 2013).

From a Freirean perspective coach education, in its present format at least, arguably does little to raise the critical consciousness of its coach learners or to help them to better understand how coaching is shaped by and in turn helps to reproduce dominant sporting ideology and experiences. This is problematic, as in their review of the exclusion and discrimination literature, Kamphoff and Gill (2013) highlight that there is an under-representation of female and ethnic minority coaches in sport. They explain that homophobia is also pervasive in sport at all levels. So it would seem that coach education should help coaches to appreciate that 'sport is not neutral' (Kamphoff and Gill 2013: 62). Rather, as Kamphoff and Gill (2013: 62) contend, the culture and organization of sport often 'leads to many of the issues experienced by women, racial minority, and gay/lesbian coaches' and, we would argue, athletes too.

Scholars are also becoming critical of the relationship between sport and neoliberalism. For example, in his highly insightful paper Coakley (2011) discusses how sport serves to reproduce neoliberalism and how neoliberal sports can shape peoples' experiences of physical activity. Coakley provides examples of how, in neoliberal society, sport is used as a vehicle to achieve certain political ends. Governments use international sporting events to promote national unity. Large corporations sponsor major events, teams, and celebrity athletes to promote the consumption of, at times, morally questionable products (e.g. fast food, soft drinks, and alcohol). He pointed out that heavily sponsored and promoted commercial spectator sports are also increasingly pervading the media and social consciousness. Sports that fail to match the ideal of highly organized and competitive activity are thus increasingly losing community support. Under neoliberal conditions, even the pursuit of seemingly positive social outcomes is accompanied by questionable consequences. For instance, Coakley talks of the displacement and involuntary relocation of marginalized populations during urban sports-related regeneration projects. He also speaks of the growing number of 'rehabilitation-oriented' programmes offered by 'sports entre-preneurs' who seek to develop within 'disaffected youths' those attributes needed to thrive in neoliberal society (Coakley 2011).

Freire (2005) was highly critical of neoliberalism and called for ethically grounded and critical forms of pedagogy that question neoliberal practices and their dehu-manizing effects. From a Freirean perspective coach education should purposely seek to raise coaching practitioners' awareness of the above-described realities. Freire (2005) reminds us that we cannot escape an ethical responsibility for our actions in the world because genetics, culture, and/or class do not determine us. Rather, we are genetically, culturally, and socially *conditioned*, not *determined*, hence the future is not fatalistically predetermined. That is, coaches and administrators have the ability not only to understand but also to transform this reality.

Freire was, however, cognizant of the fact that historical conditions lead many students to view education as a vehicle for acquiring the requisite technical knowledge to gain paid employment (Shor and Freire 1987). Because of this, Freire believed that educators needed to accept that they have a responsibility to develop within their students those scientific and technical skills and understandings required of a given job. In addition to this, though, Freire suggested that liberating educators also have an obligation to unveil and demystify dominant ideology (Shor and Freire 1987). While Freire would no doubt have encouraged coach educators to cover course content specific to the technical, tactical, and bio-scientific features of coaching, we deduce that he would likely have stressed to coach educators the importance of helping their coach learners to understand the discriminatory and dominating sporting practices that exist.

It might come as little surprise to learn that Freire (2005) was extremely critical of 'prepackaged educational materials' (Freire 2005: 15) that define the content, delivery, and assessment methods expected of teachers. For Freire these materials restrict teacher autonomy and evince a lack of trust. He considered the application of teaching packages to be ironic and contradictory, as many of them aspire to promote critical thinking and creativity while, in reality, domesticating and enslaving teachers to delivering content based on a prescribed set of guidelines. Freire would likely have been critical of existing coach education practices, as coach educators are frequently required to deliver curriculum, learning resources, and candidate assessments in prescribed formats (Cushion et al. 2010). The content and timing of courses are often articulated in detailed educator packs and through educator training courses (Nelson et al. 2014). External verifiers also regularly check delivery standards and consistency (Cushion et al. 2010). From a Freirean perspective this might be considered a tactic employed to instil and invoke fear, so that coach educators begin to internalize 'the authoritarian ideology of the administration' in acknowledgement of the fact 'that at any given moment they might be watched' (Freire 2005: 16). Freire believed that educators should actively resist such attempts to domesticate their role through the application of teaching packages and their administration.

The indispensable qualities of progressive coach educators

Freire's work also provides an opportunity for coaching to clearly focus on certain qualities needed in the coach educator. In the Fourth Letter in his book *Teachers as Cultural Workers: Letters to Those Who Dare Teach*, Freire (2005) outlined a number of virtues that he considered indispensable to the progressive teacher. According to Freire these attributes are not innate but rather acquired, over time, through practice.

- *Humility*: Central to humility is an understanding that 'No one knows it all; no one is ignorant of everything. We all know something; we are all ignorant of something' (Freire 2005: 72). Assuming this democratic, non-elitist, position permits the teacher to be ready not only to teach but also learn. It promotes listening and therefore opens up a space for dialogue to occur.
- *Lovingness*: Liberality teachers, Freire believed, need to possess a love not only of their students but also of the act of teaching. He termed this 'armed love', which he described as 'the fighting love of those convinced of the right and the duty to fight, to denounce, and to announce' (Freire 2005: 74). Without this 'armed love' Freire believed that teachers would be unable to realize their dreams and survive the demanding conditions in which they operate.
- *Courage*: According to Freire, teachers need courage to fight their fears. He explains that the political nature of the work of progressive educators can be fear inducing, as attempts to provoke the critical consciousness of students directly contest the ideology of the dominant power. Teachers, then, need to learn to harness fear by reducing the risk associated with their work while avoiding its immobilizing nature.
- *Tolerance*: Freire explains that tolerance is learning to live with and respect difference. This does not mean ignoring disrespectful acts or acquiescing to the intolerable. Freire argued that the 'act of tolerating requires a climate in which limits may be established, in which there are principles to be respected' (Freire 2005: 77).
- *Decisiveness*: The making of decisions was, for Freire, a central feature of the work of educators. This is, however, a difficult task, as it requires educators to weigh up and trade off those options available to them. Teachers must

recognize that while 'they cannot take sole responsibility for the lives of their students, they must not, in the name of democracy, evade the responsibility of making decisions' (Freire 2005: 79).

- *Security*: Whereas indecision suggests a lack of confidence, Freire was of the belief that an educator secure in his or her actions 'requires scientific competence, political clarity, and ethical integrity' (Freire 2005: 79). Being secure, then, requires educators to articulate how and why they practise in the ways that they do, to know whom and for what they support or oppose, and to permanently seek justice.
- *The tension between patience and impatience*: Freire contended that educators require both patience and impatience, as alone neither of these qualities will suffice. On its own patience can lead to inactivity and make the educator's practice ineffective. Similarly, unaccompanied and untempered impatience may lead to blind and irresponsible activism. The two, then, must live in permanent tension through the practices of the 'impatiently patient' educator (Freire 2005: 81).
- *Verbal parsimony*: This quality runs alongside Freire's discussion of the tension between patience and impatience. Being overly patient, for Freire, can stifle anger, whereas impatience can lead to a lack of restraint. Those who live impatient patience, in contrast, rarely 'exceed the limits of considered yet energetic discourse' (Freire 2005: 81).
- *Joy of living*: Freire (2005) argued that by 'completely giving myself to life rather than to death – without meaning either to deny death or to mythicize life – I can free myself to surrender to the joy of living, without having to hide the reasons for sadness in life, which prepares me to simulate and champion joy in the school' (Freire 2005: 82).

The field of sports coaching has given little thought to those qualities that coaches and coach educators might need to develop in order to become more effective practitioners. The participants of a study by Nelson et al. (2013) reported that desirable coach educator qualities include being knowledgeable, enthusiastic, experienced, well prepared, and effective presenters and demonstrators, and possessing a willingness to humbly share their opinions with others. In their exploration of the principles of humanistic psychology for discussions about 'athlete-centred' coaching and 'coach-centred' coach education, Nelson et al. (2014) have also considered the utility of those qualities (i.e. congruence, unconditional positive regard, and empathy) that Rogers (1969) believed need to exist in the relationship between the facilitator and learner (see Chapter 7). Freire's work offers a set of virtues that he considered important for those practitioners engaging in critical, liberating, and democratic education. Central to Freire's virtues is seemingly a call to liberate educators to learn how to take a balanced approach to the many tensions that they face in their work. This, arguably, includes striving not to be too dominant and forthright, while at the same time trying to avoid becoming overly passive and docile.

Paulo Freire: a practitioner commentary by Claire Maskrey

I am a coach educator for netball and have been involved in the delivery of Levels 1 and 2 coaching courses for the last seven years. I have an underlying interest in coach education and am currently undertaking my Ph.D., exploring emotions in this area. However, the first time I encountered Freire was when Lee, Paul and Ryan asked me to reflect on the ways in which his work might provoke ideas and clarify some of my current practices as a coach educator. Through my increasing awareness of the social aspects of coaching and coach education, Freire's philosophical positioning and theorizing offered a new viewpoint from which to reflect critically on my role and actions as a coach educator.

Drawing on Freire's theoretical concept of *banking* triggered a consideration of how this relationship exists when I deliver coach education courses. Rather surprisingly, I found that indeed I am sometimes perhaps exposed to 'narration sickness' as well as culpable of delivering information this way. In the training I receive as a coach educator, I am required to subscribe to a specific way of promoting how a coach should coach in both content and methods. The nature of my role means that I must deliver highly detailed course material which, on reflection, may not always coincide with my personal preferences for course content and approaches. If coaches challenge the content or deviate from it, for example when providing a demonstration or giving feedback, my job is to highlight to them the way that the course expects them to coach. It dawns on me that conveying the message of a player-centred approach when coaching within the course is perhaps not matched by the coach-centred way of developing coaches at present. As a result, I feel I am becoming increasingly aware of the way in which, currently, the coach education courses I deliver may provide a very limited consideration of the individual backgrounds and experiences that coaches bring with them to the course.

In reading Freire's concept of *problem-posing*, where the ideal is to develop interactive and dialogical learning, I feel guilty that this is something that just does not often happen in the coach education courses I am involved in. I sometimes do this sporadically, deviating from the tutor script notes, and feel it allows more engagement and pooling of knowledge, to the point where I am learning too. In some instances, I can see that this approach may have a lot to offer in coach education courses but it is perhaps unrealistic to implement fully given the time constraints and amount of content that must currently be covered. The element of retaining some degree of authority within this approach is an interesting and key point with which I agree, and is critical to ensuring that learning takes place. The way I deliver coach education is shaped by various influences. These include England Netball, the coach educator I am working alongside, and other external bodies, as well as the nature of the group of coaches on the actual course and my previous experiences over the years. I also feel that within these competing influences it can be difficult and sometimes impossible to completely leave personal preferences behind.

Through becoming more familiar with a Freirean perspective I have been able to critically consider the topics covered in coach education courses. As identified in the points raised earlier in the chapter, the course content primarily focuses on the technical performance of skills, related tactical aspects, and the way to coach. Indeed, Freire's work has raised my awareness of the absence of social, cultural, or historical aspects from the course, and as a result made me question how they could be integrated. This would potentially provide both coach educators and coaches with a greater appreciation of individuals and their experiences, and challenge dominant ideologies.

When considering the qualities that Freire suggests are indispensable to a progressive educator, I initially found some of them difficult to relate to and requiring several readings to understand. However, the two key ones that I feel I have developed to some degree whilst working as a coach educator are *decisiveness* and *courage*. Although I must follow a predetermined plan, I do look at a course as I am delivering it, and I shape the prescribed content and delivery style if required, in order to meet the greater needs of the coaches on the course. Overall, it seems evident that, on the whole, I do not possess many of the qualities in Freire's list when tutoring a coach education course. I feel there is very little chance for me to express or demonstrate *humility* or *tolerance*, mainly due to the content, expectations, and underlying requirements of the course. Rather I would criticize myself as perhaps being too patient as an educator to bring about a change in this approach. This is partly due to my casual employment as a coach educator, which could link also to the limited *security* and *verbal parsimony* that I have in the situation. I would aspire to develop many of these qualities, but in my role as a coach educator, on a casual basis, I feel I have limited opportunities to do so.

My impression is that Freire's work seems to offer interesting perspectives and approaches to achieving successful educational outcomes. His ideas have certainly highlighted how restricted I feel and how frustrated at the limited changes that I could possibly incorporate to enhance the training of coaches. I think I now may have a greater awareness of the level of *dehumanization* that is the reality of working as a coach educator in a large organization, which then filters through to the coaches I am training. At present, it certainly appears, upon reflection, that the qualities I currently employ as a coach educator are some distance from providing the critical, liberating, and democratic way of educating that Freire envisages.

Paulo Freire: critical questions

1. What is 'problem-posing' education and how is this different to 'banking' education? Which of these forms of education typifies existing practices in coaching and coach education?
2. Why does Freire consider narration to be oppressive and dehumanizing and dialogue to be liberating and humanizing? Do coaches and coach educators typically narrate or promote dialogue?
3. How should we envisage the 'coach–athlete' and 'coach educator–coach learner' relationships in light of Freire's work and why?

4. Should the preparation of coaches focus on training in practical knowledge and competencies and/or help practitioners to develop a critical appreciation of dominant sporting ideology, and why?

5. What qualities do you think coaches and coach educators need to develop in order to be effective and why? How do these relate to those virtues that Freire considered indispensable to progressive education?

References

Abraham, A. and Collins, D. (1998) 'Examining and extending research in coach development', *Quest*, 50: 59–79.

Cassidy, T., Jones, R. and Potrac, P. (2009) *Understanding sports coaching: The social, cultural and pedagogical foundations of sports practice* (2nd edn), London: Routledge.

Chesterfield, G., Potrac, P. and Jones, R. L. (2010) '"Studentship" and "impression management": Coaches' experiences of an advanced soccer coach education award', *Sport, Education and Society*, 15(3): 299–314.

Coakley, J. (2011) 'Ideology doesn't just happen: Sports and neoliberalism', *Journal of ALESDE*, 1(1): 67–84.

Cushion, C. J., Armour, K. M. and Jones, R. L. (2003) 'Coach education and continuing professional development: Experience and learning to coach', *Quest*, 55: 215–230.

Cushion, C. J. and Nelson, L. (2013) 'Coach education and learning: Developing the field', in P. Potrac, W. Gilbert and J. Denison (eds) *The Routledge handbook of sports coaching*, London: Routledge, 359–374.

Cushion, C., Nelson, L., Armour, K., Lyle, J., Jones, R., Sandford, R. and O'Callaghan, C. (2010) *Coach learning and development: A review of literature*, Leeds: Sports Coach UK.

Freire, P. (1970/1993) *Pedagogy of the oppressed*, London: Penguin.

Freire, P. (1998) *Pedagogy of freedom: Ethics, democracy, and civic courage*, Oxford: Rowman and Littlefield.

Freire, P. (2005) *Teachers as cultural workers: Letters to those who dare teach*, Boulder, CO: Westview Press.

Jones, R. L. (2000) 'Towards a sociology of coaching', in R. L. Jones and K. M. Armour (eds) *The sociology of sport: Theory and practice*, London: Addison Wesley Longman, 33–34.

Kamphoff, C. S. and Gill, D. L. (2013) 'Issues of exclusion and discrimination in the coaching profession', in P. Potrac, W. Gilbert and J. Denison (eds) *The Routledge handbook of sports coaching*, London: Routledge, 52–66.

Lawson, H. (1993) 'Dominant discourses, problem setting, and teacher education pedagogies: A critique', *Journal of Teaching in Physical Education*, 12: 149–160.

Nelson, L. J., Cushion, C. J. and Potrac, P. (2006) 'Formal, nonformal and informal coach learning: A holistic conceptualisation', *International Journal of Sports Science and Coaching*, 1(3): 247–259.

Nelson, L., Cushion, C. J. and Potrac, P. (2013) 'Enhancing the provision of coach education: The recommendations of UK coaching practitioners', *Physical Education and Sport Pedagogy*, 18(2): 204–218.

Nelson, L., Potrac, P., Cushion, C. and Groom, R. (2014) 'Carl Rogers, learning and educational practice: Critical considerations and applications in sports coaching', *Sport, Education and Society*, 19(5): 513–531.

Roberts, P. (2000) *Education, literacy, and humanization*, Westport, CT: Greenwood Press.

Roberts, P. and Freeman-Moir, J. (2013) *Better worlds: Education, art, and Utopia*, Plymouth: Lexington Books.

Rogers, C. (1969) *Freedom to learn*, Columbus, OH: Merrill.

Salazar, M. (2015) 'Reframing Freire: Situating the principles of humanizing pedagogy within an ecological model of the preparation of teachers', in M. Bigelow and J. Ennser-Kananen (eds) *The Routledge handbook of educational linguistics*, London: Routledge, 197–209.

Shor, I. and Freire, P. (1987) *A pedagogy for liberation: Dialogues on transforming education*, New York: Bergin and Garvey.

13

JACK MEZIROW

Transformative coach and athlete learning

William G. Taylor with Leol Collins

Jack Mezirow: a short biography

Jack Mezirow was born in 1923 and raised in Fargo, North Dakota. He was a bright high school student who went on to complete both his bachelor's and master's degrees in Social Science at the University of Minnesota. He later gained a doctorate in Adult Education from the University of California at Los Angeles. Mezirow's academic life centred on his interest in the nature of learning and on adults as learners. Mezirow's early thoughts on the role and nature of education were influenced by the writings and ideas of the philosopher, psychologist, and educational reformer John Dewey (see Chapter 4) and, in particular, the concepts foregrounded within the 1938 book *Experience and Education*. Much of the development of his education at this time was influenced by Dewey's thinking on the nature of democracy and the purpose of universal education. It was Dewey's belief that educational institutions, as well as the communal interactions found within them, could enable wider social reform that, above all, appealed to Mezirow.

Mezirow's wife, Edee, returned to education to complete her undergraduate degree at Sarah Lawrence College in 1973. It was with the witnessing of her experiences that these influences crystallized and paved the way for the emergence of Mezirow's commitment to develop his thinking and theories on transformative learning within adult education. Inspired by Edee's own transformation in her thinking and attitudes, Mezirow committed himself to undertake a large qualitative study of female adults who had returned to local community colleges or who had undertaken workplace learning in the USA. From this initial study, Mezirow began to see patterns within the data and concluded that most of the women had undergone a transformation in their personal attitudes and fundamental beliefs.

In 1978, Mezirow published his theory of transformative learning in the journal *Adult Education Quarterly* (1978b) and went on that same year to present it at the

National Adult Education Research Conference. Mezirow devoted the rest of his academic life to refining and adapting his ideas on the nature of transformative learning (Mezirow 1991, 1996, 1997; Cranton 1994, 1996). Interest in the work of Mezirow and the concept of transformative learning in adults has resulted in numerous journal articles and scholarly papers, more than a dozen books and over 150 doctoral dissertations (Kitchenham 2008). Mezirow died in September 2014 aged 91.

Jack Mezirow: key concepts

Within his (1978a) original paper, Mezirow suggested that many of the women whom he had studied in their return to adult education had found the experience both unsettling and enlightening and had gone through a form of transformation in their educational and personal thinking. He went on to claim that the way individuals altered their perspectives of their world and see it in a different light was not always accompanied by an epiphanic moment, but could instead be mapped as a number of phases that they might pass through. These original phases (1978a, 1978b), as outlined in Table 13.1, continued to act as the basic structure that accompanied Mezirow's thinking throughout the evolution of his ideas on transformative learning. The key elements of transformative learning, according to Mezirow (2009), were critical reflection and critical discourse. In undertaking personal critical reflection, an individual may realize that the foundations and realities of their once-held beliefs can no longer accommodate alternative ideas or apparent contradictions. Through critical discourse with self and others, they assess the truth-value of emerging alternative solutions which seem to cope with the limitations of their original set of beliefs. These considerations about the nature of the transformative experience of learning can be seen as a combination of his findings from the initial research and his commitment to, and continued interest in, the writings of Thomas Kuhn (1962), Paulo Freire (1970; see Chapter 12) and Jürgen Habermas (1971, 1984).

Mezirow's thinking about transformative learning was inspired and informed by the ideas of a number of educational theorists, social activists, and philosophers of science. Fellow American academic Thomas Kuhn (1962) developed the notion of paradigm shifts in which he argued that there was no compelling evidence for a linear development of scientific thought, rather, that changes in the way we consider scientific problems was the result of ongoing conflicts between different groups who hold differing beliefs. These groups who share similar beliefs gather around commonly held basic scientific assumptions and positions and, in turn, disagree with alternative camps on the nature and belief of fundamental scientific principles. Kuhn observed that particular groups may share commonly held beliefs and communally agree on the questions that still remain, are legitimate and yet unanswered, and that their commonly shared 'frame of reference' unites them under a 'particular paradigmatic position'. These paradigms both enable the advancement of a certain set of beliefs and restrict the development of counter claims and positions. A particular paradigm, or way of seeing the world, holds authority until it, in turn, fails to account fully for emerging contradictions that it can no longer explain within the present 'frame of reference'. The key aspect for Mezirow here was the observation that Kuhn's theory accounted for dramatic shifts in paradigms (frames of reference) and the associated thinking of those committed to them. For Mezirow, these notions echoed what he had observed in his study of adult women returnees and their experiences of educational processes and the reassessment of once held beliefs, this being a fundamental part of transformative learning.

Kitchenham (2008) suggests that we can trace the first four phases of Mezirow's early transformative learning theory to the influence of Kuhn's notion of nonlinear paradigm shifts (see Table 13.1). For perspective transformation (an individual paradigm shift) to take place, 'habits of mind' (i.e. personal beliefs about certain principles, legitimate questions, and possible solutions to individual issues) require a 'meaning scheme'; this is where individual interests and personal dilemmas are developed, pursued, and discussed to allow the previously held contradictions to be worked through and resolved. These meaning schemes, if collectively arrived at, may result in collective paradigm change. These resolutions of earlier ways of thinking, now deemed inadequate to explain an individual's experiences, are replaced by new commitments and a new personal worldview. This perspective transformation (a new paradigm) brings with it a sense of clarity and generates new considerations and novel ways of reflecting on events both present and past.

Mezirow drew on the writings of Paulo Freire (1970) in the development of the emancipatory aspects of transformative learning (see Chapter 12). Freire was very critical of the traditional modes of education of the time, believing that they resulted in learners being overly dependent on the teacher as the sole source of knowledge, as well as being limited by external control of the 'official' curriculum. These controlling structures, where passivity is encouraged and learning deemed instrumental, restrict the individual's ability to be challenged or, indeed, challenge

TABLE 13.1 Mezirow's (1978a, 1978b) ten phases of transformative learning

Phase 1	A disorienting dilemma
Phase 2	A self-examination with feelings of guilt or shame
Phase 3	A critical assessment of epistemic, sociocultural, or psychic assumptions
Phase 4	Recognition that one's discontent and the process of transformation are shared and that others have negotiated a similar change
Phase 5	Exploration of options for new roles, relationships, and actions
Phase 6	Planning of a course of action
Phase 7	Acquisition of knowledge and skills for implementing one's plans
Phase 8	Provisional trying of new roles
Phase 9	Building of competence and self-confidence in new roles and relationships
Phase 10	A reintegration into one's life on the basis of conditions dictated by one's perspective

Source: Adapted from Kitchenham 2008.

themselves at fundamental and conceptual levels. These conditions lead to a failure to develop a critical consciousness among individual learners, resulting in a disempowerment in terms of personal growth and a nullification of the emancipatory potency of education. For Freire and, later, Mezirow, the emergence of critical consciousness was a crucial factor in the ability of individuals to challenge their situation and, thus, challenge their thinking. Mezirow borrowed many of his ideas surrounding critical reflection and the growth of a critical self from individual elements of Freire's work (1970, 1973).

Another social theorist of the time, Jürgen Habermas, provided Mezirow with an understanding of 'domains of learning'. Kitchenham (2006, 2008) argues that it was the reading of Habermas' ideas on domains of learning that influenced Mezirow's (1996) paper published in *Adult Education Quarterly* and the development of his original concepts to incorporate three forms of learning into his theory. Habermas (1971) described learning as having three differing domains, each having its own particular purpose (*telos*). Learning, for Habermas, could either be categorized as (1) the technical (i.e. where learning is completed by rote, is instrumental in nature and thus aligned to a particular outcome); (2) the practical (i.e. the development of social norms and behavioural conditions), and (3) emancipatory learning (i.e. where the outcome is less about what can be repeated, or behaviours internalized, and more about the growth of the self via the introspective consideration of an individual's own place in the world, as well as the nature and origins of their knowledge). It was the emancipatory aspect contained within Habermas's last domain of learning which Mezirow incorporated into his theory.

It would be easy to suggest that the development of Mezirow's thoughts on transformative learning within adults is no more than an amalgamation of other theorists' key themes assembled to help provide descriptors for the phases of transformative learning. Mezirow, however, not only acknowledged the influences he drew from these theorists, but was also conscious that his ideas needed refinement and adaption as they became subject to increased critical consideration and as the number of educational scholars using his ideas in field-based research grew (Mezirow 2000; King 2002). One could argue that the adaptive nature of Mezirow's ideas, and the fact that he revised and added to the key concepts throughout his academic life, remains one of the strengths of his thinking on transformative learning and its effect on individuals' thoughts.

For Mezirow, transformative learning was all about change. It was about effecting change within the frames of reference of an individual that guides and constrains the way we see and consider the world. Not only do these frames of reference shape our very fundamental briefs, but they also provide justification for the rejection of ideas and concepts that are deemed non-compatible with our existing set of assumptions (Mezirow 1991). These frames of reference become established via explicit and implicit learning, and the embodiment of cultural norms, and are shaped by our own experiences and background. They are composed of two dimensions: *habits of mind* and *points of view*. Habits of mind are habitual ways of thinking about broad and abstract notions; they tend to be robust and underpin many of our central thoughts and judgements. These can be culturally, politically, educationally, and ethically acquired and form the basis for much of our commitments to particular ways of seeing the world. Points of view, however, provide individuals with a way of dealing with, and understanding, particular aspects of life that do not present themselves as expected; they allow us to cope with temporal change, accommodate low levels of conflict and deal with aspects of challenge on a day-to-day basis. They are more readily open to change as we deal with contested interaction with those around us. Mezirow tentatively suggests that the more entrenched we are within our frames of reference, the more dismissive we are of other ways of seeing the world. He goes on to suggest that not only do we discard alternative ideas, but also, such is the degree of rejection within an engrained frame of reference, that we blind ourselves to any merit or quality the conflicting idea may, indeed, possess. Positions which are adopted within a rigid and exclusive frame of reference, limit critical reflection and restrict the development of autonomous thinkers.

For Mezirow, the development of independent and responsible thinkers was the product of an individual's adoption of critical reflection as a core element of their frame of reference. Critical reflection provides not only the opportunities to review one's own set of assumptions and dispositions, but also enables one to become critically aware of the origins of such frames of reference. Adult learners may become conscious about the nature of learning and the values given by others to certain forms of knowledge and understanding. Instrumental learning for short-term gains (to pass an exam or to seek employment), though laudable at one level, fails to develop a critical consciousness or establish a long-term transformative learning experience. Learning that encourages and provides opportunities for entering into open discourse and raising criticality is more likely to lead to a transformation of frames of reference as the learner seeks, acknowledges, and adopts new and more inclusive, thoughtful frames of reference (Mezirow 1996, 1997).

Transformative learning can take several forms and Mezirow recognized that not all transformation resulted in radical shifts in personal disposition. His later work considered the importance of open discourse in encouraging individuals to challenge and to be challenged, and he saw it as an opportunity to question and validate one's own position. Not only does open discourse provide a vehicle by which assumptions may be re-examined, but it will also give rise to uncertainty. This unsettling experience, where individuals become unsure of the validity of previously held assumptions (frames of reference) and struggle to deal with contradictory and new ways of seeing the world is seen as a central element in any transformative learning. In Mezirow's later writings (1996, 2009) consideration was given to the role and nature of the educators in the transformative learning experience. The idea that education could be a form of critical pedagogy appealed to Mezirow and he wrote about the key components that adult education should include in efforts to provide an educational experience which valued and sought to enlighten, challenge, and permit transformative experiences.

Mezirow's work is not without its critics and detractors; Dirkx (1998) takes issue with the way that some accounts portray transformative learning. He suggests that transformation, in the purest sense, is a rare event and that some representations of the process miss the point in that transformative learning should be seen as a way of *being* rather than just a process of *becoming*. In doing so, the focus of subjective transformation in learning should include the emotional, spiritual, and moral aspects that are fundamental elements of who we are, and, by the nature of their importance, must be attended to if we really wish to transform not just our learning, but ourselves (Dirkx et al. 2006). Brookfield (1991) suggests that without a critical heightened awareness of the political dimensions of the context in which learning is occurring, true transformation remains an illusion. In addition, some perspectives already held, or yet to be adopted by an individual, may serve the interests of others (i.e. not just those holding them), and, thus, all learning must be considered to be conducted within political constraints. Because Mezirow, in his later works (1997), places an importance on the role of the educator to embrace critical pedagogy as a means to facilitate opportunities for critical dialogue, writers such as Burbules and Burk (1999) have gone on to challenge critical pedagogy to confront the nature of transformative learning. They argue that if transformative learning is to be seen as emancipatory, then the constraints of transformative learning and adult education themselves must be open to critical consensus and questioning.

Jack Mezirow: applications to sports coaching

A strength of Mezirow's writing and theorizing is that the key elements are not just about principles of learning, but also about the nature of adult education and the central role played by the educator in any learning experience. He goes on to say:

> Transformative learning is not an add-on. It is the essence of adult education. With this premise in mind, it becomes clear that the goal of adult education is implied by the nature of adult learning and communication: to help the individual become a more autonomous thinker by learning to negotiate his or her own values, meanings and purposes rather than to uncritically act on those of others. This goal cannot be taken for granted; education interventions are necessary to ensure that the learner acquires the understanding, skills, and disposition essential for transformative learning.
>
> *(Mezirow 1997: 11)*

For Mezirow, transformative education requires intervention and those educated to intervene. This commitment has a direct relevance for those engaged in sports coaching and in sports coach education. While many of the fundamentals of Mezirow's ideas, such as student independence, the development of criticality, and openness to new and changing ideas, have been forwarded by others writing about athlete learning in a sporting context (Kidman 2001; Light 2013), it could be argued that they have not clearly articulated and detailed the processes that individuals go through in and during learning. In addition, Mezirow (1997) contended that for effective transformative learning to take place, educators, be they coaches or coach educators, must adopt particular approaches and forms of pedagogical delivery.

For Mezirow, educators need to understand that transformative learning can take several forms and can be described as being either *objective* or *subjective reframing*. He defined subjective reframing as 'where the individual becomes critically aware of their own and others' assumptions and habits of mind' (Mezirow 1997). To achieve this, educators must provide opportunities for learners to practise recognizing frames of reference and redefine problems and issues from different perspectives. In a coaching context, we may wish to challenge others to reconsider their assumptions about the manner in which they and others most effectively engage in learning. It could be that beliefs about the need to repeat basic skills until they are 'grooved' are reconsidered in light of research findings that support skills delivery which incorporates distributed and random practice regimes. Here, the aim is not just to educate the learner about the role of variation in setting out practice drills, but also to get them to understand why they may have thought the way they do, and why they may have held on to the notion that blocked practice is the most effective mode of delivery. It may be that critical discussions regarding the way in which athletes internalize the practices of their own coaches only to unwittingly reproduce them with their charges once they become coaches, brings forward an understanding about the origins of their own assumptions. The importance here, for Mezirow, is that these critical discussions are conducted in an open and non-judgemental manner and that the collective experience of listening to others' experience allows learners to reflect on others' frames of reference and, thereby, challenge their own assumptions.

Objective reframing refers to the process in which learners might adjust their thinking in light of a realization of the political nature of some coaching preconceptions and of how this generates certain ways of thinking and sets of beliefs. The notion that biological determinism is a legitimate explanation for the lack of black managers in professional sport is an example of such. For Mezirow, learning is not always culturally and politically neutral; however, transformative learning does carry with it the opportunity for social and personal agency. Here, Mezirow sees the benefits of transformative learning as going beyond those of just the educational experience. True transformation has the potential to free individuals from the restraining conditions of other aspects of their personal lives when the resulting transfer of criticality into the social arena may allow the challenge of wider institutional conditions such a race, class, and gender. To aid these possible transformations, the role of the educator here is to facilitate opportunities for autonomous reflection and create situations which openly challenge the learner and their assumptions. These opportunities may take the form of delivering coaching sessions around problem-based learning (PBL), role play, life histories, conceptual mapping, critical consciousness raising, and using critical incidents to re-evaluate the appropriateness of current frames of reference. Each of these needs to be delivered within an atmosphere of open communication and critical discourse where the result will not only foster new ways of thinking, but also encourage a democratization of ideas and the valuing of alternative sets of beliefs.

Mezirow (2009), drawing on the experience of a doctoral programme taught at Columbia University in which transformative learning was at the heart of all engagement, re-stressed the importance of the role of the educator; the educator must seek to challenge the learner to question continuously existing frames of reference and to review and revisit habits of mind. This ongoing contesting of previously held assumptions requires a degree of mediation and management on the part of the educator so that the learner does not fall into the trap of believing in nothing or feeling that being insecure in their thinking will become a permanent condition. It is not the sense of insecurity in itself that transformative learning seeks, but rather it is the associated questioning that new challenging situations provide which is of importance. The degree to which learners are exposed to this process is ultimately a judgement call; the notion that all transformative learning will necessarily lead to autonomous, mature, and critical learners can be argued as being somewhat idealistic.

Where Mezirow's theory of transformative learning and the potency of educating individuals to be critical of their own and others' thinking may be most beneficial is in the field of coach education. It is in these situations where particularly engrained and historically robust belief systems may come to the surface. These powerful 'canons of coaching' may be restrictive in terms of holding back the learners from opportunities to be open to the consideration of novel ideas and challenges (Fenoglio and Taylor 2014). We should not underestimate the resilient nature of these frames of reference and 'signature pedagogies' (Shulman 2005); for many coaches, their coaching practice is considered indistinguishable from who they are as people. By creating a critical atmosphere and an open, inquiring discourse, individuals may feel that not only are their individual beliefs under critical examination, but also the very nature of who they are as practising coaches is now subject to question and reconsideration.

Jack Mezirow: a practitioner commentary by Leol Collins

My background in adventure sport coaching and coach education over a number of years has provided me with an opportunity to witness, facilitate, and be part of a number of coaching experiences which may be termed transformative. For ten years I held senior posts at Sport England's National Mountain Sports Centre (Plas-y-Brenin). By holding high-level qualifications in a number of adventure sports, I developed and delivered coach education programmes across the spectrum and mentored staff within the centre itself as well as further afield. For most of that time, neither the name of Jack Mezirow nor the term transformative learning was part of any staffroom conversations. Since a recent move into university and academia, I have become more familiar with the idea of education having a potential for change and possibly resulting in a transformative experience for learners.

Within adventure sports coaching, as with all coach development, transformative teaching and learning has considerable value and, I would suggest, is experienced both implicitly and explicitly in a number of contexts; however, this is not without some practical implications. Transformative approaches have a value in challenging and modifying beliefs around notions such as what we might consider good coaching to be, the nature of a coaching philosophy, and concepts of professionalism, to name just three. An educational approach that can facilitate a change in long-held and strongly valued beliefs becomes a valuable tool for the coach, coach educators, and those acting as mentors. Many of the blocks to a coach's development appear to be philosophical and individual rather than practical. I remember one particular neophyte coach I was mentoring; in their shift from a coaching philosophy of delivery being coach-led to one that was learner-centred, they became confused and unsettled. They knew the changes in delivery they needed to make, but not how to behave differently, such was their investment in their persona as a practising coach. The nature of adventure sports coaching also necessitates coaches to take part with 'adventure alongside' clients and requires adventure sports coaches to participate with their students during the act of coaching. This conflation between coaching and participation identities may lead to a general lack of clarity regarding the nature of adventure sports coaching and the nuanced and particular environments in which opinions and values are held and defended. Mezirow's idea that adult learners already come to education with a set of beliefs (frames of reference) certainly marries with my own experiences.

Within both the delivery of coaching sessions and coach education programmes, time is always an issue. The time and space in which experiences and their contexts can be reflected on is often in short supply. The practical challenge lies in the congested curricula that characterize formalized training courses that do not allow time for reflective activity. These pressures stem from both time and content requirements and can be difficult to address without compromising other practical content (often defined by an awarding body). Achieving a balanced approach in which critical reflection and the associated reapplication of ideas sits alongside more tangible aspects of the course may be difficult, as learners are often reluctant to forgo 'more important' practical aspects to allow time for additional reflection. Many of the teaching approaches suggested by Mezirow differ from those utilized in adventure sport coaching and, I would suggest, there may be a lack of permissive space for individuals to work towards transformative learning without first a commitment to do so from the governing bodies of sport.

In the act of transformation and acceptance of new perspectives, coaches may reject 'the old ways' and run the risk of 'throwing the baby out with the bath water'. Notwithstanding these problems, the innovators in some adventure sports are often held in high regard, while in other situations the maverick is viewed with suspicion and even contempt by their peers or distrusted by potential employers. A sense of conservatism brought on by the emergence of explicit risk management in adventure sports has recently been a significant factor in rejecting new approaches and has led to a risk-averse environment typical of outdoor centres and those working with young people. A colleague of mine, in returning to work after undertaking an exchange programme with another outdoor centre, felt that the institutional constraints he had returned to could no longer be accommodated within his new commitment to let children take additional risks. Challenging orthodoxy can also marginalize the trainee coach, as well as possibly damage their career development and standing in their immediate community. In this way, the creativity and adaptability that is engendered within transformative approaches can be squashed in favour of the 'tried and tested procedures of old'. So, while I can see that Mezirow's concepts can help us explore the reasons why learners sometimes struggle to take on new ideas and let go of outdated practices, the environment in which we practise can often hinder transformation and restrict the growth of individuals and their development.

Jack Mezirow: critical questions

1. How are coaches perceived and regarded after their frame of reference has undergone a transformative event? Is there a risk that the associated changes in the manner in which coaches think and practise may undermine their legitimacy?
2. Is the transformation of a coach's perspective only possible if other elements of their lives provide sufficient security and confidence to enable the unsettling nature of the process to be successfully mediated?
3. Is it possible that sports coaching culture can undertake these transformative events, or does such significant change need to start with each individual involved?
4. Are the commercial realities related to the employment of professional coaches a hindrance for those undertaking a potential radical transformation in their core beliefs?
5. Can an understanding of the transformative process not only help us make sense of an individual's journey, but also provide insights into other elements of coach education?
6. As Mezirow places so much importance on the role of the educator in generating the environment that allows transformative learning, how might coach educators be best equipped with those facilitation skills?

References

Brookfield, S. (1991) 'Transformative learning as ideological critique', in J. Mezirow (ed.) *Transformative dimensions of adult learning*, San Francisco: Jossey-Bass, 125–148.

Burbules, N. and Burk, R. (1999) 'Critical thinking and critical pedagogy: Relations, differences and limits', in T. Popkewitz and L. Fender (eds) *Critical theories in education: Changing terrains of knowledge and politics*, New York: Routledge, 45–66.

Cranton, P. (1994) *Understanding and promoting transformative learning: A guide for educators of adults*, San Francisco: Jossey-Bass.

Cranton, P. (1996) *Professional development as transformative learning: New perspectives for teachers of adults*, San Francisco: Jossey-Bass.

Dewey, J. (1938) *Experience and education*, New York: Kappa Delta.

Dirkx, J. M. (1998) 'Transformative learning theory in the practice of adult education: An overview', *Journal of Lifelong Learning*, 7: 1–14.

Dirkx, J. M., Mezirow, J. and Cranton, P. (2006) 'Musing and reflections on the meaning, context, and process of transformative learning: A dialogue between John M. Dirkx and Jack Mezirow', *Journal of Transformative Learning*, 4: 123–139.

Fenoglio, R. and Taylor, W. G. (2014) 'From winning-at-all-costs to "give us back our game": Perspective transformation in youth sport coaches', *Physical Education and Sports Pedagogy*, 19(2): 191–204.

Freire, P. (1970) *Pedagogy of the oppressed*, New York: Herter and Herter.

Freire, P. (1973) *Education for critical consciousness*, New York: Continuum.

Habermas, J. (1971) *Knowledge of human interests*, Boston: Beacon.

Habermas, J. (1984) *The theory of communicative action, vol. 1: Reason and the rationalization of society*, Boston: Beacon.

Kidman, L. (2001) *Developing decision makers: An empowering approach to coaching*, Christchurch, New Zealand: Innovative Print Communication.

King, K. P. (2002) 'A journey of transformation: A model of educators' learning experiences in educational technology', in J. M. Pettit and R. P. Francis (eds) *Proceedings of the 43rd annual adult education research conference*, 195–200. Retrieved from www.adulterc.org/Proceedings/2002/papers/King.pdf (accessed 1 February 2015).

Kitchenham, A. D. (2006) 'Teachers and technology: A transformative journey', *Journal of Transformative Education*, 4(3): 202–225.

Kitchenham, A. D. (2008) 'The evolution of John Mezirow transformative learning theory', *Journal of Transformative Education*, 6(140): 104–123.

Kuhn, T. (1962) *The structure of scientific revolutions*, Chicago: University of Chicago Press.

Light, R. (2013) *Game sense: Pedagogy for performance, participation, and enjoyment*, London: Routledge.

Mezirow, J. (1978a) *Education for perspective transformation: Women's re-entry programs in community colleges*, New York: Teachers College Press.

Mezirow, J. (1978b) 'Perspective transformation', *Adult Education Quarterly*, 28(2): 100–110.

Mezirow, J. (1991) *Transformative dimensions of adult learning*, San Francisco: Jossey-Bass.

Mezirow, J. (1996) 'Contemporary paradigms of learning', *Adult Education Quarterly*, 46(3): 158–172.

Mezirow, J. (1997) 'Transformative learning: Theory to practice', in P. Cranton (ed.) *Transformative learning in action: Insights from practice, new directions for adult and continuing education*, San Francisco: Jossey-Bass, 5–12.

Mezirow, J. (2000) 'Learning to think like an adult: Core concepts of transformation theory', in Jack Mezirow, Robert Kegan, Mary Field Belenky, Ann V. Stanton, Laurent A. Parks Daloz, Stephen D. Brookfield, Kathleen Taylor, Patricia Cranton, Judith Beth Cohen, Deborah Piper, Elizabeth Kasl, Lyle Yorks, Victoria Marsick, Edward W. Taylor and Colleen Aalsburg Wiessner (eds) *Learning as transformation: Critical perspectives on a theory in progress*, San Francisco: Jossey-Bass, 3–33.

Mezirow, J. (2009) 'An overview of transformative learning', in K. Illeris (ed.) *Contemporary theories of learning: Learning theorists in their own words*, London: Routledge, 90–105.

Shulman, L. S. (2005) 'Signature pedagogies in the professions', *Daedalus*, 134(3): 52–59.

14

ROBIN USHER

A post-structuralist reading of learning in coaching

Luke Jones, Jim Denison and Brian Gearity

Robin Usher: a short biography

Robin Usher was born in 1944. He completed his Bachelor of Arts degree in Economics and Politics at Oxford University, where he then earned a Ph.D. in Education in 1967. Usher has worked as a Senior Lecturer at the University of Southampton and currently lives in Melbourne, Australia where he is a consultant for the Royal Melbourne Institute of Technology (RMIT). Usher previously worked at RMIT as Professor of Research Education and Director of Research Training. Usher is an established educational theorist who throughout his career has critiqued the grand narratives of modernism as they apply to education, specifically by using the 'incredulity' (Lyotard 1984) of postmodernism to revisit the meaning and purpose of adult education and lifelong learning. It is not an overstatement to suggest that Usher's work should be described as a central part of a paradigmatic shift in understanding learning that has occurred over the last decade.

In 1989, Usher published *Adult Education as Theory, Practice and Research: The Captive Triangle*. Later, in 1994, Usher published *Postmodernism and Education* with Edwards. This text, using the theories of leading postmodern thinkers, established a detailed critique of the existing concepts, structures and hierarchies that framed educational discourse in the 1990s. In 1997, with the help of Ian Bryant and Rennie Johnston, Usher published *Adult Education and the Postmodern Challenge,* a text that built further upon the problematization of education through a postmodern stance. Usher's 2007 joint publication with Edwards, *Lifelong Learning: Signs, Discourse and Practices* is his most recent text. It is the reading of lifelong learning presented within this book that we apply to the sports coaching context later in this chapter.

Robin Usher: key concepts

According to Usher and his colleagues, it was apparent that, in the 1990s, the adult education system in the United Kingdom was failing those it was attempting to serve. Usher et al. (1997; Usher and Edwards 1994, 2007) saw that existing modernist approaches to adult education were proving to be inadequate due to their incompatibility with the increasingly diverse needs of learners. In an age defined by the 'decentring of knowledge' and 'multiple truth claims', alternative attitudes to learning were required. Usher et al. also recognized that the strength of modernist 'truths' about education were preventing alternative, more fluid interpretations of adult learning from flourishing. As a result, pedagogical approaches reliant on modernist meta-narratives fuelled by a quest for 'competence' (Edwards and Usher 1994: 12) meant that adult learners were not being provided satisfactory or appropriate 'learning experiences'. To rectify these shortcomings, Usher and his colleagues turned to postmodern social theory in order to develop alternative theoretical interpretations of learning that might encourage adult educators to appreciate the 'contested nature of knowledge' in the consumer age.

The key idea that underpins Usher's approach to adult education is that 'learning is neither invariant nor unchanging because "learning" is a socio-culturally embedded set of practices' (Usher and Edwards 2007: 2). Instead of endeavouring to find the 'truth' about 'how people learn', Usher saw that through the process of deciphering how truths about learning have emerged and come to prominence, adults' education experiences could be enhanced. For example, Usher asked: how are the meanings that are created about learning established? For according to Usher, it is through the study of meaning-making that an understanding of what learning actually is can emerge.

Modernity has been defined as the search for reason or knowable truth as an alternative to religion (Cahoone 2003). Adopting a postmodern stance, Usher's work in the 1990s established that since the Enlightenment, educational theory and practice have been firmly grounded in a 'discourse of modernity'. Drawing upon Foucault's (1991) analysis of the classroom as a disciplinary setting, Usher has problematized the basic teaching arrangements and techniques that comprise education. Foucault identified that historically, educational content and practices have upheld powerful modernist beliefs about learning and the human body. According to Usher et al. (1997: 10):

> Educational discourses and practices have had a powerful role in the development, maintenance and legitimization of modernity. Education has traditionally been the site where ideals of critical reason, individual autonomy and benevolent

progress are disseminated and internalized. It is here that the project of modernity is most obviously realized.

This quote highlights how the traditional perception of modern education is built around the benevolent transfer of knowledge from teacher to pupil in a linear, progressive fashion. Modernist logic has led to 'discovered knowledge' being bound into textbooks and online databases that are subsequently used as canonical resources (for example they include historical dates, scientific facts, and the bio-medical 'truth' about the human body). These bodies of knowledge were/are disseminated through traditional, overtly disciplinary classroom/laboratory settings, placing the learner as an inactive recipient in the learning process. Usher has embraced the scepticism of postmodernism and has called these sources of knowledge, and the pedagogical approaches used to distribute them, into question.

Importantly, Usher's sceptical stance allows for other conceptions of what learning is to arise and to gain recognition. For example, an alternative 'Usherian' consideration of learning might encompass 'learning as energized by desire which can follow many paths, rather than learning governed by the pursuit of universal truth (science) or unproblematic democracy (citizenship)' (Usher and Edwards 2007: 30). In contrast to a modernist perspective of learning that would advocate a progressive, linear acceptance of rational knowledge, Usher's work has sought to reconsider knowledge as a fluid and decentralized concept.

Usher has also described lifelong learning as an 'endless' process (Usher and Edwards 2007: 32), a statement that should encourage educators to recognize that how their pupils/athletes are learning is constantly changing. Usher believed that in order to keep pace with the way in which adults learn in postmodernity, the traditional practices of teaching and dominant assumptions surrounding learning have to be reconsidered. In a response to this 'failure of modernity' (Usher et al. 1997: 1) to encompass the diversity of learning experiences present and needed in any society, where curricula remain 'implicitly structured by the social engineering of the project of modernity' (Usher et al. 1997: 11), Usher and his colleagues sought to instigate a re-examination of educational theory and practice in the context of a developing postmodern society.

Usher et al.'s (1997; Usher and Edwards 1994, 2007) postmodern critiques have helped to catalyse an ontological shift in the way in which adult learning is considered in contemporary learning theory. This approach, although not universally well received (Hill 2001), has introduced tenets of postmodernism to a field previously saturated by behavioural psychology and a positivist research mindset. Historically the study of learning has been characterized by an obsession to discover 'the true nature of learning' (Usher and Edwards 2007: 4). Usher and Edwards (2007) have instead encouraged the educator to reconsider what learning is and that beliefs about what learning is need to be seen as emerging from dominant social practices. For example, Usher et al. (1997: 20) established that:

Adult educators tend to see 'lifelong learning' in a transcendental and largely psychologistic way. They thus fail to locate it in contemporary social developments, a failure which is largely attributable to inadequate theorizations about the social field in which adult education is located.

In their most recent work, Usher and Edwards (2007) have expanded upon their earlier analysis of learning to explain how learning is embedded in social practices, and not only in humans' minds/bodies as a transactional process (as traditional modernist assumptions dictate). To disrupt this problematic 'truth', Usher and Edwards argued for a more expansive perception of learning that moves beyond the production of docile, 'educated citizens' trained primarily to facilitate the economic needs of this consumer age. They strived to locate lifelong learning in a variety of practices, be they social, cultural and/or political. To achieve this, they drew upon the linguistic turn in social theory, including the work of the pre-eminent post-structural philosopher Michel Foucault.

Usher, Foucault and learning

Usher and Edwards (2002: 84–87) adopted Foucault's disciplinary analysis in order to show that 'modern forms of governance and social discipline are secured through education'. This can be attributed to what is promoted and accepted as 'rational and truthful' in curricula. Importantly, therefore, the taken-for-granted manner in which an individual learns throughout his or her life is heavily influenced by the conditions of the current 'regime of truth' that influences what is taught and in what manner. An example of this is how Edwards and Usher (1994) have revealed that since the establishment of National Council for Vocational Qualifications (NCVQ) in 1986, 'competence' in education came to exclusively mean the ability to accumulate and regurgitate facts and answers. This change led to educators ignoring 'the human qualities and wider notions of knowledge and understanding which are integral to the education of people' (Edwards and Usher 1994: 14). Drawing further on Foucault (1991), Edwards and Usher (1994) problematized the existing power relations that produced these 'truths' about 'competence' in learning. Another example of this would be how Edwards and Usher highlighted the way that disciplinary techniques employed by modernist education have 'lowered the threshold of describable individuality' and 'become a means of control and a method of domination' (Foucault 1991: 191). Using Foucault, Usher has re-emphasized that the modern educational arrangement cements a problematic assumption of what learning is, and as a consequence, this generates a normalized population of compliant, uncritical learners or, what Foucault might call 'docile' bodies.

Edwards and Usher (1994) illustrated how the dominance of certain 'educational truths' has marginalized any potential alternative understandings of how an individual might learn throughout his or her life. Foucault's well-established critique of modernity has helped Usher and his colleagues' claims, strengthening their call for educational theory to be amended to arrest the mass production of 'docile' learners. That is, learners who simply regurgitate the 'centralized knowledge' they have acquired in compliance with the (often economic) objectives of adult education institutions. Indeed, Usher's theorizing of learning could be seen as a response to Foucault's invitation to 'reverse' the modern rhetoric of progress, in this case, in the field of education.

Usher's work has used Foucault (amongst others) to reveal that educational institutions that rely on a modernist understanding of learning have the propensity to reduce all learning practices to simple transactional experiences. This is especially so in an increasingly consumerist environment where, in some instances, higher education is rapidly evolving into a product to be bought and sold. Education practitioners (including coaches), have become 'vendors in the educational hypermarket' (Usher et al. 1997: 107). The quicker and more efficiently the transaction of knowledge, and the subsequent 'equipping' of the learner can occur, the greater the margins of profit. Adult learners now exist in a time where learning and knowledge acquisition is being increasingly tied to the financial agendas of the neoliberal climate. Usher and Edwards (2007: 31) are wary of this trend where 'knowledge has become consumable', and have repeatedly warned that the reduction of education to a transactional process masks the different and multiple meanings that could be attributed to the process of learning across time and culture. Usher insisted that to comprehensively assist lifelong learners, alternative meanings associated with learning must be recognized and incorporated into the manner in which higher education operates. This should allow for the emergence of more appropriate pedagogical approaches (like the exercise we propose below), which recognize diversity and attempt to encourage critical thinking.

According to Usherian postmodern thinking, the modernist project has reduced learning to an autonomous act involving the acquisition of knowledge from a source of expertise. Consequently, the idea persists that it is the responsibility of every individual to accrue knowledge to expand him or herself as a learner. This seemingly productive status quo remains an unquestioned 'truth' in education. What possible reason could there be for this seemingly worthwhile project to be framed as a problem? There is at least one. For Foucault, learning experiences do not occur in the isolated core of an individual's mind, rather they are governed by the spaces individuals occupy and the relationships they hold. Importantly, the strength of this educational truth means that the conditions (conducive or otherwise) within which this project occurs are left unexamined as 'the way things are'. This is a problem because it not only perpetuates the myth that education occurs within a 'level playing field', but it restricts innovation and prevents alternative ways of thinking about learning from surfacing. As a result of this status quo, education in practice has given birth to 'certain kinds of pedagogical interventions' (Usher and Edwards 2007: 5). These practices include self-reflection, and importantly come with their own consequences for the learner and how learning is understood. For example, Usher and Edwards (2007: 72) explained that 'pedagogic practices have always been associated with the incorporation of individuals into discursive regimes of truth. People are governed through these regimes but also through their actions support their reproduction.' Specifically, Usher was interested in the composition and maintenance of the 'truth regime' responsible for consolidated approaches and knowledge about adults as lifelong learners.

As this quote attempts to illustrate, every social institution, including sport, has a foundation of pedagogical practices that contribute to how lifelong learning is understood.

Critiques of Usher's postmodern analysis of education

Usher's postmodern perspective on education has been widely celebrated as an important step towards better understanding what learning is in contemporary times. However, several criticisms of his postmodern stance exist and it is important that they are included here. Hill (2001) in particular is critical of Usher and Edwards (1994) for what he considers to be their hypothetical and unrealistic ideas that lack practical application to the educational context. Hill (2001) has also criticized Usher for demonstrating a profound underestimation of the intention and effects of government policy surrounding education. Another argument is that Usher has failed to produce applicable alternatives for practice in the educational field. McLaren and Farahmandpur (2001) also have concerns regarding 'Usherian' thought and have warned against the tunnel vision and myopia of postmodern thinking in education, suggesting it as incapable of producing a politically effective project. And Hill (2001: 140) has claimed that in educational theory, 'no postmodern theorist (including Usher) ... has gone beyond de-construction into considering a coherent program for re-construction'. Hill was also sceptical about the nature of the 're-configuration' of educational practices that Usher and Edwards (1994) have envisaged. Like many other postmodern thinkers, it is clear that Usher faces criticism for his lack of applicable alternative ideas.

Robin Usher: applications to sports coaching

To begin to consider how Usher's postmodern/post-structuralist sensibility towards learning could shape or influence a coach educator's practices it is important to keep in mind some of Usher's fundamental assumptions around learning. Primarily, Usher did not see learning to be something that an individual – either the learner or the teacher – must take sole responsibility for. Learning for Usher is not just a cognitive process that takes place in a person's brain or as a function of teaching. This would be to separate learning from everyday living. Rather, for Usher, learning is social and is embedded in a multiplicity of practices that we participate in daily. And it is through our participation in life that we make meaning and hence learn. Accordingly, learning is context dependent, or a function of culture; it therefore also involves work: it is not passive. Finally, when learning is understood to be social and contextual this calls into question the idea of 'best practices'.

Accordingly, for Usher, it was essential to develop approaches to learning that challenged the modernist notion of a singular truth – a best practice. In other words, Usher believed it was important to understand how learning is enmeshed within a wide range of practices not necessarily privileged by certain pre-defined goals and purposes founded on specific traditional bodies of knowledge. In the case of coach learning, this would mean challenging the canonical nature of exercise physiology, biomechanics and sport psychology and their unquestioned place in the coach development curriculum. Moreover, for Usher it was also important to make learning a space that can encompass a multiplicity and diversity of practices. In this way, learning should not be conceptualized as smooth, apolitical and linear but as complex, fluid and at times even contradictory and paradoxical. Learning becomes, therefore, a process that involves continually rethinking and questioning what one is doing. This is based on the premise that knowledge is always socially constructed and a result of complex relations of power. Therefore, for a coach educator charged with facilitating coaches' learning, to 'think with Usher' means understanding how certain practices or ideas can become dominant, such that we stop asking if they are actually effective. And when this happens, innovation or new learning is most certainly stifled.

As we have previously established, Usher's postmodern/post-structuralist understanding of learning was greatly informed by the thinking of Foucault. For example, as Foucault (1991) would say, and Usher would certainly echo, wherever and whenever learning takes place, those who are learning are required to bring forth their subjectivities for disciplining in order that they can become a particular type of person: a productive and efficient body. In our case here, that would mean a coach (the learner) leaving a learning experience having been disciplined to think in a very specific and defined way. Interestingly, a similar 'effect' occurs when coaches then go on to coach. For as most coaches report, they prefer to work with 'coachable athletes' as opposed to athletes who might question their decisions or attempt to assert their own control or identity over their sporting experiences and choices. In this way, through highly disciplinary learning practices both coaches and athletes regulate and monitor their thoughts and behaviours to conform with dominant meanings of what it means to be a competent coach and/or athlete. In other words, through a modernist or disciplinary learning logic, sport's status quo as a disciplining process is firmly maintained.

For Usher, the maintenance of such a status quo was highly problematic as he believed it can only constrain and limit individuals' growth and development through the making of docile bodies. Accordingly, the challenge faced by a coach educator who has chosen to think with Usher is: how do I develop educational practices that can help coaches become actively engaged subjects? Such an aim is, of course, difficult to achieve. For as Denison and Mills (2014) illustrated, the power of self-regulated coach competence, with its roots in various government agendas that justify the value of sport as making individuals – both coaches and athletes – into useful members of society is incredibly pervasive. More pointedly, within the strict neoliberal discourse of coach competence there is almost no space for coach educators to generate alternative views, knowledge or practices because the frameworks around which 'correct', 'normal' and 'responsible' coaching is designed and reinforced are so strong. To coach 'differently' is to risk censure or worse. As a result, truly innovative learning experiences for coaches are for all intents and purposes denigrated, dismissed and silenced as theoretical, irrelevant and academic. Accordingly, to develop flexible or open-minded coaches a coach educator must first be willing to problematize the effects produced by a rigid and disciplinary learning framework where it is seen as more important to be 'normal' than effective.

So what might an Usherian approach to coach learning mean in practice? By way of an example, we would like to share one exercise we developed that we have used with dozens of coaches from a variety of sports in a number of coach education contexts. We call this exercise 'The Formation of Coaches' Practices'. To begin this exercise we first talk to the coaches we are working with about the idea that all sports have established practices that influence how they coach. We then explain that this exercise involves examining where those practices have come from and how they have become established. More specifically, we ask each coach to consider how history and tradition – including chance and accidents – have influenced the way he or she understands how to coach. We explain that this will enable them to see how their knowledge of coaching, as well as their under-standing of themselves as a coach, is not necessarily fixed or true but the result of a number of social and cultural constructions or discourses. More specifically, it is our objective that the coaches will be able to do the following upon completing this exercise:

- Illustrate how power and knowledge are always linked in the formation of coaches' practices;
- Understand how this power–knowledge nexus, along with larger cultural understandings of 'being human' shapes bodies – their looks, dispositions, attitudes, behaviours and functions;
- Develop an awareness of the subjective nature of coaching concepts and principles;
- Critique established training practices and their effects;
- Create innovative approaches to coaching by problematizing 'all that coaching does'.

After our general explanation of this exercise's background and aims we provide the coaches with the following set of instructions.

'THE FORMATION OF COACHES' PRACTICES' – STEP ONE

In the table below list THREE established training practices in your sport and for each one record your thoughts on what you think helped shape this practice. In other words, what is the history of this training practice, where did it come from, how did it develop and why has it become so established? For example, one established coaching practice in athletics is that athletes should keep logbooks to record their workouts. This practice has been shaped by the scientific method and the belief that carefully recording one's training is the best way to predict and replicate a performance. Similarly, the use of field tests has become an established coaching practice in many team sports to measure athletes' fitness. This practice has been shaped by the belief that controlled measurements can be used to assess readiness to perform.

Established training practices in your sport	Shaped by ...
Athletes to record workouts in logbooks	Use of objective data to predict performance
Field tests to measure fitness	Fixed protocols provide accurate fitness assessments

'THE FORMATION OF COACHES' PRACTICES' – STEP TWO

While there might be many benefits associated with the training practices on your list, consider next some potential limitations and unintended consequences that could result from the practices on your list. For example, an athletics coach who has his or her athletes use logbooks to record their workouts might be unintentionally encouraging them to neglect how their bodies feel when making decisions about their training by focusing instead on what the numbers say. Likewise, a football coach who uses the beep test to determine an athlete's fitness and readiness to perform might begin to ignore other qualities that could contribute to an athlete's ability to compete. Use the table below to select ONE established training practice from your list above and record the potential limitations and unintended consequences of this practice.

Established training practices in your sport	Limitations and unintended consequences
Athletes to record workouts in logbooks	Athletes ignore their bodies' reactions
Field tests to measure fitness	Coach defines fitness as physical preparedness only

'THE FORMATION OF COACHES' PRACTICES' – STEP THREE

Now try to think of how you would avoid the limitations and unintended consequences you identified for this one training practice. What changes would you make and why? Consider any potential barriers to making these changes. For example, what would make it difficult for you to change this practice and coach differently? How would you implement this change? Could this change impact on your relationship with your athletes and others? What challenges or difficulties would it present to you? Finally, having made a change, how would you avoid creating a new set of limitations or unintended consequences?

We have found the discussion this exercise generates to be highly engaging for coaches but also extremely challenging or mind-bending. It can be disconcerting for a coach to learn that the foundations he or she believed his or her practices were based on are not as solid as he or she thought. Moreover, to see how widespread or entrenched this foundational understanding of 'how to coach' is can be disheartening when thinking about ways to begin 'coaching differently'. However, through this exercise we believe we are putting into circulation Usher's educational/learning vision. For example, we have seen coaches emerge from this exercise and begin to question the many coaching maxims that are based on a binary logic: good/bad, science/art, theory/practice, hard/soft, body/mind. Following this questioning, they begin to recognize how limited and constrained they have been by sport's modernist legacy and a disciplinary learning framework. As a result, they become more capable of challenging the various orthodoxies of their sport and more confident about thinking differently and coaching in more innovative ways.

Robin Usher: a practitioner commentary by Brian Gearity

My coaching career took off after I injured myself playing American collegiate football and an opportunity arose to become a strength and conditioning coach intern with Major League Baseball's Cleveland Indians Baseball Club. After two years in Cleveland, I became a graduate assistant strength coach, which eventually turned into a full-time position, at the University of Tennessee. There, I earned a master's degree in Sport Management, a Ph.D. in Education, and multiple certifications in strength and conditioning and athletics. During this time, I studied cultural studies of education and the sociology of sports coaching. I left Tennessee to become an assistant professor of Sport Coaching, and during this five-year period I also volunteered coaching high school (American) football for two years, youth soccer and baseball for a couple of seasons, and was a speed coach for a gymnastics center for one and a half years.

For the past year, as a program director for a master's degree in Sport Coaching and a coach educator, I've been reviewing a lot of work on learning theory, organizational learning, and instructional design. Often university courses are presented as separate and distinct from any type of larger social and historical context. As a result students can easily believe that what they have learned is exactly how things are and always have been. Professors, like coaches, are told to present themselves as omniscient and confident; yet we know that this is problematic and fails to capture the social construction of knowledge. However, as coach educators, if we were to draw upon Usher, we could teach students not what knowledge and practice are, but how they have been socially constructed. Throughout our curriculum, we could develop instructional activities guided by a genealogical analysis to demonstrate the historical, cultural and power relations of knowledge and practice.

For example, in strength and conditioning it was once believed that resistance training would make you slow and tight. People thought this because they observed massive (male) bodybuilders who were deemed too 'muscle bound' to be good athletes. With the birth of a scientific view of the body and a positivistic approach to research, and the promise of progress packaged with this Enlightenment paradigm, exercise physiologists could conduct experiments to debunk the 'myth' that the full range of motion resistance training causes the human body to be slow, tight or muscle bound. However, following Usher, we should not stop there, or be satisfied with our current understanding of the body. In my own work I have acknowledged some of the problems (e.g. coach–athlete conflict, injury, under-performance) that may occur in practice when the coach is framed as an expert. An expert who justifies his or her coaching approach with scientific 'truths' may lead to the production of athletes as docile bodies (Gearity and Mills 2013). Several potential negative effects of relying upon a scientific understanding of the body exist. For example, the idea that all bodies are the same and respond the same to training or that our training programs should draw predominantly from resistance training methods to build muscle mass and maximal strength. Therefore, aside from our dominant scientific understanding of the body, are there other ways of moving and training that could reduce or lessen the severity of injury, increase performance, or keep athletes engaged in sport? Under a competency-based approach to education and assessing student-coach achievement by their ability to conform to the expert's view of knowledge and standardized testing, we (re)produce a system of thought that is largely unimaginative, and neither creative nor innovative. Learning is reduced to a relatively stable point based on universal truths in one's mind. Therefore, because students and novice coaches lack coaching experience to reflect upon, a useful instructional practice could be to analyze and evaluate the thoughts and practices of other coaches. Such a learning activity would comply with Usher's conceptualization of social learning and relations of power. The learning outcome for this sort of activity would be to create a critical postmodern, post-structural critique of 'learning' in sport coaching. By design, this outcome is less predictable than competency-based approaches and standardized tests, but the hope is that the skill of thinking sociologically would be used over a lifetime. Indeed, lifelong learning that does little more than conform to modernist assumptions is the antithesis of an Usherian approach.

Based upon a scientific view of the body, in the 1980s many coaches eagerly used powerlifting techniques to improve strength and size, while the 1990s saw the rise of weightlifting techniques, probably due to research showing it was better at improving power than powerlifting. In the 2000s, with the rise of technology to measure athletes' heart rate, acceleration and distance, knowledge of the body has become increasingly technocratic. There is also a growing interest in rest and recovery, which suggests that previous methods were too stressful although most coaches did not think so at the time. Perhaps all parties were too caught up in their modernist assumption of scientific progress to problematize prevailing taken-for-granted assumptions? In current practice, coaches often do not have to think but merely hook athletes up to technology to be given a simple to use and guaranteed successful program. Following Usher, my point here is to show how each period has a prevailing mental model or grand narrative based on a dominant way of coaching and power relations. From a post-structural lifelong learning perspective, we should critique these 'truths' and continuously encourage coaches to think and to exercise their power not just to create docile athletes. Indeed, throughout all of these periods athletes' bodies have been tightly controlled and their own embodiment marginalized. It is a contradiction, although common practice, for a coach to simultaneously preach 'Listen to your body' while implementing technologies of dominance! But the promise for coaches to think, to coach differently, is always possible. My own experience has demonstrated that Usher's ideas on learning can be helpful for coach educators to develop coaches committed to being and thinking differently in their everyday practice.

Robin Usher: critical questions

1. How, and in what way, does Usher's interpretation of lifelong learning differ from a behaviourist or constructivist understanding of adult learning?
2. This chapter has identified that Usher's postmodern position would be sceptical of certain underlying assumptions about learning. What are these underlying assumptions?
3. What problems did Usher and his colleagues identify surrounding the association between adult education and the increased transactional nature of learning in adult education institutions?
4. Usher was critical of the 'modernist truths' that have underpinned educational practices. What are these 'modernist truths'? What are the educational practices that he was critical of?
5. How might the coach redesign a coaching programme in light of her exposure to an 'Usherian' understanding of learning? For example how might the practices chosen vary from existing dominant coaching practices?

References

Cahoone, L. (2003) *From modernism to postmodernism: An anthology*, Oxford: Blackwell.

Denison, J. and Mills, J. (2014) 'Planning for distance running: Coaching with Foucault', *Sports Coaching Review*, 3: 1–17.

Edwards, R. and Usher, R. (1994) 'Disciplining the subject: The power of competence', *Studies in the Education of Adults*, 26: 1–14.

Foucault, M. (1991) *Discipline and punish: The birth of the prison*, London: Penguin.

Gearity, B. and Mills, J. (2013) 'Discipline and punish in the weight room', *Sports Coaching Review*, 1: 124–134.

Hill, D. (2001) 'State theory and the neo-liberal reconstruction of schooling and teacher education: A structuralist neo-Marxist critique of postmodernist, quasi-postmodernist, and culturalist neo-Marxist theory', *British Journal of Sociology of Education*, 22(1): 135–155.

Lyotard, J. (1984) *The postmodern condition*, Manchester: Manchester University Press.

Mclaren, P. and Farahmandpur, R. (2001) 'Breaking signifying chains: A Marxist position on postmodernism', in D. Hill, P. Mclaren, M. Cole and G. Rikowski (eds) *Marxism against postmodernism in educational theory*, Lanham, MD: Lexington Press, 35–66.

Usher, R. and Bryant, I. (1989) *Adult education as theory, practice and research: The captive triangle*, London: Routledge.

Usher, R., Bryant, I. and Johnstone, R. (1997) *Adult education and the postmodern challenge: Learning beyond the limits*, London: Routledge.

Usher, R. and Edwards, R. (1994) *Postmodernism and education*, London: Routledge.

Usher, R. and Edwards, R. (2007) *Lifelong learning: Signs, discourses, practices*, The Netherlands: Springer.

SECTION 6
Social and ethical theorists

15

HERBERT BLUMER

Coaching and learning as symbolic interaction

Lee Nelson, Ryan Groom and Paul Potrac with Phil Marshall

Herbert Blumer: a short biography

Herbert George Blumer was born on 7 March 1900 in St Louis, Missouri, USA. Blumer completed his undergraduate degree at the University of Missouri before moving to the University of Chicago to complete his doctoral thesis, entitled 'Method in Social Psychology', in 1928. During his time at the University of Chicago, Blumer was particularly influenced by the respective works of the social psychologist George Herbert Mead and the sociologists W. I. Thomas and Robert Park. Following the completion of his doctorate, Blumer accepted a teaching position at the University of Chicago, where he stayed from 1927 to 1952. Blumer is probably best known for his seminal 1969 text *Symbolic Interactionism: Perspective and Method*, in which he advanced the theoretical perspective known as symbolic interaction, as well as openly criticizing quantitative approaches to the study of sociology and advocating naturalistic methods. While Blumer acknowledged the need for a scientific approach, he was of the belief that 'there are some features of human social life that militate against the application of scientific method, notably the need to understand subjective interpretations informing human actions and the necessity to treat social phenomena in context' (Hammersley 1990: 32).

Following his time at the University of Chicago, Blumer moved to the University of California–Berkeley in 1952, where he remained until his retirement in 1967. During his long career Blumer held a number of prestigious posts, including Secretary of the American Sociological Association (1930–1935), Editor of the *American Journal of Sociology* (1941–1952), Chairman of the Department of Sociology at Berkeley, President of the Society for the Study of Social Problems, and Vice-President of the International Sociological Association. He received honorary degrees from the University of Missouri and Southern Illinois University, became the 46th President of the American Sociological Association in 1955, and achieved Emeritus Professor in 1986. Blumer died on 13 April 1987 at the age of 87.

Herbert Blumer: key concepts

In this section, we principally draw on Blumer's (1969) book *Symbolic Interactionism: Perspective and Method*, as it was here that he arguably provided the most comprehensive overview of his thesis. Blumer opens by explaining that his intellectualizing has been significantly influenced by the works of numerous established American academics, in particular those of George Herbert Mead. While Mead and others unquestionably shaped Blumer's theorizing, he was nonetheless keen to acknowledge that he should 'bear full responsibility for the views and analyses' that he subsequently went on to present (Blumer 1969: 2).

Three basic premises

When attempting to understand Blumer's (1969) thesis it is important to appreciate that his version of symbolic interactionism rests on what were for him three *basic premises*. Each of these premises will now be discussed in turn, as these lay the foundation on which his other theoretical propositions were built. Following this we will introduce Blumer's six *root images*.

Blumer's first premise was that 'human beings act toward things on the basis of the meanings that the things have for them' (Blumer 1969: 2). Such *things*, as Blumer described them, include physical objects, other human beings, categories of human beings, institutions, and the activities of others. While Blumer was of the belief that few scholars would likely disagree with this basic premise, he highlighted how the social sciences, at the time of his writing, seemingly ignored or downplayed this basic fact. Blumer argued that psychologists frequently turned to internal explanations of human conduct (e.g. stimuli, attitudes, conscious and unconscious motives, perceptions, and cognitions), whereas sociologists referred to external factors (e.g. social position, status demands, social rules, cultural prescriptions, norms and values, social pressures, and group affiliations). Central to Blumer's (1969) critique was that both of these academic disciplines and their associated lines of thinking had a tendency to 'treat human behavior as the product of various factors that play upon human beings', and, in so doing, he believed that they failed to recognize the importance of the meaning that people place on those things with which or with whom they interact (Blumer 1969: 2–3). By placing the *meanings* that things have for human beings at the core of his theorizing, Blumer's symbolic interactionist position stood in stark contrast to those dominant beliefs in psychology and sociology at that time.

The second premise referred to how 'the meaning of such things is derived from, or arises out of, the social interaction that one has with one's fellows' (Blumer 1969: 2). In his discussion of this notion, Blumer compared his position with the two dominant views of that period, namely the belief that meaning can be found in the intrinsic nature of the thing or that meaning arises through a coalescence of psychological elements that shape an individual's perception. In contrast to these positions, Blumer proposed that meaning arises through the process of interaction; that is, the 'meaning of a thing for a person grows out of the ways in which other persons act towards the person with regard to the thing' (Blumer 1969: 4). Blumer's symbolic interactionist stance thus sees meanings as social products that are created and formed *in* and *through* social interaction (Blumer 1969).

Blumer's third premise stated that 'these meanings are handled in, and modified through, an interpretative process used by the person in dealing with the things he encounters' (Blumer 1969: 2). Here, Blumer articulated that meanings are not pristinely captured through interaction and subsequently applied to action. Rather, Blumer stressed that meaning occurs through *a process of interpretation* (Blumer 1969), and he went on to explain that this interpretive process comprises two distinct steps. The first of these steps refers to how an individual indicates to himself or herself, through internal dialogue, the thing towards which he or she is acting (Blumer 1969). The second step accounts for how the actor is subsequently required to select, check, suspend, or transform meanings (Blumer 1969). It is in light of this that Blumer argued that interpretation should not be regarded as the automatic application of meanings but as a formative process in which meanings are used and revised to guide and shape action (Blumer 1969).

Six 'root images'

Having introduced the three basic premises of Blumer's symbolic interactionist stance, we will now turn our attention to his six *root images*. When taken together, these basic ideas represent how Blumer viewed human conduct and society. Each of Blumer's six root images will now be discussed in turn.

Root image 1: nature of human society or human group life

The first of Blumer's root images states that 'fundamentally human groups or society *exist in action* and must be seen in terms of action' (Blumer 1969: 6). That is, groups comprise people participating in various activities as they encounter one another and confront the situation in which they find themselves. Here, Blumer argued that while an individual may act on his or her own, collectively, or as a representative of a group or organization, the activities engaged in 'belong to the acting individuals and are carried on by them always with regard to the situations in which they have to act' (Blumer 1969: 6). In the first and last instances, then, Blumer's symbolic interactionism requires any empirical analysis of group life to be cognizant of the fact that human society consists of individuals engaging in action.

Root image 2: nature of social interaction

The second of Blumer's root images posits that 'society consists of individuals interacting with one another' (Blumer 1969: 7). According to Blumer's analysis, there are two types of interaction, namely *non-symbolic interaction* (i.e. when an individual responds directly to the action of another without interpreting his or her action) and *symbolic interaction* (i.e. when an individual interprets the action of another before responding). While it is possible to identify instances whereby people engage in non-symbolic interaction, Blumer suggested that symbolic interaction is the characteristic mode of interaction in society. Put more simply, he was of the opinion that people seek to understand the meanings of others' actions. Social interaction, then, is a significant feature of Blumer's symbolic interactionism. As the extract below eloquently demonstrates, for Blumer social interaction directly shapes the conduct of those involved:

> human beings in interacting with one another have to take account of what each other is doing or is about to do; they are forced to direct their own conduct or handle their situations in terms of what they take into account. Thus, the activities of others enter as positive factors in the formation of their own conduct; in the face of the actions of others one may abandon an intention or purpose, revise it, check or suspend it, intensify it, or replace it. The actions of others enter to set what one plans to do, may oppose or prevent such plans, may require a revision of such plans, and may demand a very different set of such plans. One has to *fit* one's own line of activity in some manner to the actions of others.
>
> *(Blumer 1969: 8)*

Root image 3: nature of objects

In his discussion of the third root image, Blumer contended that 'the "worlds" that exist for human beings and for their groups are composed of "objects" and that these objects are the product of symbolic interaction' (Blumer 1969: 10). For Blumer, the term *objects* was used to denote anything to which a person can indicate or refer. He grouped these under three categories: (1) *physical objects* (e.g. chairs, trees, or bicycles), (2) *social objects* (e.g. students, priests, a president, a mother, or a friend), and (3) *abstract objects* (e.g. moral principles, philosophical doctrines, or ideas such as justice, exploitation, or compassion), with the nature of any object consisting of the meaning that it has for the given individual. Of course, an object may hold contrasting meanings for different individuals. According to Blumer, it is out of a process of mutual indication that common objects emerge and come to have the same meaning for a group of individuals. When considered in this way, objects are understood to be social creations formed through social interaction. Objects, according to this line of thought, have no fixed status. Through the process of interaction objects are, instead, continuously being 'created, affirmed, transformed, and cast aside' (Blumer 1969: 12).

Root image 4: the human being as an acting organism

The fourth of Blumer's root images focused on his understanding of the *self*. The self was particularly important to Blumer as he believed that possessing a sense of self permitted a person to become an object to himself or herself. Having a self enables a person to interact with himself or herself. Like other objects, the self emerges through the process of social interaction. Indeed, Blumer suggested that 'we see ourselves through the way in which others see or define us' (Blumer 1969: 13). The self has profound implications for how we understand people and their actions. In contrast to the widely held belief that the human organism responds to psychological or social factors, an understanding of the self and self-interaction led Blumer to conclude that the human organism 'is not a mere responding organism but an acting organism' (Blumer 1969: 15). The individual is required to choose his or her course of action in light of the situational factors that he or she confronts.

Root image 5: nature of human action

Blumer's fifth root image suggests that 'the capacity of the human being to make indications to himself [or herself] gives a distinctive character to human action' as it requires the individual 'to cope with situations in which he [or she] is called on to act, ascertaining the meaning of the actions of others and mapping out his [or her] own line of action in the light of such interpretation' (Blumer 1969: 15). According to his analysis, human action consists of taking into account issues such as an individual's own desires and objectives, the means available for achieving these, the actions and anticipated actions of others, his or her own self-image, and the likely result of his or her proposed line of action. The social world, when viewed in this way, is not a static entity, but rather something that is continuously made and remade as people interpret and respond to their social situation. Throughout the course of an interaction a person's line of action may be started or stopped, abandoned, postponed, or transformed.

Root image 6: interlinkage of action

Finally, Blumer's sixth root image referred to joint action; that is, group life consists of individuals collectively engaged in action. This *interlinkage* might be thought of as a large, complex network of people. While this presents a useful analogy, Blumer was critical of those who thought of networks as being self-operating systems, and presented an alternative argument:

> One should recognize what is true, namely, that the diverse array of participants occupying different points in the network engage in their actions at

those points on the basis of using given sets of meanings. A network or an institution does not function automatically because of some inner dynamic or system requirements; it functions because people at different points do something, and what they do is a result of how they define the situation in which they are called to act ... It is necessary to recognize that the sets of meanings that lead participants to act as they do at their stationed points in the network have their own setting in a localized process of social interaction – and that these meanings are formed, sustained, weakened, strengthened, or transformed, as the case may be, through a socially defining process.

(Blumer 1969: 19–20)

In his discussion of the sixth root image, he also claimed that joint action arises out of previous experiences. This helped to explain how and why people often have a prior understanding of how they should and should not conduct themselves within a given social situation. That said, for Blumer, every social situation happens anew and therefore social actors have to encounter and respond to one another in the action present.

Critiques of Blumer's work

In his book entitled *Symbolic Interactionism*, Stryker states that he has 'little sympathy with stands that Blumer takes in his elaboration of symbolic interactionism', recognizing that Blumer's ideas are in opposition to those presented in his own structural version of symbolic interactionism (Stryker 1980: 89). Like Blumer, Stryker's symbolic interactionism is grounded in the work of Mead. However, whereas Blumer sought to construct a Meadian-inspired sociology, Stryker modified Mead's ideas and introduced concepts and principles taken from role theory to deal with what he considered to be a reciprocal relationship between people and social structures. His is a version of symbolic interactionism that places much greater emphasis on the impact of social structure on social interaction than Mead's thinking, and Blumer's later interpretation, allowed. Of course, Styker's critique is not the only criticism of Blumer's theorizing. Blumer's and other symbolic interactionist positions have been attacked on a number of theoretical grounds. What Stryker's critique clearly demonstrates, however, is that there is no single and united understanding of symbolic interactionism.

Herbert Blumer: applications to sports coaching

Although Blumer's thesis did not directly address learning *per se*, Blumer's work has significantly shaped a number of learning theorists' thinking about this topic, including Mezirow (see Chapter 13) (Bron and Schemmann 2002). It is in light of this that we decided to include a discussion of his theorizing, as we believe that it offers a lens through which to consider coaches' and coach educators' actions and interactions with significant others in their respective pedagogical contexts. We will now focus on exploring what Blumer's theorizing might mean for the understanding of those interactions that occur in coaching contexts.

Root image 1: nature of human society or human group life

When considered in light of Blumer's work, coaching and coach education contexts could be conceptualized as pedagogical settings comprising various key contextual stakeholders who encounter, interact with, and respond to one another. In coaching, those interactions occurring between coach and athlete, and between coach educator and coach learner, are understandably of particular interest and significance. Coaches and coach educators are, in reality, however, required to deal with a multitude of other stakeholders. In addition to working with their athletes, those coaches that practise in elite-level sporting contexts also interact with assistant coaches, sports science support teams (e.g. fitness coach, performance analyst, physiotherapist, medic), and scouts, as well as directors of sport, chief executives, and the media. Similarly, community sports coaches interact not only with those participants who attend the various schemes for which they are responsible, but also with their respective colleagues and line managers. When applied to coach education, Blumer's theorizing also helps us to acknowledge that coach educators are required to interact not only with their coach learners but also with colleagues (especially when co-delivering courses), line managers, and potentially other key contextual stakeholders employed at their respective places of work (e.g. the national governing body of sport, the county sports partnership, the private provider, the academic institution). Importantly, then, coaching contexts comprise a multitude of individuals engaging in activity.

Root image 2: nature of social interaction

While non-symbolic interaction may occur during coaches' and coach educators' engagements with significant others, it could be contended that coaching practitioners principally seek to interpret the meanings, intentions, and actions of those with whom they communicate. That is, coaches and coach educators engage in *symbolic interaction* in an effort to understand the thoughts, feelings, and actions of others by attempting to read their body language and comprehend their verbal utterances. The information and understandings that coaches and coach educators acquire through such interpretive efforts, according to Blumer's theorizing, are subsequently used to guide and inform their conduct, planning, and decision making. It is important to acknowledge, however, that symbolic interaction is not exclusive to the interpretations and actions of coaches and coach educators. During their interactions with key contextual stakeholders, significant others are also attempting to interpret and respond to the actions and intentions of coaches and coach educators.

Root image 3: nature of objects

When applying Blumer's third root image to coaching and coach education contexts, practitioners' social realities seemingly comprise physical, social, and abstract objects. For performance and community coaches *physical objects* might include training/competition facilities (e.g. pitch, court, track, pool), sporting equipment (e.g. balls, bats, rackets, gloves, pads), and training aids (e.g. stopwatch, whistle, bibs, cones, tactics board), whereas physical objects for coach educators are likely also to include teaching spaces (e.g. classroom/lecture theatre, tables, chairs), audio-visual equipment (e.g. computer, projector, screen), and teaching aids (e.g. printouts, whiteboard and pens, workbooks). Whereas *social objects* for coaches could include athletes, parents, and colleagues, for coach educators students and co-workers are probably significant social objects. Theoretical and philosophical beliefs about learning and facilitation, as well as tactical and technical strategizing, are potentially examples of *abstract objects* that could conceivably be of importance to both coaches and coach educators. Importantly, these objects have no inherent meaning. The value that coaches and coach educators place on these objects, as well as how they talk about and utilize these objects, is learnt through their interactions with significant others.

Root image 4: the human being as an acting organism

From a Blumerian perspective, coaches and coach educators possess a sense of *self*. This sense of self allows coaches and coach educators to become an object of their own internal thoughts and permits them to participate in internal dialogue. Importantly, a coach's or coach educator's sense of self is shaped by how he or she perceives significant others to be judging his or her performance. A group of athletes that conform to the requests of their coach, openly acknowledge his or her expertise, and share with their coach how grateful they are for his or her efforts may contribute towards the coach developing a positive self-understanding. In contrast, a group of coach learners who communicate their disdain for the coach educator's course material, question aspects of the information presented by the coach educator, and provide critical feedback will likely negatively impact on the coach educator's sense of self. Of course, athletes and coach learners are not the only significant others who might shape how coaches and coach educators judge themselves. The actions and comments of those various key contextual stakeholders discussed in the first root image could conceivably influence how a practitioner reflects on his or her performance as a coach or coach educator.

Root image 5: nature of human action

When applying Blumer's fifth root image to the study of sports coaching, it is apparent that a coach's or coach educator's capacity to engage in internal dialogue permits him or her to strategically respond to those situations that he or she faces. While practising, coaches and coach educators have to give thought to their own personal desires and intentions and the means available to achieve these desired ends, as well as the actions and anticipated actions of those key contextual stakeholders with whom they interact and the professional image they wish to portray to these significant others. During their interactions, coaches and coach educators have to give thought not only to the action present, inclusive of those with whom they are communicating, but also to instances prior to the present interaction, and what implications the current situation and associated interaction might have for the future and how they are perceived by others.

Root image 6: interlinkage of action

Arguably, Blumer's sixth root image helps us to recognize that coaches and coach educators form part of a wider network of people. Sporting networks can encompass local (e.g. local sports teams and clubs), regional (e.g. county councils and sports partnerships), national (e.g. governing bodies of sport, government departments and agencies), and international (e.g. international governing bodies of sport) organizations. Importantly, from a Blumerian perspective, these organizations are not entities in and of themselves. They operate through the actions and interactions of employees (and volunteers) that take place within and between organizations. According to Blumer's theorizing, many of these joint actions, including those that occur between coach and athlete and between coach educator and coach learner, are likely to be relatively stable in terms of the way that they are enacted. Indeed, through their previous encounters coaches, coach educators, athletes, and coach learners come to acquire an understanding about how they should (and should not) conduct themselves in their social environment. In such contexts coaches and coach educators are required to 'lead from the front'. Athletes and coach learners, on the other hand, are expected to subordinate themselves to their coaches and coach educators. Coaches and coach educators are expected to design, organize, and deliver sessions aimed at facilitating the learning and development of those in their charge. It is hoped that athletes and coach learners will unquestionably follow the guidance of their coach and coach educators respectively. While this might be so, it is also important to acknowledge that coach educators and coach learners still have to interlink their actions through an ongoing process of designation and interpretation.

Herbert Blumer: a practitioner commentary by Phil Marshall

I have worked as an athletics coach and strength conditioner for almost twenty years now, and Blumer's *first root image* and the concept of group life can be observed in the wide range of coaching settings in which I have worked. For example, I have often worked with groups of athletes. The range of stakeholders, however, went far beyond just coach and athlete. Often in my work for governing bodies it included parents, administrators, management staff, physiotherapists, nutritionists, sports scientists, performance analysts, and the media.

Blumer's *second root image* is something which lies at the heart of good coaching practice. Understanding this second root image demonstrates the fine line between what he would term *non-symbolic* and *symbolic interaction*. Coaching practitioners frequently experience frustration, anger, and a host of other negative emotions. However, it is rarely acceptable to express these emotions in front of one's athletes. An example from my own practice as an athletics coach occurred during the opening race of a season. I had worked hard with a new athlete during the off-season to eliminate a range of technical faults in his running. However, in the course of this race all of those faults reappeared, despite the months of work. My initial reaction was one of frustration and anger. Had the athlete in question been close by I may have engaged in non-symbolic interaction, venting my anger with little consideration for his feelings. Instead I was able to give consideration to a range of factors in formulating my next communication with him. Here I considered my training as a coach, my own athletic experiences, previous coach–athlete interactions, the body language expressed by the athlete after crossing the line, and my knowledge of the athlete's personality and personal situation. As a result my communication became one of support and reassurance to the athlete, in a process of symbolic interaction.

I can clearly observe Blumer's *third root image* in my practice as a strength conditioner, in the equipment required for me to do my job. The weights, benches, racks, lifting platforms, and monitoring equipment all represent *physical objects*. However, perhaps of greater importance is a consideration of what Blumer called the *abstract objects*. For me they include my professional accreditations with the UK Strength and Conditioning Association and the National Strength and Conditioning Association. These accreditations and the process I went through to gain them provided me with many of the principles I use to guide my practice. Here the process of interaction with key stakeholders such as these governing bodies and other coaches, and the supporting information I draw on from the research literature, have helped to shape my practice. My understanding of many of the objects I encounter in my practice has been shaped by this process.

Sense of *self* is something that is central to coaching practice and can be significantly affected by the successes and failures of the athletes we work with. Here Blumer's *fourth root image* can be observed in my own personal experience. Early in my career I was fortunate to be asked to work with a very talented shot putter, acting as both technical coach and conditioner. This initial request had a significant impact on my sense of self and feelings of self-worth. To be approached by such a well-respected and promising performer made me feel that my skills and knowledge were valued by people at the top level of my sport. The athlete in question took part in some of the highest level competitions on offer in the United Kingdom. However, they never achieved their full potential in these major competitions. This had a negative impact on my sense of self as a coach. I questioned my knowledge and the approach I took with this athlete and ultimately our coach–athlete relationship came to an end, something difficult to accept for any coach.

Blumer's *fifth root image* has helped me to consider the impact of my actions on others' sense of self as well. In the example I used in my discussion of root image two, my chosen course of action involved a consideration not only of my own thoughts and feelings and those of the athlete but also of the other stakeholders who were present at the time. The athlete's former coach was in attendance and I was keen for the athlete to perform well in his presence. This knowledge heightened the personal pressure I felt and fuelled those feelings of anger and frustration I have described above. At the same time I was also aware of the athlete's perspective. He, too, badly wanted to show how he had progressed, following his decision to change training groups. As I moved through this process of symbolic interaction I gave consideration to his feelings of frustration and disappointment. My emotions were therefore tempered and I chose a course of action that gave consideration to the feelings of the athlete and our future working relationship.

The settings in which I have worked for almost twenty years as a coach can be effectively described by Blumer's *sixth root image*. I worked for several years as a strength conditioning coach on a national scheme aimed at providing support to talented young athletes. The training sessions delivered through this scheme, and the coach–athlete relationships which evolved from it, can be understood in terms of Blumer's first five root images. However, the scheme itself, described as a single entity, sums up Blumer's concept of *interlinkage of action*. The scheme comprised not just coach and athlete. I worked alongside physiotherapists, sports psychologists, and sports scientists. Our scheme operated as a hub for a larger regional scheme, which in turn acted as a subsidiary of a national entity. On a regional and national level the scheme had its own managers and administrators. The processes encompassed by the scheme could be seen as repetitive and stable, or what Blumer would describe as a 'form of recurrent patterns of joint action'. Athletes were identified to the scheme, referred on to administrators, and passed on to support staff in a stable and repetitive manner. Support staff screened and assessed athletes as they entered the programme, and wrote training schedules in a stable and repetitive way. However, as Blumer's sixth root image acknowledges, although this may look repetitive and stable to the outside observer, each stage of the process involved new interpretations on the part of the parties involved. For me each new athlete needed to be viewed anew, relationships had to be built and not simply replicated, the training needs of these athletes had to be considered on an individual basis, and new programmes written with this in mind. The same was true for each individual involved in this interlinkage of action. Our actions took place in a localized setting, part of a much larger and wider-reaching regional and national scheme.

Herbert Blumer: critical questions

1. In light of Blumer's theorizing, how should *group life* in coaching and coach education contexts be described? Who are the key contextual stakeholders in your coaching setting?
2. What are *non-symbolic* and *symbolic* forms of *interaction*? How might these concepts help you to understand the *nature of social interaction* in coaching and coach education environments?

3.   What *objects* might the world of coaches, athletes, coach educators, and coach learners comprise? How do these individuals come to acquire an understanding of these objects?
4.   How might a coach's or athlete's sense of *self* be influenced by their interactions? How might an interaction that occurs between a coach educator and coach learner shape their respective sense of *self*?
5.   What might Blumer's analysis of the *nature of human action* mean for how you attempt to make sense of those interactions that occur in coaching and coach education contexts?
6.   According to Blumer's discussion of the *interlinkage of action*, how should sporting organizations be conceptualized and why?

References

Blumer, H. (1969) *Symbolic interactionism: Perspective and method*, London: University of California Press.
Bron, A. and Schemmann, M. (2002) *Social science theories in adult education research*, London: Transaction.
Hammersley, M. (1990) 'Herbert Blumer and qualitative method', *International Journal of Qualitative Studies in Education*, 3(1): 31–36.
Stryker, S. (1980) *Symbolic interactionism*, Caldwell, NJ: Blackburn Press.

16

JEAN LAVE

Learning in coaching as social praxis

Christopher Cushion with Robert Townsend

Jean Lave: a short biography

Jean Lave is a social anthropologist with a strong interest in social theory. Much of her ethnographically based research concentrates on the re-conceiving of learning, learners and everyday life in terms of social practice. Her theories view learning as changing participation in ongoing changing practice. Her life work challenges conventional theories of learning and education. She completed her doctorate in Social Anthropology at Harvard University in 1968 and is currently a Professor Emerita of Geography at the University of California–Berkeley. Her studies of apprenticeship are recognized as a significant critique of educational psychology and its dominant cognitive approaches. She pioneered, and is perhaps best known for, her theory of situated learning and communities of practice with the assistance of her student Etienne Wenger. She has published three books on the subject: *Understanding Practice* (co-authored with S. Chaiklin, 1996); *Situated Learning: Legitimate Peripheral Participation* (with E. Wenger, 1991); and *Cognition in Practice* (1988). More recently her work has taken a historical turn with a collaborative, ethnohistorical research project, 'Producing Families, Trading in History: On the British merchant families engaged in the port wine trade in Portugal' – (*History in Person: Enduring Struggles, Contentious Practice, Intimate Identities*, edited with D. Holland, 2001).

Jean Lave: key concepts

Understanding learning: a critique of cognitive approaches

All theories of learning are based on assumptions and beliefs concerning the individual, the world and the relationship between the two. Importantly, assumptions about learning are inherited, and in viewing learning as a process of epistemic construction, theories are situated in work from Kant to Descartes (Packer and Goicoecha 2000). Epistemology is the systematic consideration of knowing and knowledge. Ontology is the consideration of being. Learning is chiefly considered in terms of changing knowing (Packer and Goicoecha 2000) with conventional explanations that view learning as a process by which the learner internalizes knowledge, whether discovered, transmitted from others or experienced in interaction with others (Lave and Wenger 1991). Lave and Wenger (1991) argue that the individual and cognitive focus of learning, characteristic of most theories of learning, only concentrates on the person. This paints the person as a primarily cognitive entity. That is, we have universal cognitive structures that shape our experience of reality with a 'dualist' ontology of a subjective and independent world. The human individual is 'cogito', an epistemic person unchanged by the construction of knowledge (Packer and Goicoecha 2000). Lave's work argues consistently that this focus on internalization establishes a binary or dichotomy between inside and outside, where knowledge is largely cerebral and takes the individual as an unproblematic unit of analysis. Furthermore, learning as internalization is too easily construed as an unproblematic process of absorbing the given as a matter of transmission and assimilation (Lave and Wenger 1991; Lave 1996). This dualism poses problems for a coherent theory of knowledge, learning and action as setting up the self as independent creates a gulf between the knowing mind and the world (Dewey 1966). Moreover, Lave (2009) asserts that such an approach generates silences and paradoxes with questions that cannot be asked and issues that offer no principled resolution.

Lave's work challenges dominant cognitive assumptions about learning and proposes to broaden learning as a concept to one that involves the whole person, and only partly implies becoming able in new tasks or understandings, where persons acting and the social world of activity cannot be separated (Lave 2009). Because task functions and understandings do not exist in isolation, they are part of a broader system of relations in which they have meaning (Lave and Wenger 1996; Lave 2009). The person is subsequently defined by and defines these relations; learning involves the construction of identity (Lave and Wenger 1996). From such a perspective, learning is also understood as social and embodied (practical, physical, emotional as well as cognitive).

Lave's project supports a focus on relations between sociocultural structure and social practice, and the indivisibility of body, cognition, feeling, activity and the sociocultural world (Lave 1988). Lave (Lave and Wenger 1991, 1996; Lave 1996, 2008, 2009; Lave and Packer 2008; Holland and Lave 2009) has been arguing for a conceptual shift from the traditional view of 'the individual as learner to learning as participation, and from the concept of cognitive process to the more-encompassing view of social practice' (Lave and Wenger 1991: 43). The primary focus here is on learning as social participation, not just in local events with certain people but a more encompassing 'process of being active in the *practices* of social communities and constructing *identities* in relation to these communities' (Wenger, 1998: 4).

Situated learning, legitimate peripheral participation, and communities of practice

Learning involves the construction of identities the historical production, transformation, and change of persons (Lave and Wenger 1991). However, psychological research treats identity as simply self-concept, as knowledge of self; that is, as epistemological (Packer and Goicoecha 2000; Lave and Packer 2008). But identity is linked to participation and learning in a community as a socially situated activity that must be grounded in an ontology that conceives of the person as an active being, engaged in activity, in the world (Lave 2009). Central identity-generating activities take place in practice, in which learners participate; learning is a process of becoming, of forging identities in the world where knowledge growth and change must result in changes in identity (Packer and Goicoecha 2000). Therefore, cognition alone is not an adequate way of thinking about learning – learning involves the construction of identities (Lave and Wenger 1991). The processes, relationships and experiences that constitute the participants' sense of identity and belonging underpin the nature of subsequent learning, a phenomenon captured through the notion of legitimate peripheral participation (LPP) (ibid.). LPP is a process characterized both by social structures and social relations. In this sense, learning through LPP takes place irrespective of the context 'or whether there is any intention for it at all' (ibid.: 40). Situated learning is more than learning by doing, but a position that gives 'situatedness' a dynamic and theoretical perspective. In essence, learning is viewed as part of social practice, and participation in social (communities of) practice by definition will involve learning, as the process of becoming a member of a community allows learning to take place. Being 'situated' means that people learn as they participate. They become intimately involved with a community or culture and, through interacting with the community, learn to understand its history, assumptions, cultural values and rules (ibid.).

Participation in social practice is a way of belonging to a community. Similarly, participation in social (communities of) practice will inevitably involve learning. Thus, a community of practice is not merely a repository for technical knowledge and skills; rather, it is an 'intrinsic condition for the existence of knowledge, not least because it provides the interpretive support necessary for making sense of its heritage' (ibid.: 98). Therefore, participation in a cultural practice, the knowledge associated with it and its application are all connected, while the learner's location within a community also impacts on the negotiation of meaning related to social practice.

Learning as social practice

In developing this notion further, Lave argues that the mind does not exist outside of social practice. Any focus should not be on the individual as such, but as the individual-in-action (Lave 2009). Learning viewed as simply located in co-participation in cultural practices misses Lave's point that learning is more than merely being situated in practice (Lave and Wenger 1991). Learning must be viewed as social practice (Lave and Wenger 1996). Activity evolves processes of co-construction and negotiation between participants. However, the social character of learning in many 'constructivist' approaches mostly consists in a small 'aura' of socialness that provides input for the process of internalization but is still viewed as individualistic acquisition of the cultural given (Packer and Goicoecha 2000) – learning begins and ends with the individual with a 'nod' at the 'social' or the environment in between (Lave 1996). There is no account of the place of learning in the broader context of the structure of the social world through social practice (Lave and Wenger 1996; Lave 2009).

Learning as social praxis

Lave and Packer (2008) drew on Marx's social ontology as a 'philosophy of praxis' (Feenberg 1986). Marx argues that the objective world, including its apparently 'natural' parts is socially constituted. Human beings are socially produced, including their apparently private and personal subjective innermost consciousness. Consciousness is an aspect or moment of praxis itself. The forms that consciousness takes in society are to be understood within the context of forms of social praxis (Bernstein 1971). To understand praxis we need to reject the philosophical ontological distinction between persons and things. The object or product produced is not something 'merely' external to and indifferent to the nature of the producer, the person is what they do (Lave and Packer 2008). Consequently, the very nature or character of a person is determined by what they do, or their praxis, their products are concrete embodiments of this activity (Bernstein 1971).

For Lave's work the philosophy of praxis has several implications for learning. The subject is an active agent involved with persons and artefacts in concrete settings. This subject is not separate from the settings in which it acts, but is one aspect of a structural whole: a subject engaged in situated practice, where practice has a temporal aspect. We are always thrown into a concrete situation that we cannot get out of, behind, or get completely under control (Lave and Packer 2008). Practical activity has direction, but is not instrumental. Persons in activity are located socially and differently, therefore their embodied points of view create different value in activity, because of the partial located character of such perspectives (Lave and Packer 2008). Praxis has a historical character, therefore learning must change historically as well. Therefore, a focus on practice or praxis and the development of human knowing through participation in the social world addresses the dualism that reduces persons to their minds, mental processes to instrumental rationalism, and learning to the acquisition of knowledge – a dualism that segregates those reductions from the everyday world of participation (Lave and Wenger 1996).

In drawing on theories of social practice (e.g. Bourdieu 1977; Giddens 1979), Lave emphasizes the relational interdependency of not just the individual and social world but activity, meaning, cognition, learning and knowing (Lave and Wenger 1996). By situating learning within social and cultural contexts the individual is less involved with objective de-contextualized knowledge acquisition, but is constructing knowledge through direct experience of social practice. Meaning is negotiated within practices through the ongoing interaction of that which is historical and that which is contextual. In this sense, social practice, cognition and communication in, and with, the social world are situated in the historical development of ongoing activity (ibid.). This defines the learning process as the 'historicizing of the production of persons' (ibid.: 146). Participation in social practice – subjective and objective – suggests an explicit focus on the person, but as person-in-world as a member of a sociocultural community. Knowing is activity by specific people in specific circumstances. Lave and Packer (2008) argue that knowing is part of activity – it is socially and historically situated, therefore learning is not an entirely mental operation. In a dialectically structured world, persons are produced through the processes of objectification. That subjects, understanding of themselves is mediated through other subjects and objects. This challenges the notion of internalized facts and abstract knowledge transmission (ibid.). General knowledge cannot be applied to separate and independent situations without considering the constructive relations between persons acting and ongoing activity in the world in which they are socially located and engaged (ibid.). Thus an idealized picture of unproblematic transmission of knowledge in a uniform world of shared values and uniform culture contrasts to the reality of socially located people, more or less engaged in ongoing practice, different from one another, in conflict and in unequal relations of power, involved in projects that cross situational boundaries (ibid.).

Contentious local practice

Drawing on the work of Vygotsky, and authors such as Cole, Engeström (see Chapter 10), or Hedegaard and Chaiklin, 'contentious local practice' is based on activity theory; positioning persons in practice within the ongoing, historically constituted everyday world, where participation in it helps to make it what it is, while also being shaped by the world of which they are a part (Holland and Lave 2009). Practices shape intimate identities in complex ways, but are not a matter of local practice, local institutions and local history. Local struggles are always part of a broader, historical cultural and political struggle, but in particular ways worked out in practice. Therefore, identity is worked out through contentious local practice (ibid.). Social practice theory assumes people typically act in relation to collective cultural activities rather than in direct response to internal or environmental events (stimuli) and emphasizes the historical production of persons in practice, paying attention to differences among participants and to the ongoing struggles that develop across activities around those differences (ibid.). This simultaneously foregrounds the subject or actors and persons in activities, and the historical struggle that engages them. Persons are historically produced in practice in relation to the identities, cultural genres, and artefacts that are central to the cultural activities in which persons engage. Senses-of-self form in relation to cultural activities where identities are in flux and unsettled. Therefore, people attempt to author themselves in the words of the groups in which they participate. Identity has a dialogic aspect – identity development can be characterized as forming around dialogues over difference between self and the internalized version(s) of 'the other' (ibid.). Consequently, trajectory within a community is not solely a matter of voluntary individual decisions. Informed by collective local practice, power and meaning affects everyone through their relations with each other, and those relations are not chosen but mediated through contentious local practice (ibid.).

Learning as the everyday

The 'everyday' exists on a continuum from asocial construal to a partially social view with different zones of social life with a view of social life as the fabric of social existence (Lave 2008). The asocial everyday is a residual category that produces a limited and private knowledge. This is the baseline in cognitive theorizing about learning, that suggests that learning (as acquiring knowledge) involves movement away from something toward something else – ignorance to knowledge, empty to full, novice to expert (ibid.). The alternative is the everyday as social practice – all structured and structuring in practice (ibid.). Much of what goes under the name 'learning' is not learning at all, but cultural transmission, teaching, instruction or inculcation. Learning, therefore, is portrayed as moving people to higher and greater knowledge (ibid.). However, as Lave (2008) proposes, to conceive of learning as movement towards a state of knowledgeable cultural privilege is to set apart and reify learning as a process in and of itself. To stipulate the ends towards which learning should move is an inescapably political act. Claims about learning are not apolitical or neutral. 'Rather they have the effect of accepting and justifying the contemporary social order in culturally powerful and powerfully cultural terms' (ibid.: 10). Reifying learning in whatever terms as a thing in itself, learning is something that must take place elsewhere than in the circumstances in which what is learned is supposed to be 'applied'. This creates disturbing (and specious) divisions between learning and using knowledge, and linear relations in time between learning 'before' to use 'after' (ibid.); in turn, creating a division between learning and practice. It also produces an ideology of specific institutional settings for propagating, characterizing (and studying) 'real learning', while leaving as a vague residual zones of life in which the application of the products of learning – 'knowledge', 'skill' – (not learning) is the order of the day (ibid.). The idea of learning now for other times has an idea of connectedness, but any theory of learning that has this principle is proposing that learning is produced in a site where 'real life' practice is temporarily suspended, as 'product' knowledge is to be applied in what people are doing that is not learning (ibid.).

Estranged learning

Lave and McDermott (2002) compared in detail the ideas from Marx's 1844 essay 'Estranged Labor' to social practices of learning and education, deriving a social practice of distribution and production of alienated learning – that is estranged learning. Lave and McDermott (2002) argue that named things are tied to one another in ways that sustain current arrangements in the political economy. Therefore, the logic and consequence of the arrangements are kept obscured and hidden from their participants. Objects are the product of collective human activity (learning, education, knowledge), but the history of their production is obliterated and we experience them as alien, independent of our activity and wishes (ibid.). Alienated and alienating, the production of knowledge (e.g. science, pedagogy, curricular frameworks) is separated from its distribution through educational practices (ibid.). Learning activity itself becomes a commodity that is less and less active, and increasingly passive and contemplative. Learning theory positions the object and subject in opposition, and is an alienated practice; learners are active intellectually but incapable in practice of transforming the world in any respect other than tinkering with similar 'objective' concerns, action is viewed merely as instrumental technique (ibid.). 'Phantom objectivity' is an autonomy that seems so strictly rational and all embracing as to conceal every trace of its fundamental nature: the relation between people (Lukács 1988).

> Estranged learning is estranged because it is always done for others who use it for their own purpose ... to keep themselves in place in a hierarchy of others, a hierarchy held in place by a theory of learning that denies the relevance of the distribution system while making each participant's placement its most important product ... Learning is not merely about the production of knowledge; it is by its very essence about the production and distribution of assessed knowledge. The learner produces not for himself but for his or her place in the system.
>
> *(Lave and McDermott 2002: 43)*

Jean Lave: applications to sports coaching

Understanding learning

Using Lave's concepts to understand conventional learning theory applied to sports coaching reveals a political-social dimension that generally goes unrecognized, where learning has a narrow epistemological (and individual, ahistorical, rationalistic) character (Lave and Packer 2008; Cushion 2011). In coaching, learning is generally assumed to be an entirely epistemological problem. Like the wider learning field, it has long been assigned to the conceptual-mental rather than the social material side of human being (Lave and Packer 2008; Cushion 2011). Indeed, in coaching, theories of learning are about individual psychological processes, leading to knowledge acquisition (e.g. Trudel and Gilbert 2006; Gilbert et al. 2009). Coaches are assumed to 'acquire' concepts, skills and behaviours in a state of passive alertness, ideas and seemingly abstract concepts about coaching are 'delivered'. The obvious assumption is that knowledge will be seamlessly transmitted, assimilated and trans-ferred unproblematically into coaches' practice (Gilbert et al. 2009; Cushion 2011) and by similar means, into athlete learning. Such coach learning defines what knowledge is necessary for coaches to practise and how that knowledge can 'best' be transmitted.

At the same time, the idea of 'coaching expertise' is accepted uncritically, with its assumed novice–expert continuum and a predominantly cognitive/behavioural approach to learning, again within an acquisition metaphor (Cushion et al. 2010). As Lave (1996, 2008) suggests, what is startling about such assumptions is the 'dominant but narrow and pervasive history of philosophical and psychological treatment of learning as an epistemological problem, it is all about knowledge, acquiring knowledge, beliefs, skills, changing the mind and that is all' (Lave 1996: 156). The separation between learning and social life is a division between an epistemological concern about learning and social concerns about the world in which learning takes place – learning is reified activity separate from practice. The dominant view, shared in coaching, is that social life is socially constituted but learning happens in the head (Lave 2008). Lave's work proposes an alternative for understanding coach learning that suggests that it is ubiquitous in ongoing everyday social activity and that it is a mistake to think of learning as a special kind of activity taking place only at particular times in special places arranged for it (Lave and Packer 2008).

Coaching practice is, first of all, socially and historically generated, and it is not constituted in and of knowledge. Importantly, Lave (2008) argues that the episte-mological issues of social existence are social in their construction and that episte-mological issues have no existence independent of the social practice of which they are a part, subsumed within the social ontology of human existence. Learning in coaching therefore is not movement *away* from practice, but perhaps more deeply *into* and *through* social existence; not a solely individual mental process but a social relational process (ibid.). Knowledge or knowing in coaching is creative and reproductive and is subsumed within ongoing everyday social practice (not as pre-paration for it) (ibid.). Conceptualizing learning in coaching is about how practice, participants and ways of participating change to be different. Coaching and learning are made in the medium of participation in ongoing changing social practice. Therefore, to polarize novice and expert, informal and formal, knowledge pro-duction and reproduction, educators and coaches, is to construct false dichotomies as people are located in practical, interrelated lives (ibid.).

Learning is shaped in practice through interaction in social contexts where coach learning, coaching and learning to coach are complex practices in a social world.

Taking Lave's arguments more broadly, that social practice is the primary, gen-erative phenomenon with learning as one of its characteristics, means that learning and learners in coaching should be analysed as an integral part of social practice (Lave 1996). This seems to be analogous with the evidence of how coaching – both as a social system and the knowledge associated with it – evolves from that practice (Cushion 2006). Moreover these ideas, as well as the evidence from coaching, challenge assumptions that 'formal education' is necessarily prior to, or a precondition for, learning, or that an absence of 'teaching' calls processes of learning into question (Lave 1996).

The characterization of coach learning as a social process has gathered momen-tum in recent times (Cushion et al. 2010). For example, the notion of an 'informal apprenticeship' seems to be typical of the development of most sports coaches, with time spent as athletes and coaches providing a basis for future practice (e.g. Trudel and Gilbert 2006; Cushion et al. 2010). Moreover, the progression from assistant coach to head coach and through different levels of sport is a process that may be referred to as legitimate peripheral participation (Cassidy and Rossi 2006; Trudel and Gilbert 2006). Thus, coaches are situated, and engage with 'others' as part of the social practice of coaching.

The overriding assumption of situated learning and legitimate peripheral parti-cipation is that learning takes place within a participatory framework. That is, rather than simply being in the learner's mind, meaning is mediated by the differing perspectives among co-participants; it is 'not a one-person act' (Lave and Wenger 1991: 15). The coach belongs legitimately to the context. He or she is also peripheral, thus allowing change through participation and movement, ensuring that the learning enterprise is not static (Brockbank and McGill 2007). Learning does not occur in isolation but as part of a system of relations; a community of practice (CoP) (Lave and Wenger 1991; Brockbank and McGill 2007). In coaching, Cassidy and Rossi (2006) and Cushion (2006) among others have argued the case for situated learning and CoP to be used as frameworks to understand, and as a possible design for, learning. However, as Lave and Wenger (1996) remind us, a historical-cultural theory of learning should not merely be the abstracted generalization of cases but instead a shift away from a theory of situated activity in which learning is reified as one kind of activity and towards a theory of social practice in which learning is viewed as an aspect of all activity. Importantly, legitimate peripheral participation is not an educational form, much less a pedagogical strategy or a teaching technique (Lave and Wenger 1991). It is an analytical viewpoint on learning drawing attention to aspects of learning experience. This is very different to attributing a prescriptive value to the concepts and from proposing ways to 'implement' or 'operationalize' them for educational purposes (Lave and Wenger 1996, 1991) – a direction that some scholars of coach learning seem to have mistakenly taken.

Issues with formal coach education

Notions of estranged learning show that formal coach education and learning is a market place that is estranged, alienated and mystified. There is an uncritical acceptance of a neutral process of allocation and transmission of knowledge. In formal coach education, there is a need to consider the distributive practices that alienate, estrange and appropriate the products of learning, the processes of learning and learners themselves. Why? And who for? These are important questions that are obscured by seemingly objective instrumental questions of 'what works'.

Learning and 'teaching' in coaching and coach education are problematic, requiring deeper analysis. Improving coach learning, however, takes a 'disastrous shortcut' (Lave 1996: 158) by equating learning with formal 'teaching', thus narrowing prescriptions and taking learners (coaches) and educators out of the picture. Learners and educators are participants in ongoing social practice – coaching needs to be clear on the production and transformation of *all* participants' knowledgeable identities and not mistakenly 'desubjectify' learners and educators (Lave 1996). Furthermore, prescriptions about 'proper practice' generate one form of circum-scribed participation: pre-empting participation in ongoing practice as the legitimate source of learning opportunities, the goal of complying with requirements specified from formal education engenders a practice different from the intended (Bourdieu 1977; Lave and Wenger 1991). Importantly, there becomes a distinction between a 'teaching curriculum' and a 'learning curriculum' for coaches. A learning curriculum provides situated opportunities for the improvisational development of new practice, and is a field of learning resources in everyday practice viewed from the perspective of learners (Lave and Wenger 1991). In contrast, a teaching curriculum supplies and therefore limits structuring resources for learning; the meaning of what is learned (and control of access) is mediated through a coach educator's participation, by an external view of what knowing is about (Lave and Wenger 1991). A learning curriculum evolves out of participation, engendered by pedagogical relations and by a prescriptive view of the target practice as subject matter. Therefore, it cannot be considered in isolation, manipulated in arbitrary didactic terms or analysed away from the social relations that shape participation (Lave and Wenger 1996). It could be argued that currently coaches only participate in the reproduction of coach education itself. The problems of coach education are not pedagogical at the most fundamental level, but have to do with the ways in which coaching reproduces itself and the relations that can or cannot be established within the cultural and political life of the community (Lave and Wenger 1996, 1991; Townsend and Cushion 2015).

Jean Lave: a practitioner commentary by Robert Townsend

I currently coach mainstream and disability athletes as a Community Cricket Coach with Leicestershire and Rutland Cricket Board. Previously, I have spent some time coaching cricket in Australia and New Zealand, developing cricketers from juniors through to men's and women's Premier Grade sides and Canterbury district representative squads.

My experiences mean that I can understand the chapter's argument that coaching is fundamentally a socially situated activity, enacted within a socially constituted world. In my coaching, I find myself managing a multitude of pragmatic and theoretical constraints, all of which impact my practice significantly. These efforts are based on concerns about what is needed in order to engage, include and ultimately create a space where sport is the vehicle for athlete learning. Lave's work helps me understand that I do not merely visit the social context and act out a set of pre-defined, calculated strategies that transmit knowledge to athletes. Instead, I can see the context as a generative site of learning, historically driven, practice-led. For me, doing and knowing in coaching become inventive in this sense; they are open-ended processes of improvisation with the social, material and experiential resources at hand. Lave's metaphors for learning are helpful as my practice draws on rich resources of experience, my own and that of other people, present and past. But my understanding of coaching also emerges, becoming sharper and clearer in the process. It is through participation in (coaching) practice that my understanding changes, thus my learning is a product of the taken-for-granted, 'everyday'. Lave's framework allows me to consider learning in my sociocultural, historically grounded world, and to rethink learning in social, cultural and historical terms.

Lave's ideas about situated activity make me realize that coaching is not a world that consists of neutral actors who are unaccompanied and dropped into unproblematic spaces. By situating learning in activity, in practice, this can collapse the differences between 'formal' and 'informal' coach education and enable me to recognize how I learn through ongoing interaction with significant others – athletes, mentors, peers – within a social context. My background includes a formal 'coaching apprenticeship' with a county cricket club, coaching a variety of sports and activities throughout undergraduate study, and moving on to complete a master's degree in Sports Coaching before working full-time for a year in New Zealand and Australia. Each context was a community, a different set of relations with different meanings, values and assumptions about coaching, where coaching was constructed, tentative, and legitimated through practice. My learning is being-in-practice, inseparable from actions, thoughts and emotions. In my practice, I feel the pull of old coaches' dispositions, habits, discourse, the ideologies of different coaching cultures in the way practice 'should be', and the nag of theoretical considerations in coaching. Without doubt, my membership of these different communities, cultures and spaces, and the collaboration and conflicts (of which there have been a few) with others, have provided a valuable learning experience and different ways of knowing about cricket and coaching. Here, Lave's argument that we forge our identity (and subsequently knowledge) by, and through, the systems of relations of which we are a part, rings true and enables me to reflect meaningfully on my practice, behaviour, discourse and assumptions about athletes.

Lave's work and her insistence that learning is ubiquitous in ongoing collective, cultural-historical forms of located, interested, conflictual, meaningful activity, creates important questions to consider in my practice – What knowledge do I need to function in this field? What knowledge is important for these athletes? Where has this knowledge come from? Would these athletes learn without me? How much do I actually affect learning? These questions, whilst uncomfortable, help me to try to centre practice firmly on the needs of the athlete. Importantly, the multitude of contexts and athletes I work with calls into question the uniformity of knowledge that some coach education programmes perpetuate. Indeed, considering estranged learning, for coach education to have an impact on my practice it must – as Lave argues – acknowledge the fundamental imprint of interested parties, multiple activities, and different goals and circumstances on what constitutes 'knowing' on a given occasion or across a multitude of interrelated events. In cricket coaching it becomes evident that coaches engage first and foremost in the reproduction of given, 'proper' and legitimate knowledge. Instead, Lave argues that we engage in the production of knowledge as a flexible process of engagement with the world. For me, what works for 35 six-year-olds in a primary school is entirely inappropriate for the needs of the England Learning Disability squad. Lave's work helps to blur the lines between what is proposed in isolation in coach education, and what happens in practice. This enables me to move towards an understanding of coaching as praxis and how legitimate peripheral participation shapes my understanding of the world around me. It enables me to reflect on the cultural values, assumptions and rules inherent in cricket, those that I align with naturally, and those that sit uncomfortably, and the subsequent impact on my coaching practice as I teach athletes how to play the 'game'.

Jean Lave: critical questions

1. What assumptions underpin your understanding of coach learning?
2. How do coaches learn best?
3. Is learning in coaching just about knowledge?
4. How much are social practice, norms and culture an influence on coach learning?

References

Bernstein, R. J. (1971) *Praxis and action: Contemporary philosophies of human action*, Philadelphia: University of Pennsylvania Press.

Bourdieu, P. (1977) *Outline of a theory of practice*, Cambridge: Cambridge University Press.

Brockbank, A. and McGill, I. (2007) *Facilitating reflective learning in higher education* (2nd edn), London: Open University Press.

Cassidy, T. and Rossi, T. (2006) 'Situating learning: (re)examining the notion of apprenticeship in coach education', *International Journal of Sports Science and Coaching*, 1(3): 235–246.

Chaiklin, S. and Lave, J. (1996) *Understanding practice: Perspectives on activity and context*, Cambridge: Cambridge University Press.

Cushion, C. J. (2006) 'Mentoring: Harnessing the power of experience', in R. L. Jones (ed.) *The sports coach as educator: Re-conceptualising sports coaching*, London: Routledge, 128–144.

Cushion, C. J. (2011) 'Coach and athlete learning: A social approach', in R. L. Jones, P. Potrac, C. J. Cushion and L. T. Ronglan (eds), *The sociology of sports coaching*, London: Routledge, 166–177.

Cushion, C. J., Nelson, L., Armour, K., Lyle, J., Jones, R., Sandford, R. and O'Callaghan, C. (2010) *Coach learning and development: A review of literature*, Leeds: Sportscoach UK.

Dewey, J. (1966) *Democracy and education*, New York: Free Press.

Feenberg, A. (1986) *Lukacs, Marx and the sources of critical theory*, Oxford: Oxford University Press.

Giddens, A. (1979) *Central problems in social theory: Action structure and contradictions in social analysis*, Berkeley: University of California Press.

Gilbert, W., Gallimore, R. and Trudel, P. (2009) 'A learning community approach to coach development in youth sport', *Journal of Coaching Education*, 2(2): 1–21.

Holland, D. and Lave, J. (2001) *History in person: Enduring struggles, contentious practice, intimate identities*, Santa Fe, NM: SAR Press.

Holland, D. and Lave, J. (2009) 'Social practice theory and the historical production of persons', *Actio: An International Journal of Human Activity Theory*, 2: 1–15.

Lave, J. (1988) *Cognition in practice: Mind mathematics and culture in everyday life*, Cambridge: Cambridge University Press.

Lave, J. (1996) 'Teaching, as learning, in practice', *Mind, Culture and Activity*, 3(3): 149–164.

Lave, J. (2008) 'Everyday life and Learning', in P. Murphy and R. McCormick (eds) *Knowledge and practice: Representations and Identities*, London: Sage, 3–14.

Lave, J. (2009) 'The practice of learning', in K. Illeris (ed.) *Contemporary theories of learning*, London: Routledge, 200–208.

Lave, J. and McDermott, R. (2002) 'Estranged learning', *Outlines*, 1: 19–48.

Lave, J. and Packer, M. (2008) 'Toward a social ontology of learning', in K. Nielsen, S. Brinkmann, C. Elmholdt, L. Tanggard, P. Musaeus and G. Kraft (eds) *A qualitative stance*, Aarhus, Denmark: Aarhus University Press, 17–48.

Lave, J. and Wenger, E. (1991) *Situated learning: Legitimate peripheral participation*, Cambridge: Cambridge University Press.

Lave, J. and Wenger, E. (1996) 'Practice, person, social world', in H. Daniels (ed.) *An introduction to Vygotsky*, London: Routledge, 143–150.

Lukács, G. (1988) *History and class consciousness: Studies in Marxist dialectics*, Cambridge, MA: MIT Press.

Packer, M. J. and Goicoecha, J. (2000) 'Sociocultural and constructivist theories of learning: Ontology, not just epistemology', *Educational Psychologist*, 35(4): 227–241.

Townsend, R. and Cushion, C. J. (2015) 'Elite cricket coach education: A Bourdieusian analysis', *Sport, Education and Society*. DOI: 10.1080/13573322.2015.1040753.

Trudel, P. and Gilbert, W. (2006) 'Coaching and coach education', in D. Kirk, M. O'Sullivan and D. McDonald (eds) *Handbook of research in physical education*, London: Sage, 516–539.

Wenger, E. (1998) *Communities of practice: Learning, meaning and identity*, Cambridge: Cambridge University Press.

17

PETER JARVIS

Lifelong coach learning

Pierre Trudel, Diane Culver and Jean-Paul Richard

Peter Jarvis: a short biography

Peter Jarvis was born in 1937 in the United Kingdom. He is a Professor of Continuing Education at the University of Surrey and a former Adjunct Professor in the Department of Adult Education, University of Georgia, USA. He studied sociology at Sheffield University (1969), took a master's at Birmingham (1969), and a Ph.D. at Aston (1977). For Jarvis 'learning should have life-wide connotations, or perhaps more significantly … we need to look at the whole person learning in life-wide contexts' (Jarvis 2006: 49). Therefore, we have selected some biographical events that we think may have had an impact on Jarvis' journey of becoming who he now is. When he was eight his father was killed in a road accident and from the age of ten until he left school he worked in a dairy to supplement the family's income. Unfortunately, he had to drop out of school because of low marks but then he decided to volunteer for the Royal Air Force. After three years he looked for a new life episode; he wanted to be a 'helper', thus he studied theology and became a full-time minister. During this time he studied full-time and got his first degree in Sociology and Politics. In reference to this period he mentioned that his first lecture in adult education was when he preached his first sermon (around 1955).

Jarvis has a prolific career, writing and editing over thirty books and 200 papers and book chapters. He is still very active, contributing to our learning by sharing his deep knowledge and experience of the field, as demonstrated in a recent article 'From Adult Education to Lifelong Learning and Beyond' (Jarvis 2014). Jarvis is often presented as a pioneer in the field of adult education, and his first book, published in 1983, was entitled *Adult and Continuing Education: Theory and Practice*. While adult learning was his starting point, he progressively included the concept of lifelong learning. For example, the title of the third edition of his first book (2004) was changed to *Adult Education and Lifelong Learning: Theory and Practice*. In an interview that took place at the Routledge offices in Abingdon (UK) in January 2009, when asked, 'When you look back on your career in lifelong education what are you most proud of?' the answer was: 'Starting the *International Journal of Lifelong Education*'. Among his reasons he mentioned: 'As I look back, yes, there have been a lot of people published in this journal, some of them publishing their first articles, and if we can give people an opportunity to develop themselves through a journal that, for me, is terrific.'

Peter Jarvis: key concepts

Given how deeply Jarvis goes when talking about human learning, there is significant challenge in presenting an overview of his contribution in a few pages. In line with Jarvis' theory, we must be aware that what we choose to present is influenced by our own biographies (i.e. what we know, understand, and value). Wishing to stay as close as possible to Jarvis' work, we decided to structure this section using his recently produced trilogy (Jarvis 2006, 2007, 2008) *Lifelong Learning and the Learning Society*, introduced by him as a synthesis of his previous writings, but not his final word. In an effort to capture the main concepts and how they are linked, we have drawn a figure (see Figure 17.1) that readers should refer to as they progress in their reading. However, we caution this figure is a partial map, by no means representing the whole territory of Jarvis' published world.

The first volume (*Towards a Comprehensive Theory of Human Learning*, 2006) of the trilogy is in two parts. In the first part Jarvis presents his theory of learning, using a psychological and philosophical framework. Focusing on the person to

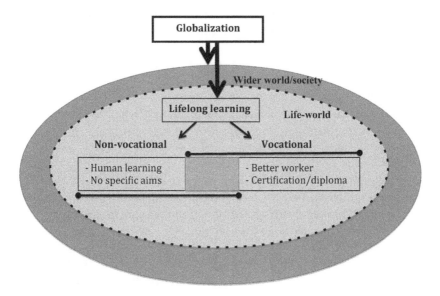

FIGURE 17.1 Mapping the main concepts of Jarvis' theory

explain the process of human learning, he walks the readers through the different stages using two complementary figures called 'The transformation of sensations: Initial and non-reflective learning' and 'The transformation of the person through learning'. These two figures are described in many of Jarvis' writings, including a recent article available online (Jarvis 2012). What differentiates Jarvis' perspective from that of others is his strong belief that human learning is an existential process and therefore, 'Learning is the process of being in the world. At the heart of all learning is not merely what is learned, but what the learner is becoming (learning) as a result of doing and thinking – and feeling' (Jarvis 2006: 6). Learning therefore is not restricted to what happens in the classroom but includes all learning opportunities (incidental and purposeful), also called episodic experiences. Before presenting Jarvis' definition of lifelong learning we need to explain a few key concepts.

Life-world: Because Jarvis' theory has a strong sociological basis, learning is considered an individual process, happening in a social context as perceived and defined by the individual – this is his or her life-world. Life-world should be understood through three elements: Space, time, and culture. Space is not only geographical since mass media and the internet now play an important role in one's social space. Moreover, a person's life-world is not static; it will change continuously, influenced by the individual's level of involvement. The life-world is part of a wider world/society that is also in permanent movement. Nowadays, we never have enough time for all the tasks and activities we want, or are expected, to undertake. For many, the challenge of implementing conscious learning activities is how to reserve periods of time for sharing knowledge, reflecting, and so on. Jarvis defines the third element, culture, as 'a social phenomenon; it is what we as a society, or a people, share and which enables us to live as society' (Jarvis 2006: 55). Jarvis discussed the importance of primary and secondary socialization. Primary socialization occurs in childhood, mainly within the family context. While often overlooked, its importance on 'our lifelong learning should never be under-estimated' (Jarvis 2006: 59). Secondary socialization involves becoming members of different groups that constitute our life-world.

Biography: An individual's biography is made up of all that the individual has previously learned (including cognitive, emotive, and physical dimensions); it will influence how the individual approaches new learning situations.

Harmony and disjuncture: Harmony is when we feel comfortable with our life-world – everything seems familiar: we are on 'cruise control'. Harmony, therefore, is a non-learning situation. Disjuncture is the opposite: 'when our biographical repertoire is no longer sufficient to cope automatically with our situation, so that our unthinking harmony with our world is disturbed and we feel unease' (Jarvis 2006: 16). Here we might ask, 'What should I do?', 'What does that mean?', and so on. In response, we can either decide not to act or we can work to find the answer/solution thereby establishing, or re-establishing harmony. Considering the continual and rapid changes in our life-worlds and wider worlds, we are exposed to disjuncture more now than ever before. But, 'if individuals disengage from the wider world so that their life-world changes less slowly than the wider world, they lose potential opportunities. They are harmony seekers' (Jarvis 2006: 26).

Lifelong learning: With these concepts explained, we can now look at how Jarvis defines lifelong learning:

> The combination of processes throughout a lifetime whereby the whole person – body (genetic, physical and biological) and mind (knowledge, skills, attitudes, values, emotions, meaning, beliefs and senses) – experiences social situations, the perceived content of which is then transformed cognitively, emotively or practically (or through any combination) and integrated into the individual person's biography resulting in a continually changing (or more experienced) person.
>
> *(Jarvis 2006: 134)*

Based on this definition, learning is existential in the sense that it derives from the need to learn and to become, but it is also experiential since it stems from a specific interaction with our life-world. However, not all episodic experiences are learning experiences. Many factors, often beyond our control, influence our access to them, how they are organized, and our freedom to participate or not. These issues are particularly addressed in volumes 2 and 3 of the trilogy.

In the second (*Globalisation, Lifelong Learning and the Learning Society: Sociological Perspectives*, 2007) and the third (*Democracy, Lifelong Learning and the Learning Society: Active Citizenship in a Late Modern Age*, 2008) volumes, Jarvis uses a socio-economic perspective to look at learning not only within the life-world but also within the much wider global context, even taking an ethical and political stand to discuss globalization. As mentioned earlier, most learning happens during an episodic experience in our life-world which 'is contained within the wider society and consequently it is not independent of the social forces generated by globalization' (Jarvis 2007: 22). The life-world and the wider world are not easy to separate (see Figure 17.1 – porous line) and comprise different levels of governments/institutions – some of which are close to us (individual/organizational, regional/local) while others are less salient (national, international). For Jarvis, globalization can take the form of a global substructure composed, among other things, of the economic and information technology systems that give transnational corporations the power to influence the wider world and the life-world. The positive side of globalization is that information and knowledge are more accessible, but the down side is that it can exert a standardizing effect on the world, meaning that individual learners, as well as local and national associations might progressively lose their sovereignty concerning what and how to learn. In addition, there is a cost related to this rapid access to information, and people from 'developing countries' are disadvantaged. Next, Jarvis explains that lifelong learning is not the same as lifelong education. Lifelong education tends to be restricted to social institutions teaching large groups of people to prepare them to assume the role of worker, that is, vocational learning. Thus, lifelong education can be a part of lifelong learning and this implies a second definition of the latter: 'Every opportunity made available by any social institution for, and every process by which, an individual can acquire knowledge, skills, attitudes, values, emotions, beliefs and senses within global society' (Jarvis 2007: 99). Therefore, 'there are broadly two quite distinct manifestations of lifelong learning – one which is private, lifelong non-vocational and often non-formal and even individual, while the other is social/public, work-life long, vocational, often formal' (Jarvis 2007: 188). It is important to notice that these two manifestations of lifelong learning will each often have functional utility in the other (see Figure 17.1 – middle box).

While some international political agencies (e.g. UNESCO) present lifelong learning with a humanistic perspective (non-vocational), others, such as the World Bank (WB) and the Organisation for Economic Co-operation and Development (OECD), take a more economic view, meaning that learning and work cannot be dissociated. Jarvis concludes his analysis saying: 'While lifelong learning is both vocational and non-vocational, it is the former that is favored rather than the latter ... , and the demands for an educated workforce mean that government is forced to give priority to vocational education, so that public money is being selectively allocated in favour of the economic interests' (Jarvis 2007: 74).

To conclude this section we can ask: Is Jarvis' theory superior to other theories in explaining the learning process? As mentioned earlier, Jarvis did provide a critique of a number of the existing theories and approaches to learning, including his own work. He also referred readers to other authors who have criticized his work (e.g. Le Cornu 2005). After decades of work, Jarvis comes to the conclusion that learning is such a complex process that it requires a multidisciplinary approach. Thus, each theory sheds some light on one or more aspect of learning but 'None of them have actually explained the whole of the learning processes, and this is the knub [sic] of the matter' (Jarvis 2006: 197).

Peter Jarvis: applications to sports coaching

Sport coach development is a very complex and intriguing process. Let us take a moment to immerse ourselves in Canadian society (the notion of 'global village' suggests that a similar situation exists in many countries) and compare high-performance coaches with family physicians, given that both groups are expected to play a pivotal role in the lives of people. It is worth mentioning that while sport coaches were traditionally given the mandate to introduce youth to sport and/or to develop athletes to their full potential, this mandate has been extended: 'Sport and, by implication, the majority of coaches are required to be part of the health and welfare intervention movement' (Taylor and Garratt 2013: 35). In the respective statements of these national associations we can see similarities regarding how they want to influence the development of their members.

> The College of Family Physicians of Canada (CFPC) ... is the professional
> organization responsible for establishing standards for the training, certification

and lifelong education of family physicians and for advocating on behalf of the specialty of family medicine, family physicians and their patients. [Mission] To support family physicians through certification, advocacy, leadership, research, and learning opportunities that enable them to provide high-quality health care for their patients and their communities.

(www.cfpc.ca/Mission/)

The Coaching Association of Canada unites stakeholders and partners in its commitment to raising the skills and stature of coaches, and ultimately expanding their reach and influence. Through its programs, the CAC empowers coaches with knowledge and skills, promotes ethics, fosters positive attitudes, builds competence, and increases the credibility and recognition of coaches.

[Mission] To enhance the experiences of all Canadian athletes through quality coaching.

(http://coach.ca/who-we-are-s16630)

However, the similarities stop here. Imagine a scenario in which most family physicians are volunteers or paid part-time and their training varies from no formal education in medicine to a few hours often taken after a few months of practising medicine. Many have decided to become a doctor after years as a patient. For those practising in highly regarded hospitals, their success records appear frequently on the front pages of the tabloids, being the main topic of discussion by the general public who openly question their competencies/knowledge when they are not performing as expected.

This comparison illustrates how sport coach development is so different to that of many other professions, and we argue that using Jarvis' work provides a helpful learning perspective, a kind of tool, to better understand how sport coaches learn to coach. It also leads to some suggestions for coach development administrators (CDAs) (Trudel et al. 2013) and new ways to support high-performance coaches in their process of becoming (Nash and Sproule 2009; Mallett 2010).

Figure 17.2 represents some of the main concepts of Jarvis' theory linked to concepts often mentioned in the literature on sport coach development. Like all human beings, coaches are involved in a lifelong learning process. The six small arrows represent learning in many different aspects and the bigger arrow in the middle learning specific to coaching. In the last decade, it has been suggested that coaching is context-specific (Côté et al. 2010) and from an extensive literature review on coaching science, Trudel and Gilbert (2006) provided the profile of a typical coach for three coaching contexts: Recreational, developmental, and elite. This implies that (a) coaches enter their coaching career with different biographies, (b) their life-worlds, especially their coaching life-world, will be different, and (c) what coaches need to know will vary and, by extension, programmes to train coaches (vocational setting) should also be different. Based on this coaching context classification and some recent coaching publications that used Jarvis' theory (Trudel

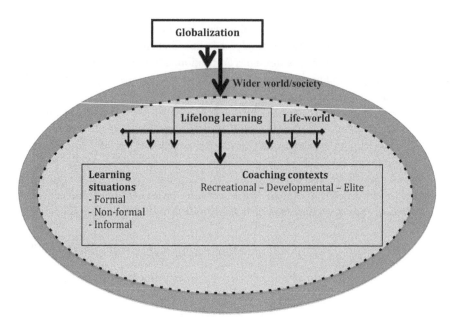

FIGURE 17.2 Jarvis' theory applied to sport coach development

et al. 2010, 2013; Callary et al. 2011, 2012; McMaster et al. 2012; Winchester et al. 2013; Cushion and Nelson 2013; Duarte and Culver 2014), we will briefly comment on the importance of three learning situations (Nelson et al. 2006) for coaches' development – situations where most of the coaching episodic experiences take place regardless of the coaching context.

Formal learning situations are coach education training programmes that provide certification. While certification is becoming more widespread, these programmes, especially in the recreational and developmental contexts, are usually delivered over one or two weekends, thus providing 'evidence that many practitioners have satisfied the governing bodies' criteria for minimum levels of coaching competency' (Cushion and Nelson 2013: 367). When asked how useful the training programme was for learning to coach, coaches' answers ranged from 'very useful' to 'a complete waste of time'. Coaches' critiques included: the content was too easy, too difficult, too theoretical, or too decontextualized. We are faced with situations where the content and/or the delivery failed to create disjuncture, the starting point in the learning process. *Non-formal situations* are opportunities (e.g. conferences, workshops) often organized by CDAs to complement their training programme. A recent move forces coaches to accumulate 'professional development points' to maintain their coaching status – lifelong education. Finally, *informal learning situations* refers to learning opportunities outside of what is required by the sport organizations/CDAs. This category is very comprehensive and includes, for example, primary and secondary socialization, diplomas obtained for careers other than coaching, experiences as an athlete, mentoring, interactions with others (e.g.

family, co-workers, coaching peers), and resources (e.g. books, websites). For many coaches this is clearly the best way to learn how to coach.

These three learning situations transpire in the coaches' life-world, their own social context. Coming back to the three components of the life-world (space, time and culture) can help to understand the expression 'Do you have ten years of experience or ten times one year?'. A sport's culture/sub-culture influences the number and the type of learning situations/episodic experiences available and how equally accessible they are to men and women. Also, coaches who limit their interactions to their coaching staffs, avoid sharing their knowledge with others and confronting different coaching approaches, and restrict their coaching life-world, are therefore more likely to repeat the same thing over and over. In other words, they are seeking to maintain harmony instead of enjoying disjuncture.

Coach development is not beyond the influence of globalization but this influence is complex and could be the topic of a full chapter. In brief, we can say that many countries have their own coach education training programme. To be able to reach the numerous coaches in the recreational and developmental contexts, such a programme often takes the form of a 'large-scale coach education training programme' (Trudel et al. 2010). Recently, there has been an initiative to try to standardize coach development around the world. The International Council for Coaching Excellence (ICCE) and the Association of Summer Olympic International Federations (ASOIF) published the International Sport Coaching Framework, 'an internationally recognized reference point for the development of coaches. It is responsive to the needs of different sports, countries, organizations and institutions and provides benchmarks for the recognition and certification of coaches' (2013: 10). To our knowledge, this framework has already been used to develop the South African Coaching Framework (Segwaba et al. 2014) and to analyse the Brazilian coach education programme (Milistetd et al. 2014). There are also initiatives from 'wealthy sports' to provide coaching materials and even specific certification worldwide. A good example is the International Rugby Board which has recently been rebranded 'World Rugby'. The vision presented on their website claims that 'World Rugby now wishes to innovate and inspire through participation, engagement, education and regulation, harnessing the sport's character-building values to excite, engage and inform new audiences in existing and new rugby markets' (www.worldrugby.org/vision). Regarding coaches in the elite/high-performance coaching context, the content of their training tends to be less publicly discussed because national sport associations/federations are constantly working to get an edge on how their coaches are prepared compared with those of other countries. Callary and colleagues (2014) gathered some information on seven national high-performance coach education programmes. While they all adapted a competency-based approach, large differences were noticed concerning (a) how many coaches are accepted and their profiles, (b) programme prerequisites, (c) curriculum delivery, and (d) evaluation processes.

We will conclude this section by providing some specific suggestions to CDAs. To apply many of the concepts and principles included in Jarvis' theory, new models for coach development must emerge, especially for coaches in the elite/ high-performance coaching context. These new models should not focus exclusively on a content-based approach – teaching preselected material 'just in case' coaches might need it – but consider introducing a needs-based approach that supports and empowers coaches by giving them more control over the time and space of their learning (coaches having access to the material as they need it – 'just in time'). In such programmes, CDAs will need to help coaches discuss relevant biographical details, particularly about their professional knowledge, interpersonal knowledge, and intrapersonal knowledge (Gilbert and Côté 2013). In Jarvis' world it will be: learning to know, learning to do, learning to live together, and learning to be. After completing this exercise, the CDAs and coaches will be in a better position to identify the best ways to support the coaches' lifelong education and, to some extend, lifelong learning. Regarding *professional knowledge* (sport related), successful high performance coaches are those who can create and innovate (Trudel and Gilbert 2013). To be successful at this, coaches need to feel comfortable living with a high level of disjuncture. It is about learning the new, not the old: 'Learning the new is about finding out about stuff that is new to the world rather than new to the individual (i.e., new ideas, new concepts, new things, new skills, new resources, etc.) – things that have yet to become codified within existing or new bodies of knowledge' (Hart 2014: 19). *Interpersonal knowledge* refers to the capacity to interact with others in the life-world and the wider world/society. Considering the complexity of coaching, this type of knowledge seems to be essential to access expertise: 'Individual expertise does not distinguish people as high performers, a larger and more diversified personal network does' (Hart 2014: 28). For both professional and interpersonal knowledge, information technology constantly provides new ways of doing things (episodic experiences) and CDAs have to be aware of these advances, often the result of globalization. Finally, *intrapersonal knowledge* involves the under-standing of oneself and the ability to reflect on one's practice; not an easy task (Knowles et al. 2014). Recently, Trudel and Gilbert (2013) argued that to help coaches become better reflective practitioners it is not enough to tell them to reflect. Rather, they suggested providing, at least initially, the support of a 'personal learning coach'. This new type of episodic experience should contribute to coaches progressively adopting new learning habits – embracing disjuncture. While learning is an individual process it happens in a social context and CDAs/sport federations play an important role in structuring the workplace (Rynne et al. 2010) by helping coaches to expand and enrich their coaching life-world.

Peter Jarvis: a practitioner commentary by Jean-Paul Richard

Like many of my peers, my development as a coach has been composed of countless learning experiences, all contributing to the person I have become as 'a result of doing, thinking and feeling'. I would like to stress the importance of feeling. Coaching is about passion. First you start practising sport as a child and without being able to say why you invest more and more time, progressively focusing on one sport. Along the way you interact with many other athletes and coaches, developing your skills and learning the sub-culture of your sport. Then one day, a coaching position is offered to you and, equipped with all your previous experiences and knowledge (biography), you jump into this new adventure with the desire to not only teach the skills but also transmit the love of sport.

Although the importance of having competent sport coaches is recognized, what coaches actually do remains a mystery to the general public. Yes, coaching is very complex and its complexity is constantly increasing with all the information now readily available. In this context, coaches have no choice but to become lifelong learners. I found Peter Jarvis' theory very useful as a tool to help me reflect upon and capture my twenty-one years of sport experience, from my first training session in freestyle skiing to the gold and silver medals of two of our athletes at Sochi's Olympic Games.

With my parents (primary socialization), I participated in several sports and started Alpine skiing with my friends, at our local club. While my parents did not ski, they would take me to the mountain. At the age of 13 I signed up for the freestyle ski club and from there I competed for six years (secondary socialization). I was forced to quit because of an injury, but given my passion for the sport, becoming a coach provided me with the opportunity to continue contributing by transmitting my knowledge to others. At age 19, I made the decision to start my own freestyle club and took on the roles of head coach and president for six years. From there I became the head coach of a freestyle team (provincial level), and during this time I instigated a programme to develop a young generation of talented skiers. This was a period of high disjuncture.

When I started my coaching career, I had to follow the compulsory coach education route, composed of seminars in which we discussed many topics related to the sport. At the end of these formal learning activities, I received a certification attesting to my level of 'professional knowledge'. Having completed these certifi- cations, I wanted to continue my development and went to a Canadian Sport Institute for a two-year programme. This learning context was a mix of classes on specific topics (formal) and opportunities to exchange with coaches from different sports on any topic (informal). Completing this programme while coaching required a lot of self-discipline and motivation but the diploma I received is a worthy recognition.

Then came the moment when I had completed all the certifications but I still had a burning desire to learn (existential). But what to do? There seems to be a black hole in the support offered to high-performance coaches as they seek to become experts. I really believe that what is needed is individualized support that takes into consideration the coach's biography and his or her coaching context. I decided to extend my coaching life-world by accepting a coaching position in Sweden. Being on my own, I looked for books and other materials to help me innovate and find solutions to the problems/questions I had (moving from dis- juncture to harmony). By confronting my earlier experiences with the Swedish culture and coaching approaches, I was able to further develop my coaching style (the three types of knowledge). At the centre of this new learning environment was my network of knowledgeable people (e.g. mental trainers, fitness trainers). Our main objective was to 'prioritize priorities' to free up time to innovate and not simply copy the best practices of others; in other words we were looking 'for the new not the old'. All these learning opportunities helped me to reflect on what I was doing; but, being pushed outside of one's comfort zone requires an open mind: a lifelong learning attitude. This attitude was important when I went back to coaching for Canada. My biography had changed and I had to 'negotiate' my new way of coaching with my athletes, coaching staff, and networks (old and new).

Recently, I decided to take on a new challenge by joining the Canadian Olympic Committee as a manager of team services. I arrived in this new working context with my own biography and the awareness that to be successful I would have to stay in tune with what is happening in the wider world and the influence that globalization can have on coaching at the high-performance level. I am convinced that to perform at the Olympic Games or other big events, Canadian coaches need to get together and feel like *one* Canadian team. Therefore we have to provide a learning environment where coaches from different sports will interact frequently – a focus on their interpersonal knowledge. The disjuncture I have at the moment is: What types of learning activities will be appealing enough that these coaches will (a) reserve time for them, (b) be willing to reflect on their practice and share their knowledge, (c) accept being challenged about their practices/points of view and, (d) see the activities as being part of their coaching rather than something added to what they are doing?

Peter Jarvis: critical questions

1. What are the differences between lifelong learning and lifelong education? How are they linked when discussing coaches' development?
2. What role does biography play in the learning process? Are coaches' biographies generally taken into consideration when developing coach education programmes (in the different coaching contexts)?
3. Considering the role that disjuncture plays in the learning process: what are the limits of many traditional coach education programmes?
4. How does globalization affect, positively and less positively, the learning of an individual? What are the main influences of globalization on coaches' development?
5. What are the three main learning situations where coaches develop their knowledge and how can coach development administrators maximize learning in each of them?

References

Callary, B., Culver, D., Werthner, P. and Bales, J. (2014) 'An overview of seven national high performance coach education programmes', *International Sport Coaching Journal*, 1: 152–164.

Callary, B., Werthner, P. and Trudel, P. (2011) 'Shaping the way five women coaches develop: Their primary and secondary socialization', *Journal of Coaching Education*, 4: 76–125.

Callary, B., Werthner, P. and Trudel, P. (2012) 'How meaningful episodic experiences influence the process of becoming an experienced coach', *Qualitative Research in Sport, Exercise and Health*, 4: 420–438.

Côté, J., Bruner, M., Erickson, K., Srachan, L. and Fraser-Thomas, J. (2010) 'Athlete development and coaching', in J. Lyle and C. Cushion (eds) *Sports coaching: Professionalisation and practice*, London: Elsevier.

Cushion, C. and Nelson, L. (2013) 'Coach education and learning: Developing the field', in P. Potrac, W. Gilbert and J. Denison (eds) *Routledge handbook of sports coaching*, London: Routledge, 359–374.

Duarte, T. and Culver, D. (2014) 'Becoming a coach in developmental adaptive sailing: A lifelong learning perspective', *Journal of Applied Sport Psychology*, 26: 441–456.

Gilbert, W. and Côté, J. (2013) 'Defining coaching effectiveness: A focus on coaches' knowledge', in P. Potrac, W. Gilbert and J. Denison (eds) *Routledge handbook of sports coaching*, London: Routledge, 147–159.

Hart, J. (2014) *Social learning handbook*, Italy: Lulu Press.

ICCE and ASOIF (2013) *International sport coaching framework, version 1.2*, Champaign, IL: Human Kinetics.

Jarvis, P. (1983). Adult and Continuing Education: Theory and Practice. London: Routledge.

Jarvis, P. (2004). Adult Education and Lifelong Learning: Theory and Practice. London: Routledge.

Jarvis, P. (2006) *Towards a comprehensive theory of learning*, London: Routledge.

Jarvis, P. (2007) *Globalisation, lifelong learning and the learning society: Sociological perspectives*, London: Routledge.

Jarvis, P. (2008) *Democracy, lifelong learning and the learning society: Active citizenship in a late modern age*, London: Routledge.

Jarvis, P. (2012) 'Learning from everyday life', *HSSRP (Human and Social Studies Research and Practice)*, 1(1): 1–20. Available at http://hssrp.uaic.ro/continut/1.pdf

Jarvis, P. (2014) 'From adult education to lifelong learning and beyond', *Comparative Education*, 50(1): 45–57.

Knowles, Z., Gilbourne, D., Cropley, B. and Dugdill, L. (eds) (2014) *Reflective practice in the sport and exercise sciences: Contemporary issues*, Abingdon: Routledge.

Le Cornu, A. (2005) 'Building on Jarvis: Towards a holistic model of the processes of experiential learning', *Studies in the Education of Adults*, 37(2): 166–181.

Mallett, C. J. (2010) 'Becoming a high-performance coach: Pathways and communities', in J. Lyle and C. Cushion (eds) *Sports coaching: Professionalisation and practice*, London: Elsevier, 119–134.

McMaster, S., Culver, D. and Werthner, P. (2012) 'Coaches of athletes with a physical disability: A look at their learning experiences', *Qualitative Research in Sport, Exercise and Health*, 4(2): 226–243.

Milistetd, M., Trudel, P., Mesquita, I. and Nascimento, J. (2014) 'Coaching and coach education in Brazil', *International Sport Coaching Journal*, 1: 165–172.

Nash, C. S. and Sproule, J. (2009) 'Career development of expert coaches', *International Journal of Sport Science and Coaching*, 4(1): 121–138.

Nelson, L. J., Cushion, C. J. and Potrac, P. (2006) 'Formal, nonformal and informal coach learning: A holistic conceptualization', *International Journal of Sports Sciences and Coaching*, 1(3): 247–259.

Rynne, S. B., Mallett, C. J. and Tinning, R. (2010) 'Workplace learning of high performance sports coaches', *Sport, Education and Society*, 15(3): 315–330.

Segwaba, J., Vardhan, D. and Duffy, P. (2014) 'Coaching in South Africa', *International Sport Coaching Journal*, 1: 33–41.

Taylor, W. G. and Garratt, D. (2013) 'Coaching and professionalization', in P. Potrac, W. Gilbert and J. Denison (eds) *Routledge handbook of sports coaching*, London: Routledge, 27–39.

Trudel, P., Culver, D. and Werthner, P. (2013) 'Looking at coach development from the coach-learner's perspective: Consideration for coach development administrators', in P. Potrac, W. Gilbert and J. Denison (eds) *Routledge handbook of sports coaching*, London: Routledge, 375–387.

Trudel, P. and Gilbert, W. (2006) 'Coaching and coach education', in D. Kirk, M. O'Sullivan and D. McDonald (eds) *Handbook of research in physical education*, London: Sage, 16–539.

Trudel, P. and Gilbert, W. (2013) 'The role of deliberate practice in becoming an expert coach: Part 3 – Creating optimal settings', *Olympic Coach Magazine*, 24(2): 15–28.

Trudel, P., Gilbert, W. and Werthner, P. (2010) 'Coach education effectiveness', in J. Lyle and C. Cushion (eds) *Sports coaching: Professionalisation and practice*, London: Elsevier, 135–152.

Winchester, G., Culver, D. and Camiré, M. (2013) 'Understanding how Ontario high school teacher-coaches learn to coach', *Physical Education and Sport Pedagogy*, 18(4): 412–426.

18

NEL NODDINGS

Caring, moral learning and coaching

Laura Purdy, Paul Potrac and Rūtenis Paulauskas

Nel Noddings: a short biography

Nel Noddings was born on 19 January 1929 in Irvington, New Jersey, USA. She obtained a bachelor's degree in Mathematics and Physical Science from Montclair State College and a master's degree in Mathematics from Rutgers University. She began her educational career as a schoolteacher and spent seventeen years working with elementary and high school pupils. Throughout her teaching career, Noddings also held a variety of administrative positions (i.e. Mathematics Department Chairperson, Assistant Principal) alongside her teaching duties. Her experiences in these roles enabled her to not only become familiar with various classroom-related issues, but also the demands and dilemmas that are a feature of the wider school context. During this period she also undertook a Ph.D. in Educational Philosophy and Theory at Stanford University. Following the completion of her doctoral work, she took up faculty positions at Stanford University, Columbia University and, latterly, at Colgate University. Here, her own experiences of being taught by, and working with, caring teachers proved a significant influence on her research and scholarly thought about student–teacher relations.

Noddings enjoyed a prolific academic career, which included the authorship of over eighteen books and more than 200 articles. Indeed, she is recognised as one of the premier philosophers of moral education (Bergman 2004). Her insightful and articulate scholarly work has been widely lauded in the academy and she has been the recipient of numerous accolades and awards. For example, she was elected as the president of the John Dewey Society, the National Academy of Education, and the Philosophy of Education Society. She also received a medal for distinguished service from Teachers College (Columbia University), the Award for Distinguished Leadership in Education (Rutgers University), was the recipient of the American

Educational Research Association Lifetime Achievement Award, and is currently the
Lee L. Jacks Professor of Education, Emerita, at Stanford University.

Nel Noddings: key concepts

In her writings, Noddings advocated a position whereby learning should not solely
be considered in terms of how much an individual knows about a particular academic
or technical subject or topic. Instead, she believes that it should also focus on what
people do with the knowledge that they acquire and develop. Importantly in this
regard, she asks us to consider how we have 'become a better person because of it?'
(Coleman et al. 2011). Indeed, Noddings believes that the purpose of education
'should be to produce competent, caring, loving and lovable people' (Noddings
1992: 8).

For Noddings, education is best understood as 'a constellation of encounters,
both planned and unplanned, that promote growth through the acquisition of
knowledge, skills, understanding and appreciation' (Noddings 2002: 283). It is a
view, then, that positions the student as 'infinitely more important than the subject'
(Noddings 2002: 20). In her various publications, Noddings has argued for moral
education to be recognised as an essential feature of educational curricula (e.g.
Noddings 1984, 1992, 1998, 2002, 2012a, 2012b). In this respect, she contended
that educators 'should produce not only moral people', but that they should also
provide 'an education that is moral in purpose, policy, and method' (Noddings
1992: xiii). According to Noddings, the foundation of morality is in caring and
educators should, therefore, consequently strive to create learning environments
that promote and encourage students to care for all that they see around them.
This includes themselves, other people, animals, objects, and ideas.

At the heart of Nodding's theorising is the belief that human beings have an
innate need to 'be understood, received, respected, and recognized' by others
(Noddings 2002: 26). Indeed, she believes that *caring* and being *cared for* are fundamental features of everyday social life. Here, Noddings understands caring to be 'a
set of relational practices that foster mutual recognition and realization, growth
development, protection, empowerment and human community, culture and
possibility' (Gordon et al. 1996: xiii). In her consideration of caring, Noddings
differentiates between *caring for* and *caring about*. The former refers to a person
caring directly for another, while the latter is concerned with an individual
subscribing to a state of mind where he or she nurtures caring ideas or intentions
(e.g. being concerned about human suffering in poor or war-torn countries).
Interestingly, Noddings (2002) believes that it is important for an individual's *caring
about* to be ultimately transformed into *caring for* if there are to be meaningful
improvements in terms of how people relate to, and responsively treat, one
another. In her words:

> The key, central to care theory, is this: caring-about (or, perhaps a sense of
> justice) must be seen as instrumental in establishing the conditions under

which caring-for can flourish. Although the preferred form of caring is cared-for, caring-about can help in establishing, maintaining, and enhancing it. Those who care about others in the justice sense must keep in mind that the objective is to ensure that caring actually occurs. Caring-about is empty if it does not culminate in caring relations.

(Noddings 2002: 23–24)

While Noddings (1992, 2002) recognised that caring is something that cannot be achieved in a formulaic manner, she outlined three key elements that she believes are a feature of a caring relationship. These are a carer, a recipient or one who is cared for, and recognition by the recipient that he or she is being cared for. The latter point is particularly important, because if the cared-for denies that he or she is being cared for, then there is, ultimately, no caring relationship (Noddings 2005a, 2005b). Similarly, although she recognised that caring 'requires different behaviours from situation to situation and from person to person' (Noddings 1992: xi), there are, from her perspective, several common characteristics that are evident within caring encounters. These include *engrossment* and *motivational displacement* on behalf of the carer.

Engrossment refers to 'an open, nonselective receptivity to the cared-for' by the carer (Noddings 2002: 16). This involves the carer trying to see, hear, or feel what the other person is trying to convey. At the same time, the carer needs to bracket his or her own self-interests (i.e. *motivational displacement*) to focus on the particular needs, wants, and interests of the cared-for. It is a sense of being 'present', being willing to listen, and conveying interest in the cared-for. In doing so, the carer experiences a motivational shift or a 'sense that [the carer's] motive energy is flowing toward others' (Noddings 1998: 41). The ultimate goal here is that the cared-for feels that the one caring is receiving him. The cared-for also has a contribution to make to this caring exchange. This specifically relates to their acknowledgement that the carer's efforts have been received. This might be manifested in the cared-for's demonstration of gratitude to the carer, but it can also include the cared-for pursuing an agree-upon objective with renewed determination energy, asking of further questions, including the carer in the cared-for's projects, or, more simply, recognition in the form of a nod or a smile (Noddings 2012a, 2012b).

For Noddings (2002), there are moments when people care for others quite naturally. She refers to this as *natural caring* and suggests that caring in this form 'does not require an ethical effort to motivate it' (Noddings 2002: 2). For example, if parents see their child in distress, they naturally want to provide help and assistance. In contrast to *natural caring* is her notion of *ethical caring*, which requires a conscious effort or choice on behalf of an individual to care for another. For example, a passer-by might respectively think that 'I must' help an individual who has fallen to the ground in pain even if there instinctive preference is to walk past the person on the ground. Importantly, Noddings (2002) suggests that, while the capacity to care might vary from one individual to another, the adoption of a caring approach to others and life in general is something that can be taught and learned through moral education.

Moral education refers to the intentional bringing about of moral growth (Arnold 1994) and contributes to the development of attitudes and skills that are required to sustain caring relations and 'the desire to do so' (Noddings 1984: 21–22). In essence, for Noddings, it is the process of how educators can help students to learn to care and to be cared for. According to Noddings (1984), moral education has four essential components. These are *modelling, dialogue, practice* and *confirmation*. The first component, *modelling*, enables the carer to demonstrate how to care by creating caring relations with the cared-for. The second important component of moral education is *dialogue*. Genuine dialogue, talking, listening, sharing, and responding, invites the carer and the cared-for to be exposed to ideas and understandings other than their own (Noddings 1992). *Dialogue* also helps maintain caring relations as it enables the carer and cared-for to connect through language and shared experience (Noddings 1992). *Dialogue* also allows the carer to shift the focus of the interaction in light of the cared-for's needs (Noddings 1992). Without *dialogue*, those who want to care must infer the needs of the cared-for (Noddings 2002). This can be problematic, as carers may fail in their quest to establish caring relations because they do not feel that the one being cared for is receiving them. The third component of moral education is *practice*. For Noddings, it is through practice that attitudes and ways of thinking are shaped. Noddings values *practice*, as it is through opportunities to collaboratively practice care that individuals learn how to care and contribute to a community in which all are involved in a variety of tasks. The fourth component is *confirmation*, which is an act of affirming and encouraging the best in others in order to develop positive relationships (Buber 1965). In caring relations, *confirmation* is the result of establishing trust. Noddings (1992) suggests that the carer achieves *confirmation* by developing a relationship in which the carer gets to know the interests, values, and goals of the cared-for. In her words:

> When we confirm someone, we identify a better self and encourage its development. To do this we must know the other reasonably well. Otherwise we cannot see what the other is really striving for, what ideal he or she may long to make real.
>
> *(Noddings 1998: 192)*

Through their engagement in the process of moral education, Noddings (1998, 2003) argued that individuals could be encouraged to critically reflect on a number of issues related to their thoughts, feelings, and actions to others. Her notions of the *ideal self*, the *ethical self*, the *physical self*, and the *diminution of the ethical ideal* could inform such reflection and discussion. In this regard, the *ideal self* is concerned with the frequency and extent to which an individual genuinely cares for, and is committed to, the well-being and development of another individual or group. The *ethical self*, meanwhile, refers to the relation or distance between an individual's actual self and his or her *ideal self*. In this regard, the *ethical self* is concerned with an individual's feeling of 'I must do something' in situations where they would prefer not to act in a caring fashion. Often, this involves an individual's willingness to work through their doubts, apathy, or aversion because they believe that this is the right thing to do, especially given the role that they occupy (e.g. a nurse working with a patient or patients) (Noddings 2003; Lundqvist and Nilstun 2009). Relatedly, the *physical self* is concerned with an individual's thoughts regarding what leads them to feel pain or pleasure. For Noddings, an individual's views on these topics often precede the act of caring for others and, crucially, can influence the way that caring is manifested. On occasions, a carer's needs regarding the physical self may, for example, overshadow their willingness to understand, or receive, the needs of the cared-for. Finally, the *diminution of the ethical* ideal relates to an individual's decision to act against their own commitment to care (Noddings 2003; Lundqvist and Nilstun 2009). In this regard, an individual may find the act of caring burdensome and subsequently choose to exclude a person or persons. Equally, the *diminution of the ethical self* can also occur when an individual's emphasis is on being seen to conform to institutional guidelines regarding expected behaviour, rather than genuinely and reflexively committing oneself to a caring philosophy. Here, in the context of nursing, Noddings (2003: 116) noted:

> Institutions sometimes demand loyalty and affirmation of certain beliefs. Insistence on obedience of rules contributes to destroy genuine caring and tends to reduce individual responsibility and the reflection necessary for the nurse to make decisions.

Like all educational theories and ideas, Noddings' work has not been received without some criticism. In this regard, concerns have been raised regarding Noddings' lack of emphasis on caring for oneself. While Noddings insists that a person takes care of her/himself, this understanding of self-care is premised upon being better at caring for others. This has drawn the attention of critics who have argued that if self-care is done as a service for others, there is a danger of merging. That is, '[s]he (the carer) has identified her own interests and projects so closely with those of the person for whom she cares that she stands in danger of losing herself altogether' (Lindemann Nelson 1992: 11). As such, there is a danger of burnout in the work of caring. Indeed, Lindemann Nelson and Carse (1996) recommend considering limits on the extent to which one individual has a duty of care for others. In addition to critical consideration of the potential impacts of caring on the carer, other scholars have proffered some concerns that relate to the potential oppression of the cared-for. For example, Hoagland (1990) questioned the carer's dominant position of making decisions regarding what is good for the cared-for, with the cared-for often having little control over the nature of the caring that is received.

Nel Noddings: applications to sports coaching

Having briefly considered above some of the key ideas and concepts from Nodding's theorising about learning, this section explores some of the ways in which her work could be utilised to potentially underpin and guide a coach's pedagogical practices. It is important to note that Noddings did not write directly about sports coaching. As such, this section should be considered to represent our collective interpretation of just some of the ways that her work could be utilised to support learning and practice in coaching settings. In shaping this section, we have primarily drawn upon Noddings' (2012b) paper addressing the caring relation in teaching, as we believe it has considerable utility and transferability in terms of stimulating our thoughts about coaching practice.

From our perspective, the most striking feature of Noddings' work is her challenge to us to consider the overall purpose of our educational efforts. In this regard, she believes that education should entail more than preparing learners to demonstrate their knowledge and understanding of particular academic concepts and ideas in various standardised tests and examinations (Noddings 2005a, 2012b). Instead, it should also include the development of their commitment to care for, and co-operate with, others. This is something that she considers to be an essential human capacity in a time of increasing global interdependence (Noddings 2012b).

In the context of coaching, Noddings' sentiments above seemingly suggest that a coach's educational role goes beyond the teaching and learning of particular techniques and tactics to include a consideration of how they might create an environment where caring relations might flourish (Noddings 2012b). That is, the challenge for coaching practitioners is not limited to facilitating athletes' learning of a variety of performance-related issues and topics, but it also entails creating a pedagogical climate where coaches 'can best meet individual needs, impart knowledge, and encourage the development of moral people' (Noddings 2012b: 777). This perspective on educational activity certainly resonates with a variety of community sport initiatives where coaches are asked to provide sporting interventions that promote social cohesion and community spirit, help reduce crime, loneliness, and social isolation, and contribute to the development of good citizens (Ives et al. in press). Similarly, while limited in terms of the amount of scholarly consideration afforded to it, the role of, and potential for, caring and moral learning in the context of elite level sport has also received some insightful attention (e.g. Walton 1991; Jones et al. 2004; Jones 2009).

Importantly, the facilitation of moral learning entails a willingness on the behalf of the coach to accept the role as a moral, as well as a sporting, educator (Noddings 2012a, 2012b). In terms of day-to-day practice, then, coaches would need to consider, and engage with, various social and moral issues with athletes whenever they arise. These might include, but are not limited to, exploring issues related to anger, envy, fear, inauthentic behaviour, and cheating, as well as the possible strategies that athletes could utilise to manage them (Noddings 2012b). Realistically, such pedagogical interventions would require the coach to have a knowledge base that extended beyond the 'nuts and bolts' of sporting performance. Indeed, coaches wishing to pursue moral learning through sport would likely benefit from educational provision and continuing professional development opportunities that supported them to help athletes to learn about, and make connection with, 'the great existential questions as well as questions of current social life' (Noddings 1999: 215).

Relatedly, the quest to help individuals develop a caring attitude in their wider social, professional, and civic lives also entails coaches modelling, facilitating, and rewarding a caring approach in their coaching practices. For Noddings, this entails much more than merely 'telling them [athletes] to care' and giving 'them texts to read on the subject' (Noddings 1998: 190). Instead, it is important that coaches not only model a caring approach in their everyday interactions with athletes, but that they also provide opportunities for athletes to practise and reflect upon caring acts and behaviours (Noddings 1998, 2012b). This could, for example, include being polite and courteous, showing sympathy for others (e.g. taking an interest in injured athletes' rehabilitation), recognising other pressing concerns in the lives of athletes (e.g. school examinations), and spending some time talking with and getting to know all of the athletes in a particular group or squad.

For Noddings (2012b), the development of caring relations is also dependent on an educator's ability, as well as willingness, to listen to the ideas and thoughts of those in their charge. In the context of coaching, then, this may mean coaches consciously pursuing strategies where they encourage individual athletes to share their views and feelings on a particular topic or issue. (Noddings 2012b: 774). Equally, coaches may wish to listen to athletes as they work together in pairs or small groups. In this scenario, coaches may wish to join in the dialogue, make suggestions, or bring the whole group together to discuss and clarify matters that they have heard across the smaller groups. However, coaches should avoid simply telling athletes the answers. Rather, from our perspective at least, Noddings' (2002: 287) work encourages coaches to engage in true dialogue that is characterised by 'mutual exploration, a search for meaning, or the solution of some problem'.

Of course, given the frequently asymmetrical power relations that exist between coach and athlete, some athletes may be reluctant (or even frightened) to engage in such activity (Jones et al. 2011; Noddings 2012b). As such, it is essential that athletes come to recognise that their thinking will be respected if such dialogue is to evolve in a meaningful way. In order to develop and sustain positive interactions and trusting relationships with learners, coaches may benefit from giving consideration to how they respond to the mistakes and misunderstandings of others. Here, Noddings (2012b) argued that educators have much to gain by not attaching blame to individual and collective errors. Specifically, she believes that educators can use such instances to improve their own explanations, as well as the learners' understanding of particular issues and topics. Equally, coaches may also wish to reflect upon the extent to which they treat athletes in a respectful and supportive manner, as well as how they encourage athletes to also relate to each other in such ways (Noddings 2012b).

Through the process of listening to athletes, a coach may hear an individual talk about an issue (e.g. a child doesn't like being made to play football) that goes beyond the assumed needs of learners which underpins a particular coaching programme or curriculum (Noddings 2012b). In such scenarios, Noddings (2012b: 772) believes that educators should be able to respond to the expressed needs of the learner (or cared-for) for 'emotional support, moral direction, or shared human interest'. It is important to recognise that, in these circumstances, Noddings is not advocating for an abandonment of assumed needs (e.g. the coaching curriculum). Rather, she believes that a caring approach entails also recognising and responding to the expressed needs of the cared-for. In the scenario presented above, this might mean the coach engaging with a child to identify and, where possible, tackle what the individual does not like about playing football.

Finally, coaches might wish to draw upon Noddings' concepts of the *ideal self, the ethical self*, the *physical self*, and *the diminution of the self*, to help frame their personal introspection regarding how they view and enact their coaching role. For example, Jones (2009) suggested that coaches could critically consider the extent to which they care for and care about the welfare and development of their charges, inclusive of the challenges, fears, and anxieties that they might encounter in relation to the achievement of the latter. Similarly, coaches may also wish to reflect on the importance that Noddings (2002) attaches to educators being seen to think and act in a consistent manner in their attempts to facilitate moral learning and create a caring coaching climate. Here, Noddings noted:

> The fundamental aim of education is to help [learners] grow in desirable ways ... To be effective it must be genuine; that is, an exemplar must not consciously exhibit one form of behaviour and then – caught off guard – act in a way that contradicts what he or she has modelled ... Modeling may be more effective in the moral domain than in the intellectual because its very authenticity is morally significant.
>
> *(Noddings 2002: 287)*

Of course, some coaches might challenge the practicality of engaging with these issues on top of all other demands that are made of them. However, Noddings' response to teachers asking similar questions is that moral learning and the establishment of a climate of care should not be considered as something that is 'on-top' of other aspects of a coach's work (Noddings 2012b: 777). Instead, she not only argued that it is 'underneath' all that educators do, but she also believes that, when a caring climate is established and sustained, other aspects of learning and performance improve or are enhanced. This final point is certainly something that has been hinted at in the existing coaching literature (e.g. Jones et al. 2004; Jones 2009). For example, in drawing upon the work of Noddings (1984, 1992) and Bronfenbrenner (1978), Jones (2009: 383) argued that coaching behaviours and practices that convey the message that 'I am interested in you' could boost the self-actualisation and the situational competence of athletes. Indeed, in a caring environment, an athlete may feel a sense of security, belonging, and freedom from the constraining fear of failure (Jones 2009).

Nel Noddings: a practitioner commentary by Rūtenis Paulauskas

This section is based upon an interview with Dr Rutenis Paulauskas, a former elite level basketball coach, and considers his views on caring practice. Rūtenis is a former professional basketball coach who has worked with teams such as Lokomotiv (Russia), BC Lietuvos Rytas (Lithuania), Dynamo Moscow region (Russia), and CSKA Moscow in addition to serving as Head Coach of the U19, U18, and U16 Lithuanian men's national teams. In 2007 he became Head Coach of the women's Euroleague team TEO Vilnius (Lithuania) and was the Head Coach of the Lithuanian women's national basketball team in 2008– 2009.

Rūtenis believes caring coaching involves understanding 'who' the player is and taking into consideration their unique circumstances. In doing so, the carer can construct a physical and social environment in which the player can perform at the highest level. He sees a caring coach as one who 'focuses not only on their performance in the sport, but also outside of it'. As such, he views his role as not only developing a player's sports skills, but also their personal skills. For Rūtenis, *caring for* a player begins in the recruitment phase. During this time, he is not only interested in how the prospective player is playing and her or his potential, but also who she or he is as a person. As such, when considering signing a player, Rūtenis speaks to other players and coaches to find out more about the prospective player. Relating this to Noddings' work, Rūtenis' information-seeking in the recruitment phase can be viewed as instrumental in establishing the conditions under which a relationship of care can flourish. One of his former players commented, 'It was a good starting position for our relationship because he brought me to his team ... He liked my talent and he saw the possibility of making me into a very good player.' As such, the player recognised that he was being *cared for,* an essential component in a caring relation. Upon signing with the team, Rūtenis develops the caring relation by *caring for* the player. In his words, 'when I recruit a player I have to take care of them. I will make sure the player gets playing time, I will protect him or her if the management wants to drop them, they will get their salary.'

Rūtenis also demonstrates *engrossment* within his caring encounters with the players. He noted that in professional sport *caring encounters* could occur in a variety of situations. These can include training sessions, travel to games, and training camps. During this time, Rūtenis takes advantage of the time with players to learn about their needs, working habits, interests, and talents. In these encounters he tries to *see, hear, or feel* what the player is saying. The information gleaned in these encounters enables him to recognise the individuality of the player and consider his or her individual development within the team. This includes recognising the demands of balancing professional sport and family responsibilities or studying, acknowledging issues or successes in their personal lives and helping them solve problems and/or supporting them through injury. In doing so, he recognises that caring 'requires different behaviours from situation to situation and from person to person' (Noddings 1992: xi). For example, Rūtenis recalled working with two talented players. The first player was able to focus on her training full-time. As such, Rūtenis could rely on her to be prepared for practice and to recover properly (i.e. eat properly, rest). Consequently, Rūtenis could design training programmes for her that had an increased physical load. The second player had two young children. At times when childcare was not possible, Rūtenis encouraged her to bring the children to training sessions.

> I understood that it was so difficult for her and I had to recognize that she was a player, she was a mum and she was also a wife. Normally children were not allowed in the gym, but I could not say 'no, it's not possible to bring your kids into the gym'. I had to take them, I had to accept them in order to take care of her and her family.

Here, Rūtenis recognised the player's life outside of sport as something that could not be ignored and, while he cared for both players, their different needs resulted in different care. Additionally, he believes that *caring for* the players can lead to improved performance as care is the starting point in the development of trusting relations between coach and player and amongst the team. To Rūtenis, trust is a contributing factor to a team's success. He recalled a team which had a high level of trust:

> I was so close to my players and they trusted me so much and they tried and tried to help win each game – they fought for every ball, they struggled every time and we got excellent results … They trusted me so much and we won so many games.

Although Rūtenis has provided examples of how he cared for his players, he noted that it was not always easy for a professional coach. In this respect, he recalled points in his career when the pressure of maintaining his job had an impact upon his ability to care. 'I was under huge pressure … and I was put in the position in which I had to choose between keeping my job or dropping a player … I felt that I had to stop caring … I felt that I lost myself.' In this situation, Rūtenis experienced a *diminution of the ethical ideal*. That is, Rūtenis had the intentions to care for the players, but the context caused him to act against his commitment to care. Here, Noddings would also suggest that the demands of his role resulted in him being over-extended and unable to experience care as a natural impulse.

While Rūtenis found himself in a position where he could not *care for* the players, he was able to rely upon and orchestrate others to care for the player. In this way he relied upon the network of people in the players' lives (i.e. partners, families, friends, agents, and fans) and the other members of the coaching team. Rūtenis stated: 'if you have good staff, if you have good assistants, if you have good doctors, physiotherapist, they can help you'. At times, being cared for by others as opposed to the coach was not viewed negatively by the players. Rather, the players recognised how the context in which they were working could impact upon the coach's ability care for them. One stated:

> Caring is very difficult in professional sports. It's not like with family and friends, it's different. It's a big business. The coach is responsible for the team, but behind the coach is the management, GM or director, who is pushing the coach and there is huge pressure.

Although in this section the coach has been positioned as the 'one-caring' and the player is in the role of 'cared-for', the roles can be reversed. For example, some retired players become general managers. These former players can care for the coach by employing them and protecting their contracts in the event of a move to fire them. Additionally, some players might become sponsors who fund their former coaches' clubs or support their interest in developing the next generation of players.

One area missing in Noddings' discussions is the evolution of care as the result of a person's career development. During our discussion, Rūtenis recognised that over his career his caring had changed. For example, early in his career he recalled receiving a phone call in the middle of the night from a player whose car had run out of petrol and consequently was stranded. Rather than calling his teammates for assistance, the player called Rūtenis, his coach. Rūtenis responded by bringing petrol to the player. Ten years later if a player called him for the same reason he believes that he would respond in a different way, 'I would say "Look, you shouldn't be driving your car in the middle of the night – you have earned a $100 fine." In this way I wanted to protect them, to let them know they shouldn't be driving in the middle of the night!' Certainly, for coaches, the 'evolution' of care is an area worthy of further investigation.

Nel Noddings: critical questions

1. How do Noddings' views on the role of education and the educator challenge traditional beliefs on coaching and learning in your chosen sport?
2. How might coaches in community and professional settings implement a caring pedagogy? What might they do and why?
3. What issues and challenges might coaches encounter in seeking to facilitate the moral learning of athletes? How might they be addressed?
4. Should Noddings' work on relational caring and moral learning be included in formal coach education provision? Why? Why not? How might her ideas be integrated into coach education curricula?

References

Arnold, P. J. (1994) 'Sport and moral education', *Journal of Moral Education*, 23(2): 75–89.
Bergman, R. (2004) 'Caring for the ethical ideal: Nel Noddings on moral education', *Journal of Moral Education*, 33(2): 149–162.

Bronfrenbrenner, U. (1978) *The ecology of human development: Experiments by nature and design*, Cambridge, MA: Harvard University Press.

Buber, M. (1965) *Between man and man*, New York: Macmillan.

Coleman, K., Depp, L. and O'Rourke, K. (2011) *The educational theory of Nel Noddings*, retrieved from www.newfoundations.com/GALLERY/Noddings.html (last accessed 17 June 2015).

Gordon, S., Benner, P. and Noddings, N. (1996) *Caregiving: Readings in knowledge, practice, ethics, and politics*, Philadelphia: University of Pennsylvania Press.

Hoagland, S. L. (1990) 'Some concerns about Nel Noddings'caring', *Hypatia*, 5(1): 109–114.

Ives, B., Gale, L., Nelson, L. and Potrac, P. (in press) 'Enacting youth sport policy: Towards a micro-political and emotional understanding of community sports coaching work', in A. Smith and K. Green (eds) *The Routledge handbook of youth sport*, London: Routledge.

Jones, R. L. (2009) 'Coaching as caring ("The smiling gallery"): Accessing hidden knowledge', *Physical Education and Sport Pedagogy*, 14(4): 377–390.

Jones, R., Armour, K. and Potrac, P. (2004) *Sports coaching cultures: From practice to theory*, London: Routledge.

Jones, R., Potrac, P., Cushion, C. and Ronglan, L. T. (eds) (2011) *The sociology of sports coaching*, London: Routledge.

Lindemann Nelson, H. (1992) 'Against caring', *Journal of Clinical Ethics*, 3(1): 8–15.

Lindemann Nelson, H. and Carse, A. L. (1996) 'Rehabilitating care', *Kennedy Institute of Ethics Journal*, 6(1): 19–35.

Lundqvist, A. and Nilstun, T. (2009) 'Noddings's caring ethics theory applied in a paediatric setting', *Nursing Philosophy*, 10(2): 113–123.

Noddings, N. (1984) *Caring: A feminine approach to ethics and moral education*, Berkeley: University of California Press.

Noddings, N. (1992) *The challenge to care in schools: An alternative approach to education* (2nd edn), New York: Teachers College Press.

Noddings, N. (1998) *Philosophy of education*, Philadelphia, PA: Westview Press.

Noddings, N. (1999). Caring and competence. In G. Griffin (Ed.), The Education of Teachers. Chicago: National Society for the Study of Education.

Noddings, N. (2002) *Starting at home: Caring and social policy*, Berkeley: University of California Press.

Noddings, N. (2003) *Caring: A feminine approach to ethics and moral education* (2nd edn), Los Angeles, CA: University of California Press.

Noddings, N. (2005a) *The challenge to care in schools* (2nd edn), New York: Teachers College Press.

Noddings, N. (2005b) *Educating citizens for global awareness*, New York: Teachers College Press.

Noddings, N. (2012a) *Philosophy of education* (3rd edn), Philadelphia, PA: Westview Press.

Noddings, N. (2012b) 'The caring relation in teaching', *Oxford Review of Education*, 38(6): 771–781.

Walton, G. (1991) *Beyond winning: The timeless wisdom of great philosopher coaches*, Champaign, IL: Human Kinetics.

19

CONCLUSION

Recognizing the dimensions and tensions of learning in coaching

Lee Nelson, Paul Potrac and Ryan Groom

Introduction

Having separately explored the work of various theorists in the preceding chapters of this book, we conclude by comparing and contrasting several aspects of their respective approaches to learning and education. In particular, this chapter is principally organized around the four inter-related themes of (a) 'nature of reality and knowledge', (b) 'freedom and determinism', (c) 'the learning self', and (d) 'learning and its facilitation'. It is not our intention to compare and contrast all of the theories considered in this book. Rather, using various examples, we wish to articulate some of their similarities, inter-relationships, and differences. To date, there has been surprisingly little consideration of these issues within the coaching and coach education literature base. From our perspective this is a somewhat problematic situation, especially given the centrality of learning within both of these settings and, relatedly, the field's claim to the status of a profession. As such, we hope that the discussion presented herein will not only contribute to a more nuanced and critical understanding of learning and education in sports coaching, but it might also assist coaches, coach educators, and relevant policy makers to reflect critically upon their own pedagogical belief systems, choices, and actions.

Theme 1: 'nature of reality and knowledge'

The first tension relates to theorists' underpinning philosophical beliefs about the nature of reality (i.e. ontology) and the nature of knowledge (i.e. epistemology). According to Schuh and Barab (2008), learning and instructional theories tend to be underpinned by contrasting philosophical understandings of ontology and epistemology. For example, *behaviourism*, which includes the work of Skinner (see Chapter 2), is understood to subscribe to an objectivist ontology and epistemological empiricism. That is, reality is considered to exist separately from the individual, while 'knowledge comes from experience and through the senses' (ibid.: 68). In contrast to behaviourism, the *cognitive constructivist* approach of Piaget (see Chapter 8), subscribes to ontological realism and epistemological rationalism. Here, reality is acknowledged as being separate from the mind, and knowing involves a correspondence between the world and an individual's mind, with reason being the primary source of knowledge (ibid.). In practice then, behaviourism focuses on describing specific observable outcomes that are considered to be indicative of learning, while cognitive constructivism is concerned with a person's unique and individually constructed view of the world (ibid.).

There is, of course, a further range of ontological and epistemological philosophies and choices that coaches and coach educators may wish to consider. For example, Vygotsky's social constructivist work (see Chapter 9) is based on the belief that reality exists in the process of individual interpretation. From this perspective, there are no absolute truths as knowledge is something that is socially and experientially constructed (ibid.). Equally, Lave's exploration of learning and cognition in everyday life (see Chapter 16) subscribes to a *situativity theory* perspective, which recognizes that learning not only takes place within the practice of a community, but that the practice of the community also shapes the learners in a reciprocal way (ibid.).

Finally, Freire's *critical* theoretical perspective is founded on a dialectical understanding of ontology and epistemology (see Chapter 12). Specifically, Freire believed that reality is a complex, unfinished, and evolving process involving interactions between human beings and the world (Roberts 2000). It is a position that holds there is an external world as well as our conscious understanding of it, and that both exist in a dynamic relationship (ibid.). Epistemologically, Freire believed that knowledge is actively constructed within particular social relations and is, as a result, reflective of particular ideological and political formations (ibid.). Knowledge, according to Freire, then, should be understood as continuously evolving and being reconstructed through dynamic encounters with the world and others (ibid.).

Theme 2: 'freedom and determinism'

The second tension is concerned with the different beliefs that theorists have about freedom and determinism. To illustrate this point, we compare and contrast the philosophical positions of B. F. Skinner (see Chapter 2), Carl Rogers (see Chapter 7), and Albert Bandura (see Chapter 3). Skinner is known for his assertion that 'man is not free' (Skinner 1953: 447). Indeed, he was highly critical of any attempts to explain human behaviour via inner psychological processes and interpretations. Instead, Skinner's *radical behaviourism* proposed that a person's behaviour should only be explained in relation to genetic and, more importantly, environmental determinants. In this respect, individual behaviour should not be considered autonomous, purposeful, and responsible in nature, but determined and ultimately controlled by its environment.

Rogers' *humanistic* stance presents an alternative position to that of Skinner's behaviourism. Contrary to Skinner, Rogers (1969: 494) contended that 'the best vantage point for understanding behavior is from the internal frame of reference of the individual self'. For Rogers, freedom is important as it allows people to commit to a process of personal change. In this respect, Rogers held a subjective and existential understanding of freedom. That is, he considered freedom to be 'something that exists in the living person quite aside from any of the outward choices of alternatives which we so often think of as constituting freedom' (Rogers 1969: 268). While Rogers (1969) recognized that his subjective and existential understanding of freedom was different to that proposed by Skinner and other behaviourist thinkers, it should also be noted that he did not consider his position to be a direct contradiction of the deterministic stance. Rather, Rogers (1969: 269) saw the freedom of which he spoke 'as existing in a different *dimension* than the determined sequence of cause and effect'. This position led him to conclude that we are faced with a *paradox* that we must learn to accept, whereby from one perspective man is a complex machine and from the other man is subjectively free.

Bandura, meanwhile, presents an integrated perspective on freedom and determinism. His *social cognitive theory* is agentic in that it proposes that 'people are contributors to their life circumstances not just products of them' (Bandura 2008a: 87). However, his theorizing does not present people as purely autonomous agents, nor does it suggest that their behaviour is wholly determined by situational circumstances and influences. Rather, Bandura (2008a) argues that 'human functioning is a product of a reciprocal interplay of interpersonal, behavioural, and environmental determinants' and that from this perspective the 'notion of "free will" is recast in terms of personal contribution to the constellation of determinants operating within the dynamic triadic interplay' (ibid.: 93). When viewed through the lens of social cognitive theory, freedom is not conceived as the absence of coercion and constraint in the choice of action. Instead, Bandura is of the belief that individuals are contributors to determining conditions. Somewhat paradoxically, then, according to Bandura's (2008a: 97) thesis, there is no absolute freedom, as 'to gain freedom individuals have to negotiate consensual rules of behavior for certain activities that require some relinquishment of autonomy'.

Theme 3: 'the learning self'

The third tension is concerned with the various understandings of the self that are presented in the theorizing of learning. Here, we believe that Tennant's (2012) insightful analysis provides a useful analytical framework for understanding multiple interpretations of the self and their place within learning and education. In particular, his articulation of the socially constructed self, the autonomous self and the storied self provides the basis for our consideration of the different ways in which scholars of learning, education, and interaction have discussed the self in their respective work.

The socially constructed self

We begin with *the socially constructed self*, as this embracing category encapsulates a considerable proportion of the theorists featured in this book. It includes but is not limited to Bandura (see Chapter 3), Lave (see Chapter 16), and Vygotsky (see Chapter 9). For example, according to Bandura (2008a, 2008b), people are not born with a sense of self. Rather, a person's sense of self is socially constructed through his or her transactions with the environment. Importantly, Bandura (2008b: 19) does not consider the self to be 'a homunculan overseer that resides in a particular place and does the thinking and acting'. Instead, he argues that the self *is* the person. Bandura (2008a, 2008b) openly questions conceptual understandings that posit the presence of multiple selves. Indeed, he considers the notion of multiple selves to be philosophically and conceptually untenable, as it raises significant questions about which self is the ultimate arbiter and where one should stop the fragmentation of the self. While Bandura (2008a, 2008b) eschews the notion of multiple selves, he considers identity formation to be an important feature of human agency. Bandura (2008b: 22) uses the term personal identity to refer to 'one's self-characterization', something that he believes 'affects how people structure their lives and relate to the everyday world around them'. Self-representation, for Bandura (2008a, 2008b), is not monolithic, but instead is something that should be conceptualized as being multifaceted in nature. While an individual's personal identity will almost inevitably be multifaceted, Bandura stresses that in each case it is the one and the same person who manifests this complex personal identity. Such personal identities, from a Bandurian perspective at least, are derived not only from how an individual lives and reflects on his or her life, but also from 'how one is treated by significant others' (ibid.: 22).

In their exploration of situated learning Lave and Wenger present an alternative social reading of identity formation. For Lave and Wenger (1991: 53) identities are 'long-term, living relations between persons and their place and participation in communities of practice'. Central to their theorizing is participation in social practice. Learning, as an aspect of social practice, implies becoming a member of a social community and engaging in the activities of that community. Learning, according to Lave and Wenger's perspective then, refers to developing into a different person, a person able to participate in new activities, through social relations. Indeed, Lave and Wenger (1991: 53) remind us that 'to ignore this aspect of learning is to overlook the fact that learning involves the construction of identities'. Common to all of the above-discussed theories, then, is a belief that the self emerges from and is maintained and developed through social interaction.

The autonomous self

According to Tennant (2012: 35), *the autonomous self* is 'characterized by agency, choice, reflection, and rationality' and 'stands in contrast to the automaton' who acts out 'behaviors and social roles […] as if he or she were simply shaped or conditioned by social forces'. Humanistic thinkers such as Carl Rogers (see Chapter 7) and Abraham Maslow (see Chapter 6) subscribe to a notion of the self that is capable of agency and choice developed through introspective reflection. In many respects Rogers' understanding of the development of the self shares many similarities with the views of those theorists expounding a socially constructed understanding of the self. Indeed, in his theory of personality and behaviour, Rogers (1951: 498) contended that 'as a result of interaction with the environment, and particularly as a result of evaluational interactions with others, the structure of the self is formed'. In other words, the 'I' and 'Me' emerge in the person's perceptual understanding as a result of social interaction. Where his understanding of the person arguably departs from those positions previously discussed is that Rogers (1957: 200) did 'not discover man to be, in his basic nature, completely without a nature, a *tabula rasa* on which *anything* may be written nor malleable putty which can be shaped into *any* form'. Rather, Rogers (1961: 194) claimed that 'an inescapable conclusion from a quarter-century of experience in psychotherapy' was that 'when we are able to free the individual from defensiveness, so that he [or she] is open to the wide range of his own needs, as well as the wide range of environmental and social demands, his [or her] reactions may be trusted to be positive, forward-moving, constructive'. He believed that, at an organismic level, people are driven by a tendency toward actualization (Rogers 1951, 1961, 1977).

Similarly, Maslow rejected behaviourists' ambivalence toward understanding the self. For Maslow, the self was of central importance when attempting to understand the *essence* and *intrinsic* characteristics of human nature (what he described as a specieshood). Maslow's conception of the self was also at odds with the work of Sartre, who believed that man was entirely a product and arbiter of his own unfettered will (Maslow 1968). Maslow acknowledged the significant influence of biological or *raw materials* upon the self (e.g. gender), which shape one's identity through a process of *introspective biology* (i.e. the method by which we search for identity), and the sense of a *real self* or *subjective biology*, in which we uncover and discover what we are throughout our life course (ibid.). Through this process of self-reflection and discovery self-acceptance and self-making about our commonness and our uniqueness are negotiated (ibid.). While people may differ, in gender for instance, emotional experiences remain species-wide phenomena (ibid.). Maslow further explained that through the process of self-discovery and the journey toward understanding our own uniqueness and individuality, we often recognize our similarities to others (i.e. our *specieshood*).

The storied self

In his discussion of *the storied self*, Tennant (2012) contends that 'the idea of narrative is appealing to educators', as learning can be understood as a narrative process, and that, as educational resources, narratives can bring about personal change. He goes on to suggest that teachers are often required to respond to those stories that learners bring to the classroom, and potentially challenge these narratives in order to explore with their learners 'alternative stories about the self' (ibid.: 90). Arguably, the work of Goodson and colleagues (see Chapter 11) aligns with this perspective of the learning self. In their theory of narrative learning, Goodson et al. (2010: 127) contend that narrative learning 'can be evidenced in the substance of the narration but also in the act of narration'. In their *Learning Lives* project, from which their narrative theory evolved, Goodson and colleagues defined identity as the way a person sees themselves in the world. The authors go on to state that their definition, and its accompanying understanding, implies more than cognitive concerns, as it acknowledges that people often understand their sense of self in ways that combine emotional, physical, and relational aspects. They also suggest that people's identities are often tacit in nature, as when asked to comment on themselves people tend to leave much out. Theirs is a stance that supports notions of multiple identities, as they discovered that 'people see themselves differently in different situations' (Biesta et al. 2011: 95). People, according to the perspective of Goodson and colleagues, enact multiple roles that touch and overlap with each other. As such, they reject the idea of a 'true self', recognizing instead that for some people some identities change while other identities remain the same. While Biesta et al. (2011) are concerned with a dynamic understanding of the self, they acknowledge that 'the nature of the self places boundaries around what learning is possible or might become possible, and therefore influences the likelihood of some learning rather than other learning within those boundaries' (ibid.: 95).

In their postmodern deconstruction of the self, Usher (see Chapter 14) and colleagues (1997) argue that understandings of, and practices within, adult learning and education have traditionally been underpinned by a set of taken-for-granted conceptions of the self. From their perspective adult learning has principally focused on autonomy, which refers to 'the government of the self by the self, a freedom from dependence, a situation where one is influenced and controlled only by a source within oneself' (Usher et al. 1997: 78). Usher et al. take issues with an autonomous understanding of the self and associated pedagogical practices. According to them (1997: 79) such interpretations of the self might be better conceived as the 'classic scientific self', which they consider to be an 'individualized, undifferentiated, and essentially abstract entity' and a 'self-contained individual having no transactions with and unaffected by anything "other" to itself'. Usher et al. (1997: 82) also critiqued Rogers' and Maslow's understanding of the relationship between self and the person's organismic being (see 'The autonomous self' above). In this regard, they argued that at the heart of the humanistic perspectives can be found an individual–society binary in which 'individual autonomy and empowerment lies in liberating oneself from the social and its oppressive effects'.

Usher et al. also offer a critique of the critical pedagogy tradition (see Chapter 14). While acknowledging that critical pedagogy places emphasis on social rather than personal autonomy, they contend that critical theory is, in fact, not so different from other traditions in that it too focuses on the outcome of freeing people from oppressive social relationships. Each of these perspectives, according to Usher et al. (1997: 84), wrongfully assumes an understanding of 'a self that is a unified consciousness with the power of self-presence and the capacity to act rationally'.

In light of the above critiques, Usher et al. offer a postmodern reading of the self. For them the postmodern self is 'a decentered self' that is 'caught in meanings, positioned in language and the narratives of culture' (Usher et al. 1997: 88). It is a self that 'cannot know itself independently of the significations in which it is enmeshed' and thus, they claim, 'there is no non-linguistic or non-historical position, no originary point, where persons can gain a privileged access to the world or to themselves' (ibid.). The authors go on to argue that such a stance requires postmodernists to hold a storied understanding of the self. In the authors' own words:

> Representations of the self, instead of being seen as 'truths', need to be seen more usefully as stories, often very powerful stories, which perform a variety of social functions, including the construction of selves with appropriate character- istics. In being positioned through narratives we get a sense of ourselves, but this sense is always changing. When we tell stories about our experiences, these are not stories simply about ourselves as entities that exist independently of the story, although they may appear to be. They are not stories about emanating from essential selves, but stories that help in the construction of selves.
>
> *(Ibid.)*

Theme 4: 'learning and its facilitation'

Finally, it would appear that many of the theorists discussed in this text present contrasting implications for understanding learning and its facilitation. Indeed, according to Merriam and colleagues (Merriam et al. 2007; Merriam and Bier- ema 2014) behaviourists, humanists, cognitivists, social cognitivists, and con- structivists present alternative understandings of the learning process, locus of learning, purposes of education, and role of the instructor in learning. Accord- ing to Merriam and Bierema (2014: 26), behaviourists, including Skinner, con- tend that 'human behavior is the result of the arrangement of particular stimuli in the environment'. Those behaviors that are reinforced are likely to continue, whereas those that are not reinforced will likely disappear. From this perspective, behavior is shaped by the environment and learning manifests in behavior change (Merriam et al. 2007).

The role of the behaviourist-informed educator, then, is to arrange the environ- ment to elicit behavioral change in the desired direction (ibid.). When applied to the context of sport, coaches and coach educators would seek to organize settings whereby desired behaviours could be positively reinforced as close to the behavioural response as possible (see Chapter 2). Coaches and coach educators aligning to this orientation would be less interested in the internal thought processes of their players and coach learners, focusing instead on their externally observable behaviours (see Chapter 2).

For Merriam et al. (2007), the *humanist* orientation of Maslow (see Chapter 7) and Rogers (see Chapter 6) is radically different to that of Skinner's behaviourism. Rather than focusing entirely on overt, external, behaviour this perspective con- siders 'the whole person including body, mind, and spirit, and the development of humans for growth and development' (ibid.: 30). It is, according to Merriam and colleagues, an orientation which recognizes that learning is a function of motivation and responsible choice, and has an affective as well as cognitive dimension. Educators conforming to this stance seek to facilitate the development of the whole person in order for them to become self-actualized (ibid.). Humanist-informed coaches and coach educators would actively involve their athletes and coach learners in every stage of the learning process, including the topics to be covered and the methods of delivery, as well as the means of assessment employed (see Chapter 7). That is, they would assume the role of facilitator rather than teacher (see Chapters 6 and 7). During pedagogical interactions with athletes and coach learners, coaches and coach educators would seek to prize, accept, and trust learners, and be empathetic to learners' experiences while remaining congruent to themselves (see Chapters 6 and 7).

In their exploration of learning theory, Merriam and colleagues align the work of Piaget (see Chapter 8) with both the *cognitivist* and *constructivist* orientations. According to Merriam et al. (2007), cognitivists are particularly interested in internal processes – how the mind makes sense of the external environment, the impact of prior knowledge, and those developmental stages that learners progress through. Coaches implementing this approach would seek to create interactive learning environments that foster co-operation, in an attempt to promote the social, moral, and intellectual development of their athletes (see Chapter 8). Here, coaches would give thought to how their athletes learn and how they might promote adaptation through assimilation and accommodation, and would try to align their coaching activities with their athletes' stages of development (see Chapter 8). While Piaget is often considered to be a cognitivist, similarities have also been identified between his theorizing and that of constructivist theories, leading authors such as Schuh and Barab (2008, see above) to label Piaget a cognitive constructivist.

Whereas cognitive constructivists tend to focus on the individual learner and how his or her cognitive schemes adapt to his or her physical environment, social constructivists place greater emphasis on the dialogical and social nature of meaning making (Merriam et al. 2007). For example, Vygotsky's writings illuminate the importance of mediation to learning in coaching and coach education settings. In this regard, his work arguably challenges coaches and coach educators to consider not only how they exteriorize psychological tools to learners, but also how they might subsequently orchestrate, monitor, and evaluate the learners' use and mastery of these particular tools (Karpov 2014). When discussing the constructivist orientation Merriam and colleagues also make reference to the theorizing of Dewey (see Chapter 4), Vygotsky (see Chapter 9), and Lave (see Chapter 16). Here, we can see that the classification of theorists' work is not without its difficulties. For example, while Merriam and colleagues locate Lave's work in the constructivist orientation, Schuh and Barab (2008) identify her theorizing as *situativity theory* perspective: an orientation distinct from constructivism.

According to Merriam et al. (2007: 297), social cognitive theorists, including Bandura (see Chapter 3), argue that learning 'occurs through the observation of people in one's immediate environment' and is 'a function of the interaction between person, environment, and behavior'. From this perspective, the instructor's role is to help learners to acquire new behaviours through a process of modelling (Merriam et al. 2007). When attempting to implement a social cognitivist approach, coaches and coach educators would attempt to facilitate the learning of athletes and coach learners by providing demonstrations (see Chapter 3). Here, they would employ strategies to gain the attention of their learners, provide example demonstrations with accompanying verbal prompts, break models down into constituent phases where appropriate, present their learners with opportunities to rehearse the modelled behaviours, provide correct feedback where necessary, and strive to reinforce correct performances (see Chapter 3).

In addition to those orientations outlined by Merriam and colleagues, we would also like to discuss the *critical* and *post-structuralist* perspectives. While these two positions share a critical understanding of learning, arguably humanist ideas can be found in the underpinning philosophical roots of the former whereas the latter overtly rejects this position. For us, the critical orientation includes the work of Freire and Mezirow. Central to Freire's thesis was his critique of 'banking' education: teaching that seeks to deposit information into students through narration (see Chapter 12). Freire was critical of such pedagogical approaches, as he believed that they served to domesticate and inhibit creative and critical thought (see Chapter 12). To overcome this critique he urged educators to embrace problem-posing education, an approach that is embedded in the life-worlds of its learners and that embraces dialogue and promotes critical thought (see Chapter 12). Similarly, the work of Mezirow encourages educators to create situations that challenge learners to reflect more critically on their own and others' values, beliefs, and assumptions, in order for them to become more autonomous thinkers (see Chapter 13). For critical theorists, education should help learners to deconstruct existing understandings and dominant ways of thinking. Educators, then, are seen to play an active and political role within this process.

Like the critical orientation, Usher's post-structuralist stance also questions those teaching and learning methods and techniques that educators have traditionally utilized (see Chapter 14). However, Usher also went on to critique the modernist, Enlightenment discourse that he considered to be the foundation of much teaching and learning theory, including that of the critical orientation (see Chapter 14). As has previously been discussed, Usher was critical of the belief that education produces individual autonomy and emancipation. Rather, drawing on the linguistic turn in social theory, in particular the work of Foucault, he called for an understanding of learning located in social, cultural, and political practices (see Chapter 14). As such, whereas those coaches and coach educators applying a critical stance would seek to help athletes and coach learners to understand and problematize dominant ways of thinking in the name of humanization, post-structuralist educators would fervently question the pursuit of this outcome. Instead, educators conforming to a post-structuralist stance would focus on helping their athletes or coach learners to better understand how certain ideas and practices became and remain dominant in sport.

Final thoughts

In this chapter we sought to identify and explore some of the differences that exist between contrasting theories of education, learning, and interaction. For some, we suspect that thinking about such issues might appear somewhat bewildering and confusing, and perhaps even 'off-putting'. Indeed, we do not doubt that some readers would have liked us to end this book with a definitive understanding of learning and, relatedly, the presentation of specific guidelines designed to inform the practices of coaches and coach educators. While we certainly understand such wants and desires, we believe that the field can only develop by grappling with these debates, issues, and dilemmas. Indeed, from our perspective, there are no 'quick fixes' or 'cast-iron' guarantees, nor one 'best way' in pedagogical activity. Instead, coaches, coach educators, and relevant policy makers ultimately have to make choices about what they think learning is and how it might be pursued, as well as interpret and respond to their subsequent engagements with learners in the field. As such, we hope that the issues discussed in this concluding chapter (and the book as whole) not only illustrate the breadth of the theoretical choices and perspectives available, but also shed some light on their underpinning foundations and core tenets. Indeed, we hope that the consideration of such issues can assist in the 'what', 'when', 'how', and 'why' decisions that coaches, coach educators and policy makers regularly have to make regarding learners and learning.

References

Bandura, A. (2008a) 'Reconstrual of "free will" from the agentic perspective of social cognitive theory', in J. Baer, J. C. Kaufman and F. Baumeister (eds) *Are we free? Psychology and free will*, Oxford: Oxford University Press, 86–127.

Bandura, A. (2008b) 'Toward an agentic theory of the self', in H. W. Marsh, R. G. Craven and D. M. McInerney (eds) *Self-processes, learning, and enabling human potential: Dynamic new approaches*, Charlotte, NC: Information Age Publishing, 15–49.

Biesta, G., Field, J., Hodkinson, P., Macleod, F. and Goodson, I. (2011) *Improving learning through the life course*, Abingdon: Routledge.

Goodson, I. F., Biesta, G., Tedder, M. and Adair, N. (2010) *Narrative learning*, London: Routledge.

Karpov, Y. (2014) *Vygotsky for educators*, Cambridge: Cambridge University Press.

Lave, J. and Wenger, E. (1991) *Situated learning: Legitimate peripheral participation*, Cambridge: Cambridge University Press.

Maslow, A. H. (1968) 'Some educational implications of the humanistic psychologies', *Harvard Educational Review*, 38(4), 685–696.

Merriam, S. B. and Bierema, L. L. (2014) *Adult learning: Linking theory and practice*, San Francisco: Jossey-Bass.

Merriam, S. B., Caffarella, R. S. and Baumgartner, L. M. (2007) *Learning in adulthood: A comprehensive guide*, San Francisco: Jossey-Bass.

Roberts, P. (2000) *Education, literacy, and humanization*, Westport, CT: Greenwood Press.

Rogers, C. R. (1951) *Client-centered therapy*, London: Constable.

Rogers, C. R. (1957) 'A note on "the nature of man"', *Journal of Counseling Psychology*, 4(3): 199–203.

Rogers, C. R. (1961) *On becoming a person*, New York: Houghton Mifflin.

Rogers, C. R. (1969) *Freedom to learn*, Columbus, OH: Charles E. Merrill.

Rogers, C. R. (1977) *Carl Rogers on personal power: Inner strength and its revolutionary impact*, London: Constable.

Schuh, K. L. and Barab, S. A. (2008) 'Philosophical perspectives', in J. M. Spector, M. D. Merill, J. V. Merrienboer and P. Driscoll (eds) *Handbook of research on educational communications and technology*, Mahwah, NJ: Lawrence Erlbaum Associates, 67–82.

Skinner, B. F. (1953) *Science and human behavior*, New York: The Free Press.

Tennant, M. (2012) *The learning self: Understanding the potential for transformation*, San Francisco: Jossey-Bass.

Usher, R., Bryant, I. and Johnstone, R. (1997) *Adult education and the postmodern challenge: Learning beyond the limits*, London: Routledge.

INDEX

Taylor & Francis eBooks

Helping you to choose the right eBooks for your Library

Add Routledge titles to your library's digital collection today. Taylor and Francis ebooks contains over 50,000 titles in the Humanities, Social Sciences, Behavioural Sciences, Built Environment and Law.

Choose from a range of subject packages or create your own!

Benefits for you

» Free MARC records
» COUNTER-compliant usage statistics
» Flexible purchase and pricing options
» All titles DRM-free.

Benefits for your user

» Off-site, anytime access via Athens or referring URL
» Print or copy pages or chapters
» Full content search
» Bookmark, highlight and annotate text
» Access to thousands of pages of quality research at the click of a button.

REQUEST YOUR **FREE** INSTITUTIONAL TRIAL TODAY | **Free Trials Available** We offer free trials to qualifying academic, corporate and government customers.

eCollections – Choose from over 30 subject eCollections, including:

Archaeology	Language Learning
Architecture	Law
Asian Studies	Literature
Business & Management	Media & Communication
Classical Studies	Middle East Studies
Construction	Music
Creative & Media Arts	Philosophy
Criminology & Criminal Justice	Planning
Economics	Politics
Education	Psychology & Mental Health
Energy	Religion
Engineering	Security
English Language & Linguistics	Social Work
Environment & Sustainability	Sociology
Geography	Sport
Health Studies	Theatre & Performance
History	Tourism, Hospitality & Events

For more information, pricing enquiries or to order a free trial, please contact your local sales team:
www.tandfebooks.com/page/sales

 Routledge Taylor & Francis Group | The home of Routledge books | **www.tandfebooks.com**